+DS151 .A2 K613 1983+

DS
151
A2
K613
1983

Kol, Moshe, 1911-
    Mentors and friends

Mentors
and Friends

Moshe Kol

A Publication of the Herzl Press

New York • Cornwall Books • London

© 1983 by Rosemont Publishing and Printing Corporation

Cornwall Books
4 Cornwall Drive
East Brunswick, NJ 08816

Cornwall Books
27 Chancery Lane
London WC2A 1NF, England

Cornwall Books
2133 Royal Windsor Drive
Unit 1
Mississauga, Ontario, L5J 1K5, Canada

Library of Congress Cataloging in Publication Data

Kol, Moshe, 1911–
   Mentors and friends.

   Abridged translation of: Morim ya-haverim.
"A publication of the Herzl Press."
Includes index.
   1. Zionists—Biography. 2. Israel—Biography.
3. Kol, Moshe, 1911–   . I. Title.
DS151.A2K613   1983   956.94'001'0924 [B]   82-71073
ISBN 0-8453-4741-1

Printed in the United States of America

Contents

Preface 7
Biographical Sketch of Moshe Kol 9
Rabbi Alter Kolodny 13
Chaim Weizmann 24
Nachum Sokolow 30
Yitschak Ben-Zvi 35
Zalman Shazar 39
Yitschak Greenbaum 45
Moshe Glickson 61
Pinchas Rosen 76
Levi Eshkol 91
Moshe Sharett 97
Berl Katznelson 106
Yosef Sprinzak 115
Pinchas Sapir 123
Henrietta Szold 129
Vera Weizmann 140
Rose Halprin 148
Rebecca Sieff 151
Kurt Blumenfeld 155
Selig Asher Brodetsky 159
Abba (Albert) Schoolman 163
Yechiel Charif 167
Moshe (Ossi) Biderman 177
Daniel Brisker 182
Abba Barditchev 186
David (Dado) Elazar 193
Glossary 199
Index 201

Preface

The three-volume Hebrew edition of *Morim Ve-Haverim* (Mentors and Friends) elicited a most favorable reaction from the Israeli public. The encouraging reviews it received prompted me to publish a volume in English devoted to those mentors and colleagues with whom I traveled a long ideological and political road, and to personalities who influenced me during decades of fruitful cooperation with them. Even when I differed with some of these Zionist and national personalities I continued to esteem them, value them, and learn from them.

The General Zionist and Liberal movements have made no effort to describe the achievements of their outstanding members or to record their great merits in preparing the infrastructure of the state and in fulfilling the Zionist vision. My efforts over a number of years to create a special collection to present the personalities of our movement to the people and to the young generation met with little encouragement. Back in the thirties, I prevailed upon Dr. Moshe Glickson to publish two volumes of his ideological writings entitled *Im Hillufei Mishmarot* (With the Changing of the Guard). We also began to publish the *Yesodot* collection, which was devoted to Zionist philosophy, so that the young generation could learn more about it. Over the years I helped Yitschak Greenbaum to publish his speeches in the *Sejm*, the Polish parliament, and at Zionist Congresses, in the hope that by doing so the people of Israel would come to know more about this powerful personality.

My books, *Morim Ve-Haverim*, are a modest attempt to present to the reader the leaders and builders of our movement and our educational enterprises—our youth villages, which today are grouped within the framework of *Yesodot*.

Today we are witnesses to the ideological shallowness of the Zionist camp. The Zionist movement faces a grave crisis, and finds itself at a parting of the ways: today there is no difference between a sympathizer with Israel and an officially declared Zionist. Indeed, those who sympathize with the cause of Israel sometimes reveal a closer identity with the Jewish State than do the Zionists themselves.

At this time of lost faith and superficial ideals, it is perhaps worthwhile for the Zionists in the Anglo-Saxon world to learn of the General Zionist, Liberal, and Labor personalities whose contributions to the achievements of Zionism were so great—men who were real partners in the establishment of the state. These men inspire by their example; from them one can learn the meaning of personal identification with Zionist fulfillment and how one may find a place in the great national edifice.

Through the nineteen years of my responsibility for Youth Aliyah, I was privileged to work with women leaders who built the women's Zionist organizations, with women of international standing, and women with noble aspirations who saw in Youth Aliyah a humanitarian educational movement transcending the borders of one nation. To those outstanding personalities among the Zionist women who gave me their support and confidence, I have devoted chapters in this book. It is the first time that the achievements of these Zionist women leaders and the working leadership among Israeli women receive such recognition.

In the many years of my Zionist activity since the eighteenth Zionist Congress in Prague in 1933, the first I attended, and ever since I was elected a member of the General Zionist Council in 1937 and a member of the Jewish Agency Executive from 1947 to 1966, I have had the privilege of being inspired by great Zionist personalities and of cooperating with outstanding leaders. Among them were the builders of the Zionist Labor movement who became later the leaders of the entire Zionist movement and of the Yishuv. During World War II, I was a member of the Histadrut Executive and head of the Labor Exchange, and I was fortunate enough to have gained an insight into these personalities. Some of them are described in this book. Many more are included in the Hebrew edition.

Zionists in the English-speaking countries—the majority of the world movement today—must ask themselves, "Where do we go from here?" The lives, the principles, and the epic struggles of the people about whom I have written in this book may help to provide an answer. I hope that the moral stocktaking of those who read these pages will produce favorable results. If this English edition is received with the same sympathy and appreciation as were the Hebrew volumes, I will have been amply rewarded.

The publication of this book was made possible thanks to the help of the late Doctor Albert P. Schoolman and my friends of the Children of Youth Aliyah Committee of Great Britain, to whom I am deeply grateful. Special thanks to Dr. Mordecai S. Chertoff of the Herzl Press, who edited the book, and to Yael Guiladi for the English translation.

Jerusalem, 1982

Biographical Sketch of Moshe Kol

Moshe Kol was born in Pinsk, Russia in 1911, to a comfortable middle-class family. His father was a successful wine merchant, his grandmother an enterprising haberdasher, and his grandfather a man of affairs who busied himself with the problems of schooling local Jewish youngsters.

Kol was one of the leaders of the Zionish Youth Movement in Poland. He settled in Palestine in 1932. Since then he was held a variety of prominent offices in the Zionist movement and in the Israel Government. He was one of the signers of the Declaration of Independence. He served as minister of tourism for over ten years, and was a member of the Cabinet Committee of Defense, Economics and Colonization. He was head of Youth Aliyah for nineteen years. During his tenure, more then 100,000 children and youth came from 85 countries, among them 20,000 orphans. For many years he served as vice-president of the International Federation of Children's Communities under the auspices of UNESCO, and chairman of the Mutual Aid Committee of the International Union for Child Welfare under UNICEF, which helped children in developing countries.

Mr. Kol was one of the founders and leaders of the World Confederation of General Zionists, and is currently chairman of the Independent Liberal Party and vice-president of the Liberal International. He is the honorary treasurer of the Israeli Archaeological Society, and chairman of the Hanoar Hazioni youth villages.

Among his published works are *Arachim*, which deals with the ideology of the Zionist Labor Movement, and a volume of Youth Aliyah that has appeared in Hebrew, English and French. He contributes regularly to the Israeli press and to journals both in Israel and abroad. The present volume is excerpted and translated from the original three-volume Hebrew edition of *Mentors and Friends*, published 1968–1977.

Mr. Kol is married and the father of three daughters, all of whom are married and living in Jerusalem with their families.

Mentors
and Friends

Rabbi Alter Kolodny

My grandfather, Rabbi Pinchas Eliyahu Halevi Kolodny, was known in Pinsk by the name of Alter Kolodny. As a very small child, he fell gravely ill and, in accordance with Jewish custom, his name was changed to Alter ("Old Man" in Yiddish), a remedy that would bless him with a long life. Forty-six years have passed since his death, and I still see him in my mind's eye as though he were alive; indeed, I believe I will see him thus to my dying day. Only a few weeks after my arrival in Eretz Israel he passed away. I well remember the deep melancholy that enveloped us when grandfather and I parted. He was then confined to the sickbed from which he was not to rise again. I pretended to be cheerful, although I was filled with a deep presentiment that I would never see him again. I am sure he shared this feeling, but he tried to conceal it from me.

To his credit it may be said of my grandfather that he possessed in good measure the noblest of virtues—learning and courtesy—and that he deserved the respect he enjoyed. All that he learned and achieved in his life he acquired entirely through his own efforts: he was the authentic self-made man. He amassed his rich and varied knowledge at great pains, spending sleepless nights over his books. At that time there were few Jews who, like him, allied learning with courtesy in the right proportions.

Rabbi Alter Kolodny was well known in the Pinsk community, which was famous for the many important personalities and community workers it produced. Grandfather inspired widespread respect and esteem. In the commemorative volume entitled *A Thousand Years of Pinsk* (published in New York in 1941) there is a chapter describing the Pinsk Talmud Torah. Grandfather is mentioned as having served as its head until 1914, although he actually did serve for many more years thereafter. I remember that period extremely well. My parents' home was not far from the Talmud Torah building, and after the town's great synagogue burned down a regular minyan was held there. The members of our family were among those who prayed at that minyan. At that time I followed closely everything grandfather did.

In *A Thousand Years of Pinsk* we read that "He was particularly devoted to the education of poor children. Rabbi Pinchas Eliyahu Kolodny, an educated man, in addition to his fine qualities of character, served as pedagogical adviser [to the Talmud Torah] and for twenty years took care of religious and general education in Pinsk." At the Talmud Torah, which was housed in a fine wooden building, hundreds of poor schoolchildren were educated. Through its broad, high windows, light flooded into the classrooms.

Talmud Torah board members were elected at general meetings. Most of them were involved in public affairs; some of them were learned, but the majority lacked all understanding of educational matters. Grandfather was an authority on pedagogy and was recognized as such, even by the teachers. It was he who introduced the newest and most up-to-date educational methods. The school was spotlessly clean, thanks to my grandfather, who was himself immaculate and took great pains with his own appearance as well as that of his family.

Grandfather was a unique combination of the religious Jew and the modern man. He was able to maintain, without contradiction, both his religious character and his modern ideas.

There were periods when we lived in neighboring houses, and at times in the same house, and I would watch him every morning as he went after prayers—and a copious breakfast—to the Talmud Torah, where he worked until midday. At that time he no longer had to work for his livelihood, for he enjoyed a permanent income from rental of some shops in a building at the end of the main street in Karlin. Occasionally he did give lessons in accounting or provide legal advice to plaintiffs appearing before the rabbinical court. Almost all of his free time was devoted to community affairs, from which he derived great satisfaction. He was well versed in the Bible, the Talmud, and the Halacha and acted as legal adviser both to the rabbinical court and in affairs pertaining to the state judiciary, even though it was known that he was not a lawyer. He was gifted with sound common sense and his well-balanced opinions and legal advice were much in demand. He was well known as an accounting teacher, and he trained many students who later became independent accountants. In his later years he worked on an accounting textbook in Yiddish. He had completed the text and used to read chapters from it to his pupils. The manuscript was never published and was lost—probably along with the other manuscripts that remained after his death—when our house was destroyed during the Holocaust.

Few people would have imagined that my grandfather was also an expert in growing vegetables. He had a plot of ground beside his house that was devoted entirely to agricultural experiments, mainly with vegetables. He worked in the vegetable garden himself, and all of us—his sons, his grandsons and the rest of his family—gave him a hand. During my initial period as a member of Kibbutz Hamefales in Kfar Saba, I worked at vegetable gardening. I had learned all about it from my grandfather. Every year, in early spring when the snow began to melt, grandfather would prepare wooden frames with glass windows and build a small hothouse. In the boxes he planted vegetable seeds which, when they sprouted, were transplanted to the vegetable garden. Winter in Pinsk was severe, and it took hard work to block every hole so that the cold would not penetrate the wooden frames and the glass. Around the boxes we used to pour sand, and on the windows we put sacks and straw to keep as much of the heat as possible inside and to make sure that the seeds would germinate. The plants that grew in the hothouses were not just for our own use; grandfather used to sell them to other people who wanted to grow vegetables in their gardens. We grew potatoes, carrots, beetroot, tomatoes, cabbage, cauliflower, onions, radishes (both large and small), and other vegetables whose names were unknown to most of the Jewish inhabitants of Pinsk. I remember the amazement provoked at the time by the white cauliflower that grew in our plot: it was so very white that some women believed it had milk in it and therefore could not be eaten with meat. Grandfather used to buy the seeds locally, although he sometimes ordered them from out of town. I always used to find catalogs from the world's famous seed merchants in his house. He also studied, and taught, how to combat the various pests that afflicted the vegetable garden. In his last years he did not content himself with growing only plants and vegetables; he added seed raising. He would leave the fruits of the vegetables until they were overripe, and then he would extract the seeds and bring them into the house. Or again, he would hang branches of fruit in the yard to dry. Inside our house all kinds of green plants were hung up on the windows to dry, and green tomatoes were put on the window sills until they reddened.

The house was full of vegetables and seeds—no place was free of them. Grandfather had a special affection for his vegetable garden, and always wanted to introduce innovations. When I began to plant flowers in a corner of the garden in the courtyard, he was patient with the novelty, but when the flowerbed expanded and took up a sizable portion of the garden he was not too pleased. He liked flowers, especially sweet-smelling ones, but at the same time he husbanded every piece of land, no matter how small, so that he could grow on it the vegetables he loved.

He greatly expanded the vegetable growing and spent a lot of time reading the relevant professional publications, in Russian and other languages. He even wrote a pamphlet in Yiddish on vegetable growing and had it printed at his own expense in Pinsk. He distributed some copies free and sold others at a good price to those who came to buy plants or seeds from him.

In an introduction to the pamphlet, which he called *Gardening* and which was written and printed at the end of World War II, he wrote:

> The World War, with all its attendant miseries and shortcomings, also brought good and useful things in its wake. One of these useful things is the planting of vegetable gardens. It is well know that a vegetable garden in the yard beside the house is useful for a number of reasons: first of all materially—beetroot, radishes, onions, cucumbers, etc., which are home-grown are cheap, and furthermore, have the additional advantage of being available whenever required; secondly, hygienically—the yard is always clean and covered in greenery; thirdly, the contact with nature. Since I had both a theoretical and a practical knowledge of vegetable growing, and since I wished to help people with no experience in this area to make use of their gardens, I decided to publish a small pamphlet in which I would set out in brief the most important and essential information on how to work and care for a vegetable garden. It is true that not all soils are suitable for vegetable growing, but since this pamphlet is intended for home owners who wish to plant gardens in their yards and are unable to go in search of suitable soils, I shall regretfully omit information regarding the soil, its qualities and characteristics and ways to improve and enrich it. I shall simply list the vegetables and explain how to prepare the land for each type.
>
> I would like to take this opportunity to express in a few words the importance of vegetable growing in general. I disagree with the view that the interest in vegetables that has arisen during the war will pass once hostilities are over. On the contrary, I believe that the interest in vegetable growing is real and will persist for a long time. What is more, I hope and believe that many people who engaged in vegetable gardening during the war no matter how small their plots, will do so in the future not for material gain but simply to supply their personal needs; and when they see the utility and realize the importance of this activity, their desire to engage in vegetable growing permanently will be awakened. I also hope that this small pamphlet will serve as a way to increase among our Jewish brothers interest in vegetable growing, and that they will derive satisfaction from their labors.

This small pamphlet, seventy pages long, awakened great interest even among various Jewish circles in other countries. With the help of my aunt Chasya, grandfather's youngest daughter, the pamphlet reached a number of publishers. It was published in 1919, after some slight touching-up by Michael Davidson, by the Yiddischer Folkes Verlag in Kiev and Saint Petersburg. In 1921, my aunt sold the copyright to Klal Verlag in Berlin. (By mistake the name Pesach Kolodny was printed as the author, instead of Pinchas Eliyahu Kolodny.) Thus, the little booklet enjoyed wide distribution both in Russian and in German, and undoubtedly reached many other Jewish groups.

There were only a few cherry trees beside our house but next door to grandfather's there was a large orchard. Grandfather liked to sit in the shade of a cherry tree and contemplate his thriving vegetable garden. From this vantage point he also watched over the beds to make sure they were not destroyed by the birds, and he often set up scarecrows to frighten them away.

In the evening, grandfather used to sit up late reading. He was a book lover, devoted to religious literature, but he also read modern books in Hebrew, Russian, and Yiddish. Almost every day he spent some time writing. He wrote rapidly and his style was clear and simple, unencumbered by rhetoric. He used to write stories in Yiddish, inspired by Jewish life in the town and its environs. In those stories he evoked characters and events from his own life. He also wrote plays. Few knew Yiddish and wrote it as he did. From time to time he enjoyed reading his works aloud to us and to friends and acquaintances who visited the house. Fortunately, most of his writings were saved at the very last minute, a few weeks before the Nazi invasion of the city and its destruction. I hope that these works will one day be published. They would constitute an important source of information on Jewish life in Pinsk.

Grandfather was a music lover and played the violin. He saw to it that his sons, my father and my uncle, also learned to play. Indeed, Uncle Abraham had quite a talent for it. Grandfather also liked to lead the congregation in prayer during the minyan at the Talmud Torah, and was the most popular prayer leader in the community—he almost qualified as a cantor. He generally led the Mussaph prayer on the Sabbath of the new moon (Rosh Hodesh), Kol Nidrei (on the eve of Yom Kippur), and on similar occasions. He displayed a particular talent for accentuating the passages in the liturgy that were sung. Since he understood the language of the hymn, he knew where to place the emphasis, what to draw out and what to cut short. He therefore had no particular liking for those readers who pushed their way into leading the congregation, who not only did not have pleasant voices but had no understanding of the words they uttered and took the soul out of the liturgy.

Grandfather was a *mitnagged* and never showed any spiritual affinity with Hasidism. He enjoyed listening to the prayers chanted by a famous cantor who came to take the service in the great synagogue, but he was never drawn to the Hasidic airs. His status at the Talmud Torah, his fine reputation within the Jewish community in Pinsk, and his relations with the Russian and Polish intelligentsia gave him a special status among the citizens of our city. In summer, he would sit at home beside the open window and passers-by would stop for conversation. Others came to visit, to talk, or for advice. Pinsk was composed of two communities, Pinsk and Karlin. Grandfather's communal activities were well known mainly in Pinsk. However, in Karlin he owned a large building in which he rented out shops. Among them was the shop run by my parents. Grandfather liked to stroll around and look at houses, spend some time in the shops, talk to the neighbors and discuss business in my father's shop. Karlin was not far from his sphere of interest, but both his spiritual world and his public life revolved entirely around Pinsk.

Grandfather never belonged to any political party. He had absolutely no spiritual affinity with them because his religious world was essentially tolerant. When I was studying at the Tarbut Gymnasia I used to bring books to read at home, and grandfather liked to look at them from time to time. Thus, he also came in contact with modern Hebrew literature. He was greatly interested in biblical research and criticism, and enjoyed keeping abreast of the new commentaries.

The year before he died, he found me reading Professor Joseph Klausner's *Jesus of Nazareth,* and expressed his desire to read it, too. It took him several weeks—when one of the Talmud Torah workers came to visit him he would stop reading and quickly cover the book with newspapers. I once asked him why he did this and he replied simply: "You and I both know that one can read Klausner's *Jesus* and not be harmed, Heaven forbid, religiously. One can agree or disagree with many of the assumptions and conclusions made by this writer and historian. However, if one of the Talmud Torah workers were to see me holding such a book in my hand, he would think Heaven knows what, and perhaps, even, God forbid, that I have become a heretic. Just imagine what would happen if the rumor spread that I, Alter Kolodny, had with my own eyes been reading Klausner's *Jesus!*"

In the twenties he visited his daughters and sons-in-law in Moscow, a great experience for him. He found them all engaged in science and the study of mathematics, French, psychoanalysis, etc., and was delighted to find that there were no party workers among them. He was heartbroken, though, by the destruction of Jewish religious and national life. On his return, he spoke of his conversations with Litvakov and the other members of the Jewish section of the Communist party; he stung them as sharply as he could and attacked them bitterly. He also attended the Jewish theatre, and he witnessed the decline of Yiddish journalism and literature. On no account could he accept the new Yiddish spelling. On the one hand, he was delighted with the important scientific positions held by my uncles and aunts, but on the other he was depressed at the sight of the assimilation and the destruction of Jewishness that he saw.

As a man who understood the spirit of his generation and recognized the importance of education, he paid great attention to the education of his children. My father was a graduate of the Kharkov dental school, though he did not practice his profession until the last years of his life. Rachel, grandfather's elder daughter, was sent to Paris to study French language and literature at the Sorbonne. Her husband, Bezalel Schneider, studied mathematics and became a lecturer in mathematics at Moscow University and published research papers and books on the subject. Chasya, the younger daughter, studied psychology and she also published many books. Grandfather was not content with educating his sons and daughters; he also took care of the education of his grandchildren. In his view, education was the best investment a man could make for the future. Primary and secondary education were not enough, he believed, and he aspired to a higher education for all of us.

I can see him now, the handsome figure of a learned Jew, an expert in legal matters, a teacher of accounting, a vegetable grower, a writer, an educator and public worker, a music lover and prayer leader. He was a versatile personality who stood out in his town and community and enjoyed the confidence of most people. His financial position was solid, although he was far from being considered wealthy. But, above all, he was deeply concerned about the education of his children and grandchildren.

When grandfather's autobiography reached me in 1927, my admiration for him increased tenfold. The volume was written in Yiddish verse and dedicated to his two daughters, Rachel and Chasya. The following paragraphs are a brief summary.

Grandfather was born in 1857 of a very poor, religious family. His parents had a house of three small rooms, two of which they rented to lodgers. The entire family lived in the front room, which also served as a bakery and from which the bread was sold. This income was one of the family's sources of livelihood. Many of the customers were given their bread on credit, so instead of making a profit, the family lost money. The admiration in which grandfather held his mother comes through clearly in the autobiography; she seems to have had a great influence on his life. Once he asked her why she worked so hard when all that remained was a deficit. She replied: "The most important thing in life is not money; it is more important that the poor should eat and be satisfied." On Saturdays and festival days great-grandfather used to bring many visitors home from the synagogue to eat at his table. He was a poor and simple Jew; he traded at the market and paid exorbitant interest on the loans he took, and it is doubtful whether he ever made a profit on his transactions. His wife kept the accounts. Grandfather wrote that his mother had the head "of a minister" and an astonishingly good memory. She gave generously to charity and was kindhearted and refined and contented with her lot—even with her poverty. She used to say to her son, my grandfather, "My son, you must know and study everything. It will be of great help to you in the future."

When grandfather was four years old he was already going to school at the heder as was the custom in those days. There he learned to read the prayer book, the *Chumash* with Rashi's commentary, and later the Gemara, the Tosafot, and other commentaries. He was a very talented student. When he was fourteen he was accepted at the government school, but he remained there for only a short time. After he left school he began to work as a gardener—he hoed, laid out flower beds, sowed, and raised produce. He was not content with the physical labor alone, but studied gardening and vegetable growing as well. This was where his love of vegetable growing began. It found practical expression many years later and became one of the activities he enjoyed most. It also proved to be extremely profitable. At the same time he began to learn accounting. When he was twenty he married; he was then a bookkeeper in a tobacco factory in the town. His in-laws were wealthy to begin with, but they later lost their fortune. Grandfather received a dowry of 200 rubles, in cash. Grandmother Pessl (my sister Paula, who was murdered by the Nazis, was named after her) was a frugal housekeeper. Her household expenses came to only one ruble per week and grandfather wrote that they lived together like a "king and queen."

At first grandfather traded in grain. He and his partner bought a horse and cart and drove through the townlets and villages buying and selling grain—until they lost all their money when the horse was wounded in the flank and had to be sold. Grandfather then began to trade in pigs' bristles, but after he had bought a substantial stock, a plague of cholera broke out in Russia and the borders were closed. The stock could not be moved. Grandfather then decided not to continue as an "independent" businessman and looked for a suitable job as a bookkeeper. He found one at the tobacco factory. The wages were low—three rubles a month—but his mother urged and encouraged him to take the job, arguing that if he did well he would be given a better job at a higher salary. Grandfather wrote that before he accepted the position he wept bitterly. It was apparently infra dig for this young householder, who already had a family, to work for strangers and earn a mere three rubles per month. When he came to the factory he met the customs officer, who tested him to see if he really did know arithmetic, fractions, and decimals (previous bookkeepers had been fired for their lack of such knowledge). Grandfather wrote that they knew as much about bookkeeping as do "chickens about men." He kept the factory books faithfully and was praised for his work.

The customs officer once asked him if he knew how to draw. He was surprised at the strange question. He was told that extra stories had to be added to the building to expand the factory; suitable plans had to be drawn up. Grandfather agreed to prepare the plans even though he knew absolutely nothing about such things. He worked extremely hard, wrote and erased, made complicated calculations, and spent days and nights over the job until he finally produced a number of building plans, all of which the man liked. Grandfather was given a few rubles as a bonus. From then on he began to rise in the world; his income increased steadily, and grandmother was delighted.

Next door to the tobacco factory was the office of a notary who was looking for a clerk with a fine and very small handwriting. The notary was both very pedantic and very mean and he wanted someone who would economize on stationery. The factory management recommended grandfather, and he was hired as a clerk by the notary at a monthly salary of five rubles plus certain bonuses which were never clarified. Naturally, he considered this an important advancement.

At that time (1881) the railway was being built in Pinsk, and many contracts, surveys, etc., were being drawn up. Grandfather worked day and night and earned a fine salary. In the course of his work at the notary's office he learned the profession, conscientiously studied the relevant laws, and practiced accounting. Meanwhile, a new notary had arrived in Pinsk to replace grandfather's employer and grandfather had to pass examinations all over again. This meant additional effort, but once he had successfully passed the examination he became master of the office. People crowded at his door to ask for advice. He served the notary faithfully as cashier, adviser, and manager all in one. This situation continued until an order came from the Council of Ministers prohibiting Jews from working in notaries' offices. The notary was in no hurry to dismiss grandfather, and he could have continued in his job, but a Jew informed on him. A special order was issued by the minister prohibiting his employment. In the end, however, much good was to accrue to him from his dismissal.

In those days it occurred to grandfather to open up his own office as a legal adviser. He could draw upon all the experience he had gained at the tobacco factory and in the notary's office. These were good times for him. Although he worked hard, night and day, even to the detriment of his health, he ended up a wealthy man. In 1901, after the great fire in Pinsk, many people came to him to draw up their contracts, prepare building plans, seek advice on the arrangement of mortgages, the registration of plots, and so forth. He then decided to do something for his own family: he acquired a plot of land and built on it a block of shops, which for many years provided him with a source of income and enabled him to devote himself to public affairs.

That same building, and the house in which grandfather lived (and our family with him), was to bring tragedy to us all. When I emigrated to Eretz Israel, I asked my father to sell the buildings and come to join me. Real estate prices in Pinsk were low at the time and my father postponed his decision from year to year in the hope that prices would rise. Catastrophe struck: World War II erupted and the entire family was wiped out.

For many years, however, the building served as a solid basis for grandfather's livelihood. He opened a wine and spirits shop there. He later extended the business to include dried fruits, and also dealt in rice, candles, and almonds. He developed connections with Persia, Bukhara, and other countries that exported wines and dried fruits. His commercial ties expanded greatly, but it all lasted only until the outbreak of World War I. In 1914, his business was in ruins and the money he had amassed lost its value.

I well remember the days of currency devaluation, when bank notes were used as wallpaper in the kitchen. Money had no value. The stock that had remained in the shop provided grandfather with a livelihood during the war. The fees from his legal advice and from the lessons in bookkeeping, and the income from the vegetable garden provided the rest. The shop later passed into my father's hands. He continued grandfather's business, temporarily abandoning his dental practice.

Grandfather was a man who achieved greatness by his own efforts. The story of his life reads like a fairy tale, the tale of a poor young Jew who succeeded in bettering himself by dint of his own efforts and became an educated man, brimming with learning and wisdom.

These chapters of his life added to the affection and esteem in which I held him; for me, he was both symbol and model, and that was the reason it was so hard for me to take my leave of him when I emigrated to Eretz Israel in 1932. He did not attempt to hold me back; he knew that my future was not in Pinsk, nor even in Poland. Before I made my aliyah we had a photograph taken together. He considered me his spiritual heir. There was a great similarity between my fields of interest as a youth and his own. On the photograph he wrote: "The departing generation greets the rising generation."

I often feel how greatly I was influenced by my grandfather, and how many traits of his noble character I inherited. If I have devoted nearly fifty years of my life to the education of youth, to Zionism, to pioneering and agricultural achievements, and if I have had the privilege of heading the Youth Aliyah enterprise for nineteen years, I have no doubt at all that this was an inheritance from my grandfather. Grandfather cared for the children of the poor Jewish classes in Pinsk like a father; it was he who showed me how to work with my hands and brought me into contact with the land.

If I were to make an objective appraisal of my grandfather—not looking at him through the eyes of a loving grandson—I would say only this: he was an extraordinary personality, rare in the annals of the Jewish people in eastern Europe. There is much to be learned from his experience and way of life, much that can serve as a source of inspiration for future generations.

Chaim Weizmann

In my native town of Pinsk, tales and legends circulated about Chaim Weizmann's student days and his early Zionist activity. My parents knew the entire Weizmann family, including Chaim, and gave me their impressions and memories of those times. Zionist activists in Pinsk also told me of their experiences with him during the period Weizmann spent in our town. Later, as the elected head of the Zionist Youth district in Polesia, I used to visit Motele, where Weizmann was born, and there I would hear from the old Jews about their Chaim and his parents. Naturally, the Jews of Motele and Pinsk were proud of Chaim Weizmann for achieving greatness among the Jewish people, and for helping to realize the Zionist ideal through his inspiring personality and powerful leadership.

I became acquainted with Chaim Weizmann on my immigration to Eretz Israel at the end of 1932. At that time he would appear at mass meetings in the Emek or at the People's Hall in Tel Aviv, conquering his audiences with his personal charm. But that was only a spectator's acquaintance. Not until I began to participate in Zionist congresses—beginning with the eighteenth in Prague in 1933—and in meetings of the Zionist General Council after my election to it in 1937, did I come into personal contact with him. On the executive council of the World Confederation of General Zionists, I was the representative of the Zionist Youth, the General Zionist Pioneer, and the Zionist Workers in Eretz Israel, and as such, I was a member of the inner circle of the confederation's leadership. The Progressive General Zionists (Zionists A) were faithful followers of Chaim Weizmann, and frequent meetings were held between him and the highest echelon of the confederation, to which I already belonged as a very young man. At those meetings Weizmann enjoyed speaking the spicy Yiddish of Pinsk, and in his intimate conversations and exchanges he emphasized his folk roots in the Jewry of Pinsk.

When I began to participate in meetings of the confederation executive in London—meetings that were headed by Rabbi Y. K. Goldblum, Professor Selig Brodetsky, and Levi Bakshtansky—I heard from them about Chaim Weizmann, his political struggles with the British Government, and his activities at the highest political levels in Great Britain from the mid-thirties until World War II.

The Zionist world traversed stormy periods when fierce opposition to Weizmann was organized by the Revisionists, headed by Ze'ev Jabotinsky, and the Radicals, headed by Yitschak Greenbaum. The opposition's main attack was against Weizmann's cooperation with the mandatory government. Those were difficult days for Weizmann, for the British government had repudiated its promises and was placing obstacles in the way of Jewish immigration to Eretz Israel and the acquisition of land for settlement. The trouble grew worse from 1936 on, those trying days of Arab violence against the Yishuv.

Although Weizmann fought with the British governments to implement the mandate in the spirit of the Balfour Declaration, he did not want to break off relations with them, for he knew that we had no other partner following the rise of the Nazis to power in Germany and their declaration of a war of liquidation on the Jewish people. I observed Weizmann at the pinnacle of his debates with political opponents at the Zionist congresses, at meetings of the Zionist General Council and in smaller committees. Given his captivating personality, it was easy to understand how he could win over statesmen and other personalities to the Zionist cause. No man better represented the Jewish people's fight for redemption and independence; no man expressed as he did the pain, the anxiety, and the fear for the fate of European Jewry at that time.

Chaim Weizmann's speech to the Peel Commission on the danger that was menacing six million Jews remains one of the most moving documents of the times; it is an expression of the power and Jewish faith of this great leader. Weizmann sought compromise and agreement with the Arab people. From the day of his historic meeting with Faisal, he never abandoned hope for the possibility of compromise. At various times he was prepared to accept flexible formulae for shaping our political future in the land of our ancestors, but he never abandoned the goal of the return to Zion and the rescue of Jews through the rebuilding of their historic homeland. Motivated by a belief in the future of the Jewish state, he worked toward its realization through constructive creation: settlement based on the redemption of "dunam after dunam." He did not accept high-flown formulations of political definitions, placing his faith instead in construction of the Zionist infrastructure by activity that would lead to the creation of the Jewish force. He therefore conceived the idea of partition—the establishment of a Jewish state in part of Palestine, to make possible the rescue of those Jews who were in danger. I was greatly influenced by Weizmann in the 'thirties. When his collected speeches and letters appeared (entitled *Devarim*), I published extensive appraisals of each volume in the *Zionist Worker* and in *Kibbutz Magazine;* I wanted our members to become familiar with the principles of his Zionist theory.

On the brink of World War II, I witnessed Weizmann's tragic appearances following the British government's betrayal of the Zionist enterprise in its desire to curry favor with the Arabs during the rise of Nazism and fascism. Weizmann was deeply apprehensive over the fate of the Yishuv. During the war he wanted a Jewish force to arise and fight the Nazi oppressor. To this end, he put pressure on Churchill to establish a Jewish brigade within the British Army. He knew that such a force would be of great significance after the war was over. Weizmann opposed terrorism; he feared that the activities of the dissident organizations would bring about an open breach with Great Britain and would endanger the peace of the Yishuv. He believed in the moral basis of our struggle on the battlefields and within the country, but opposed personal terrorism—at great risk to himself.

Weizmann traveled to the United States during World War II in order to enlist the support of American leaders for the future of the Yishuv, and for Jewish independence once the war was over. Ceaselessly he demanded that Roosevelt and Churchill, their ministers and advisers, and other Allied statesmen, grant to Zionism and the Jewish people their rights. He drew up plans for after the war and at the same time waged a tough, bitter debate within the Zionist camp. More than one crisis erupted between him and Ben-Gurion. During the war, Weizmann tried to convince the Allied leaders to rescue Jews, to bomb the extermination camps. He was consumed with anger and pain at the indifference shown by the anti-Nazi front toward the liquidation of European Jewry.

Weizmann suffered many disappointments at the hands of the Zionist movement and the Jewish people—hence his resignations and later reelection to the presidency of the World Zionist Organization. During those events I was able to observe Weizmann as he fought on both the external and internal fronts. I was convinced that no other leader of his stature had arisen among the Jewish people. He was a man who, as Ben-Gurion put it, bore two crowns: one as the sovereign leader of political Zionism; the other as a scientist, whose activity led to the establishment of the Hebrew University on Mount Scopus, the planning of the Sieff Institute, and later the foundation of the Weizmann Institute in Rehovot for the development of science and research in the Jewish state.

Once we reached the definitive parting of the ways with the British government at the end of World War II, and Bevin implemented his anti-Zionist policy, foiling attempts to bring the survivors of the Holocaust to Eretz Israel, the question of the establishment of a Jewish state in part of Palestine arose again. Weizmann wanted to avoid a confrontation between the British Army in Palestine and the fighting organizations of the Yishuv—which at one time included the Haganah, Etzel, and Lechi. When the struggle against Bevin's anti-Zionist policy grew more fierce, and illegal immigrant ships that reached the coast of Palestine were sent to Cyprus, Weizmann expressed the full measure of his anger against the hostile British authority, mobilized world opinion, and enlisted the support of political leaders in Europe and the United States against the machinations of the British government and its wanton cruelty. Once again, Weizmann used all his force of persuasion to bring about an international poltical decision in favor of the establishment of a Jewish state in part of Palestine, an idea he had conceived back in the days of the Peel Commission.

When Great Britain announced its abandonment of the mandate, and the United Nations special committee was appointed to examine the Palestine problem, Weizmann worked for a decision to that effect. As the end of the British Mandate approached, Weizmann demanded the declaration of a Jewish state.

He had no hesitation in the matter, although rumors spread through the Yishuv that he had opposed the declaration. When the state was born, Weizmann was not in Israel: he had gone to the United States to ensure more satisfactory borders for the new Jewish state and, indeed, he elicited important decisions from President Truman, notably the inclusion of Eilat and an outlet to the Red Sea within Israel's territory. Weizmann did not sign the Declaration of Independence, and Ben-Gurion did not agree to his signature being affixed to it later. This hurt Weizmann deeply, and he recalled it bitterly on more than one occasion. But when he was elected first president of the State of Israel it was clear to the entire people that he was worthy of symbolizing the constituted Jewish sovereignty, for no man had done more than he to achieve it.

During his presidency, Weizmann was already a frail and ailing man. Nor was he satisfied with the powers allocated to the president. He had become accustomed to an American-style presidential regime when he was president of the World Zionist Organization and, in effect, the "prime minister" of the state-in-the-making. But in the State of Israel, Weizmann was a president with practically no effective power. This was one of the most difficult periods in his life. He had great difficulty in adapting himself to his new position and there were times when he asked to resign.

In the relationship between Weizmann and Ben-Gurion there were periods when they reached the summit of friendship, cooperation, and mutual esteem; others of serious crisis such as often arise between two strong personalities, each of whom believes in his course and methods of action and seeks to win for himself the decisive place in the history of his people. Weizmann and Ben-Gurion may have complemented one another, and they traveled a long way together in their basic approach to the realization of Zionism. But when their ways parted, partly through misunderstanding, partly because of contradictory approaches, their exchanges were sharp and wounding.

I knew Weizmann for more than fifteen years. The fact that his wife, Vera was one of the leading friends and supporters of Youth Aliyah from its inception, and that I was in close cooperation with her, gave me the opportunity to view the Weizmann home more closely and to observe the president's personality. I was greatly influenced in the evolution of my Zionist thought by Weizmann's political conceptions and his integral, synthetic Zionist approach. Even though I sometimes disagreed with him, as I did at the Zionist Congress held after World War II, Chaim Weizmann greatly influenced my course in Zionism and the crystalization of my outlook on the realization of its principles.

Chaim Weizmann steered the ship of Zionism for thirty years. His achievements for our people were tremendous, but in the history of Zionism he will always be remembered for the most outstanding of them: the Balfour Declaration, which paved the way for the British Mandate over Palestine. Thanks to the Balfour Declaration, the World Zionist Organization acquired semisovereign status: it established national organs, became responsible for the direction of immigration and the redemption and settlement of the land, and created an economic, cultural, social and defense infrastructure that was to serve as the basis of the independent state. All that was built between 1917—the year the Balfour Declaration was issued—and the War of Independence and the declaration of the state was made possible by the promises made to us in the Balfour Declaration and in the British Mandate, whose task was to bring about the realization of the declaration.

We struggled bitterly with the British government as it backed down from the obligations it had assumed to assist in the establishment of the Jewish National Home, in the end repudiating its obligations. But thanks to the mandatory regime that was created in Eretz Israel, and the status of the World Zionst Organization and the Jewish Agency, we were able to accomplish much. It was those achievements that enabled us to win the War of Independence. The Jewish people did not adequately exploit the conditions that were created after the Balfour Declaration, and Chaim

Weizmann cried out, "Jewish People, where are you?" But what was established, the Yishuv that was growing and consolidating itself, would not have been possible without the Balfour Declaration and the Mandate. Weizmann's achievement enabled us to advance toward statehood. His policy of constructive Zionism proved itself. Declaratory Zionism would not have brought us independence.

The retreat of the British government under Arab pressure weakened Weizmann's status vis-a-vis the people and the movement, for he symbolized the cooperation between our people and our movement and the British and mandatory governments. Despite all the difficulties, both internal and external, progress was tremendous.

Nachum Sokolow

Florian Sokolow's book, *My Father, Nachum Sokolow* (The Zionist Library, 1970), is outstanding for its description of one of the greatest figures in the Zionist movement, a man who played an important part in the preparation of the road to our national independence. The book portrays Nachum Sokolow as I saw him at the beginning of the thirties, at the Zionist congresses in Prague and Lucerne in 1933 and 1935, and at other Zionist assemblies in that period.

When I was a young man Nachum Sokolow made a great impression on me. He was a Zionist leader of broad horizons, familiar with both Jewish and universal culture, a Zionist diplomat of the first order who could win over his interlocutor by his personal charm and his pleasant conversation, a prolific writer and journalist, and an orator and lecturer in several languages. There were few Jewish leaders of his caliber. I heard much about Sokolow when I was a member of the Zionist Youth leadership in Warsaw. I also met him there during one of his visits to the Polish capital. He was received with great pomp and ceremony by the Polish leaders: they regarded him as a son of Polish Jewry who had achieved international standing and wielded great influence in western capitals. At a meeting of the central committee of the World Zionist Organization in Poland, Nachum Sokolow told us that we must plan wisely for our fight against the British government's immigration decrees and white papers, and that we must take the international situation into account. He explained that it was no use fighting on several fronts at once; it was preferable to choose one main front and concentrate the bulk of the struggle there. When Hitler came to power in Germany, and the Nazi movement rocked the foundations of German and central European Jewry, menacing its very existence, Sokolow declared that the principal front was against the Nazis. Our struggle against the mandatory government would have to be selective, he said, for we would not succeed in fighting a war on two fronts simultaneously. We tried to convince

Sokolow that the menace hovering over European Jewry obliged us to increase immigration to Palestine, which in turn meant bringing pressure to bear in London on the mandatory government that was obstructing and limiting immigration. Sokolow's opinion was that we must examine carefully the arms we disposed of in these struggles; fine phrases and calls of alarm alone were not sufficient to force the Nazis to abandon their demonic plans. If we wished to organize world opinion to put pressure on Great Britain, we would have to proceed cautiously, for the partnership with Britain was the basis of our work in Eretz Israel and was vital in the struggle to rescue German Jews and, in putting pressure on the Nazi regime, to restrain its more violent elements.

Sokolow was elected president of the World Zionist Organization after Weizmann resigned in 1931, at the beginning of the tragedy of European Jewry. To assume the presidency at that time was to shoulder a heavy responsibility. The World Zionist Organization faced serious internal strife; on the one hand were the Revisionists led by Ze'ev Jabotinsky, on the other, the labor movement and the General Zionists with their different approaches and nuances. Sokolow endeavored to preserve the unity of the movement during those difficult times, and employed his political talent and his qualities of leadership to moderate the internal struggles so that we would be able to stand firm on the external fronts.

Nachum Sokolow was president of the World Zionist Organization for four years. At the nineteenth congress, in Lucerne, Chaim Weizmann resumed the presidency. Sokolow's position was difficult: he was elected honorary president of the World Zionist Organization, but his request to be present at meetings of the executive was rejected. At the congress I heard about the talks that had been held on this issue between Chaim Weizmann and a distinguished delegation of his friends—who were also friends and admirers of Sokolow—and I was very upset by Weizmann's refusal. It had seemed to me that the relations between these two men, who had worked together for so long, had not soured when Sokolow accepted the presidency. Proof of this was Weizmann's agreement to head the Committee for German Jewry, and to assume the task of mobilizing the means for their rescue and settlement in Eretz Israel during the period of Sokolow's presidency. I suppose I was too naive to plumb the depth of the relationship between the two men. Weizmann apparently never forgave Sokolow for having accepted the presidency after the seventeenth congress had passed a vote of no confidence in Weizmann.

After the Lucerne congress, Sokolow resumed his activity on behalf of the Keren Hayesod and pursued his literary and journalistic work. His articles, which appeared at that time in *Ha 'aretz*—then under the editorship of Moshe Glickson—as well as in other newspapers, were fresh and clear, outstanding for their wealth of ideas and captivating form of expression. I took a particular interest in Sokolow's literary and journalistic work at that time. As a student in Jerusalem after my arrival at the end of 1932, I earned a partial living working for the weekly paper, *The General Zionist*, edited by Shalom ben Baruch in Jerusalem. One of my tasks was to proofread Sokolow's articles. His handwriting was extremely difficult to read and the printers made many mistakes. Thus I took my first steps in journalism in Eretz Israel, and it was during that period that I met some of Jerusalem's finest writers and journalists. When Sokolow visited Eretz Israel I avidly absorbed his words at the meetings and assemblies he addressed. I was charmed by his personality, which for me symbolized the glory of Polish Jewry, the marvelous synthesis of authentic Jewish and western cultures.

Florian Sokolow's book gives us a glimpse of the Polish Jewish townlets of Wishogrud, Makov, and Plotsk, where Nachum Sokolow was born and raised. While he was still a youngster his genius manifested itself: he taught himself foreign languages so he could read the world's greatest literary masterpieces in the original text. Nachum Sokolow continued to visit the vibrant Jewish communities of the towns and hamlets of Poland whenever he had the chance, either as a journalist, a Zionist worker, or an emissary of the Zionist funds. He loved the Jewry in whose midst he had grown up. His talent as a Hebrew journalist had been discovered when he was still a youth, and attracted the attention of Chaim Selig Slonimski, founder and editor of *Hatsfira* (The Epoch).

In time, Sokolow came to share editorial responsibility with Slonimski, later becoming the paper's sole editor. He filled its columns with articles, reports and reviews of world events and Jewish problems, opening up broad horizons for his readers and enabling them to take an informed interest in the great problems confronting their people.

When Sokolow moved to Warsaw, his home became a center for conversation and debate, for the delivery of lectures, and for the exchange of views among the finest writers, philosophers, and national and Zionist leaders of Polish Jewry. For many of them, Sokolow's drawing room was the nursery where they formulated their views and took their first steps in leadership.

Here one could find Y. L. Peretz, David Frischman, Yitschak Greenbaum and many others who, in time, were to become the editors of Jewish and Hebrew papers, writers and poets, thinkers, artists, and statesmen. There were debates here between nationalist Jews and assimilationists, with the host, Nachum Sokolow, taking the lead, discreetly making his mark on those present, drawing the youth around him and influencing his guests by his personality and his comprehensive knowledge.

Nachum Sokolow's wife was of great help to her husband. She ran the *Hatsfira* when he was away—for weeks or months at a time—visiting various European countries. Sokolow continued to send back his articles and reports on those countries, describing cultural institutions and political centers, and sketching portraits of the personalities he met. Mrs. Sokolow bore the financial burden, took care of the family, and did her best to help Nachum Sokolow fulfill the tasks, which became more numerous as time went by.

Sokolow was dazzled by his visits to Paris and Rome. Since he knew both French and Italian, he was enthralled by the cultural and art treasures of these great cities. He loved France, its people, and its culture. The French statesmen, writers, and personalities who met him were conscious of this special attitude and reciprocated with their friendship. They helped him in the accomplishment of his tasks. Italy, with its works of art, won his heart. He tried to share all his experiences and reactions with the readers of *Hatsfira*, to make them feel as if they had been with him.

On his arrival in London, Sokolow sensed that the British capital was to play a great role in the history of our people and in the realization of our national destiny. He was received with exceptional honors in the British capital, by both the leaders of the press and of the Jewish community, and his personal ties multiplied both there and in the other capitals he visited. It was the same in Berlin, a great center of Jewry, where he met personalities and statesmen whom he was later to commemorate in his book *Ishim* (Personalities). Sokolow felt that he should settle in London. Despite his love of Warsaw Jewry and of Poland, the decision to move to London was imperative.

When the days of crucial decision arrived, and the struggle commenced for a declaration to be made by the British government in favor of a Jewish National Home in Palestine, Sokolow was among the leading activists—together with Chaim Weizmann, Lord Rothschild, Lord Samuel, and the heads of British Jewry—who worked for the ratification of the historic document that was to become known as the Balfour Declaration. At the same time, at the end of World War I, it was necessary to obtain similar political agreements and declarations from the French and Italian governments. That mission was entrusted to Sokolow. He achieved an extraordinary success when the French government wrote to him expressing its agreement with the British government's declaration. Sokolow also succeeded in his mission to the Pope;

his conversation with the head of the Catholic church appears almost in its entirety in Florian's book. Subsequently, Sokolow obtained declarations of support for the Jewish National Home in Palestine from the governments of Poland, Romania, and other states. There was a great flurry of activity prior to the appearance of the Jewish delegation before the victorious allies in Paris. It was a historic moment, one in which Sokolow played an important role. His connections in the European capitals were quite extraordinary, and many statesmen envied him his ability and success. Indeed, his diplomacy in those pre-statehood days produced important results.

A great part of his life was devoted to missions on behalf of the Keren Heyesod, the fund which was to make possible the construction of the Jewish National Home, the establishment of agricultural settlements, and the consolidation of a Jewish economy in the ancestral homeland. His appearances in the United States attained the pinnacle of success, for here he met all those who had been brought up on his articles in *Hatsfira* and had later emigrated to the United States. Sokolow's fame as a Jewish leader preceded him, and in every American Jewish community crowds flocked to hear him. It was the same in South Africa, where the Lithuanian Jews welcomed him enthusiastically. Thus, Sokolow reaped a great success in all the far-flung Jewish communities he visited on his fund-raising missions and on political and Zionist business.

Sokolow's visits to Eretz Israel were great experiences for him. Here, he felt the pulse of the new creation for which he strove, and with which he was linked in every fiber of his being. He was received with warmth, affection, and esteem. His appearances at mass rallies in Tel Aviv and Jerusalem, at new settlements or in established villages, drew young and old from all sections of the population. These visits gave him the encouragement he needed to continue his role as leader, for his inspiration came from the land of Israel, which he loved and for which he labored and lived. But throughout his life no one ever thought of building a home for him within the national home.

Florian Sokolow's book, written by a loving son, sculpts the figure of Nachum Sokolow life-size. He tried to be as objective as possible. We owe him our thanks for reviving for us the cherished, wonderful figure of his great father.

The Zionist Executive should fulfill an obligation it has to one of the presidents of the World Zionist Organization, and one of the great leaders of our people: it should devote resources to the care of the Sokolow archives, his diaries, his interesting letters, and his unpublished writings. Grants should be given to students to carry out research into areas in which Sokolow played a central role. Nachum Sokolow's literary and spiritual heritage requires attention and should be published in full.

Yitschak Ben-Zvi

Yitschak Ben-Zvi, the second president of the State of Israel, was the personification of pioneer values, Jewish tradition, love of the people and the homeland, simplicity of manner and modesty. He was deeply attached to the historic path of Israel's Labor movement, of which he was one of the founders and builders. Yitschak Ben-Zvi embodied the best of the new Israeli who enhances the annals of our people. In addition to being a statesmen, he was a historian of Eretz Israel and carried out research into its past. Already at the beginning of his Zionist career in his hometown of Poltava in the Russian Ukraine, he was among the young colleagues of Dov-Ber Borochov, ideologue of the Zionist workers movement.

His public activity began when Ben-Zvi came to the defense of Jews against Russian rioters in his hometown. In Eretz Israel he was one of the founders of the Haganah and of its precursor, Ha-Shomer. As one of the founders of the movement, he was able to adapt the philosophy of the Zionist workers movement to the emerging reality in Eretz Israel, and participated in the establishment of the Histadrut (the General Federation of Labor).

Ben-Zvi was popular among all sections of the population. He took an interest in all the communities of Israel, doing much to bring them together and unite them into one people. All his life he took an interest in the most minute details of life in various communities. Ben-Zvi knew how to foster relations with the Palestinian Arabs and did his utmost to bring Jews and Arabs closer through goodwill and mutual assistance. He paid particular attention to the problems of the Arab workers. Ben-Zvi is also considered one of the founders of archeological and historical research in Eretz Israel. When he traced the origins and remains of far-flung branches of the Jewish people, he sought to uncover the traces of our past in our land, doing so discreetly and modestly, without publicity.

I met Yitschak Ben-Zvi in the thirties, when I used to come to the

National Council Executive to meet Eliyahu Berlin, one of the leaders of the progressive democratic Zionists in what was the General Zionist camp. Ben-Zvi, then president of the National Council, and Eliyahu Berlin, its treasurer, were great friends. They were both leaders of Knesset Israel and pillars of the National Council, which represented the Yishuv in Eretz Israel. From our first meeting I was deeply impressed by Ben-Zvi's personality, his pleasant manner, and the way he drew me to him. I met his wife Rachel, too, also a founder of the labor movement, and one of the promoters of agricultural training institutions for youth. Like her husband, Rachel was one of the leaders of the workers' movement and among the founders of the Haganah. In their wooden dwelling in Rehavia I observed the simple pioneering way of life of the Yishuv leaders, outstanding personalities on the Jerusalem scene. I came to know Yitschak Ben-Zvi better over the years, particularly after I had read his studies and learned of his struggles within the Jerusalem Municipality. I was full of admiration for the way in which he represented the Yishuv to the high commissioner and the mandatory government. I observed Ben-Zvi during the great struggles of those trying, turbulent days when the mandatory government repudiated its promises, closing the gates of the country to prevent the rescue of European Jewry and betraying the historic mission it had assumed in the land of the Bible.

During World War II, Ben-Zvi was a partner in all the efforts to rescue Jews from the Nazi hell. He knew no respite, but he did things his own way based on an attachment to the basic principles of Zionist policy, which sprang from the pure sources of a great past. Ben-Zvi made use of the many languages he knew. Since his arrival in Eretz Israel he had learned Arabic, and in 1909–10, as a student in Istanbul, he had learned Turkish. He acquired English during his stay in the United States after his expulsion from Eretz Israel, and it was there that, together with Ben-Gurion, he founded the pioneer movement. He continued to study, drawing inspiration from the sources of the past. His special qualities manifested themselves during his years as president of the National Council, during his membership in the Knesset after the establishment of the state, and during his term as president of the State of Israel.

When Ben-Zvi was elected president after the death of Chaim Weizmann, the wooden presidential home became the symbol of the new pioneering Israel that believed in the loftiest Jewish and human values. A new tradition was established: representatives of the communities and sects from the various Diasporas gathered there to talk about their life and customs, sing and perform, and reveal their unique cultural assets. The entire people knew that the president was *their* president, a part of them, and bonds of love grew between the presidency and the people of Israel as it gathered together from its places of exile. At the president's wooden home, gatherings were held of scholars who were doing research on Eretz Israel, of writers and poets, rabbis, simple folk, representatives of pioneering border settlements, and military personnel. Diplomats who come to the presidential residence were deeply impressed by the modesty and simplicity of the dwelling, the like of which they had not seen in other countries. Rachel Ben-Zvi employed her energy and her personality to leave that imprint on the presidential home. During Ben-Zvi's presidency I was head of Youth Aliyah. Absorption and education matters brought me into close contact with Rachel, and the presidential home became an august meeting place for Youth Aliyah leaders and trainees who came for conventions. On more than one occasion workers from Youth Aliyah abroad gathered there, receiving encouragement in their great work from the highest moral authority in the State of Israel.

Indeed, the presidential home during Ben-Zvi's term rendered outstanding service to Youth Aliyah. We regarded it as our home, and it was open to us when we organized nationwide events, during observance of World Jewish Children's Day, and whenever international seminars on children and youth were held in Israel. President Ben-Zvi himself participated in various events thoughout the country. He attended the inauguration of Kfar Juliana, named after the queen of Holland; inaugurated with us the synagogue at Ramat-Hadassah-Szold, an absorption and transit center for Youth Aliyah children, and was quite at home in Youth Aliyah institutions all over the country. During his visits he spoke words of encouragement and appreciation for the manner in which the immigrant children were educated and rehabilitated.

Yitschak Ben-Zvi was familiar with Youth Aliyah from the training farm in Talpiot that his wife had founded and continued to direct with great ability. He had also been in contact with the youth village that was established in Ein Karem immediately after the War of Independence— well before his incumbency as president—when Rachel was living there. He would visit, meet the immigrant children and youth, and spend much time with them. Youth Aliyah may be said to have been spiritually close to Ben-Zvi. It was an enterprise whose content and development he had known from the time he collaborated with Henrietta Szold, then a member of the National Council Executive, who was responsible for the social welfare department and youth education. Yitschak and Rachel Ben-Zvi's home was, in no small measure, Youth Aliyah's home.

I had the privilege of many discussions with Ben-Zvi about research on Eretz Israel, problems of settlement, and state and educational, and religious questions. We prayed together at the Hanassi synagogue in

Rehavia where I sat beside him and saw him pray with devotion. On many occasions during the reading of the Torah I heard his explanatory comments.

After the death of Israel's second president I was among the first to propose the establishment of a Ben-Zvi memorial in the form of a research project on Eretz Israel to be devoted in particular to the study of the Yishuv of which Ben-Zvi had been one of the founders and promoters. The intention was to establish a center for the study of all that had been created in the past century, from the days of Mikve Israel down to the present. It is a pleasure to see that the Yad Ben-Zvi has made significant progress in the fulfillment of these goals. With the installation of the presidential residence in its permanent premises, the wooden building was transferred to Yad Ben-Zvi, giving great impetus to its activity. Ben-Zvi's writings were republished and widely read. Material about him was disseminated through the Yad in conjunction with the Ministry of Education and Culture. The great activity that surrounds meeting devoted to the study of Eretz Israel and the Yishuv will continue to remind the citizens of Israel today and for generations to come of the significance of Yitschak Ben-Zvi's lofty personality as Israel renewed its independence, and of his contribution to the realization of the vision of redemption and of our renewed sovereignty in our homeland.

Yitschak Ben-Zvi's warm, vibrant personality will continue to inspire the people of Israel and the state, and will serve them as a model.

Zalman Shazar

Zalman Shazar, third president of the State of Israel, was unique. A prominent figure in the Labor Zionist movement, in the Yishuv, in the state, and in world Jewry, his personality was a marvelously harmonious combination of spiritual values that sprang from contrasting sources far removed from each other. Shazar was well versed in both the Written and the Oral Law. On the one hand, he was a brilliant orator who could captivate his listeners with a style that was in the best tradition of Jewish preachers; on the other, a highly competent lecturer on scientific and literary subjects. He was a talented writer, with clarity of style, profundity of thought, and simplicity of expression. But Shazar had a poetic soul, too, and he gave expression to it in Hebrew and Yiddish poetry. His last book, *Livyat-Niv* (Nuances of Expression), contained selected Hebrew poems. When I received my copy, he was already confined to his sickbed.

From his youth, Shazar (Rubashov) studied the Torah at home and with teachers at the heder and the yeshiva. Steeped in Jewish learning, he was an expert in the Talmud, in the Halacha, and in the ramifications of the generations of rabbinical literature. As a historian, Zalman Shazar approached the history of the Jewish people with personal knowledge and perception. His book, *Orei Dorot* (Lights of the Generations) proves that in his studies of the history of the Messianic movement, he sought the sparks of redemption, the longing for Jewish national revival, in the darkest periods of our people's history.

At the same time, Shazar was a fine theoretician of the ideology of socialist Zionism and a faithful interpreter of the philosophy of Ber Borochov, one of the leading thinkers of the Labor Zionist movement. A skilled polemicist, he could deal with anti-Zionists—those who in one way or another denied Jewish nationalism, or Jewish socialists who were cut off from the sources of their people and hated their Jewishness. As a socialist philosopher, he did much at sessions of the Second (Socialist) International (founded in Paris in 1889) to win friends for Zionism.

Zalman Shazar enjoyed revealing the illuminating aspects of the great periods in the history of Jewish settlement in Israel. His papers on the period of Rabbi Joseph Caro and the holy Ari of Safed, and on the Golden Age of Tiberias in the days of Don Joseph Nassi and Doña Gracia, make delightful, spellbinding reading.

Shazar was a Hasid, and with all his being he lived the Hasidic movement, its currents and its courts. He himself was a member of the Habad group. A faithful follower of his rabbi, he was well versed in Hasidic literature and in the history of the struggle between Hasidim and Mitnaggedim in the days of the Gaon of Vilna and his disciples. When he hummed the tunes of Rabbi Shneour Zalman of Ladi, Shazar was spiritually uplifted. The Hasidim of Habad considered him one of them, and were proud of him. His visits to Kfar Habad became exciting folk experiences. When he was President of the State, Shazar ignored the criticism voiced against him for going to visit the Rabbi of Lubavitch, instead of waiting for the rabbi to call on him, and pay the respects due to the President of the State of Israel. Shazar decided that the President of the State would visit the President of Habad. His fidelity to Hasidism was rooted in his childhood: it came from his father, his grandfather, his milieu, and from the Habad philosophy, which he studied deeply and to which he remained faithful.

Shazar was simultaneously a propounder of the socialist Zionism of the labor movement and one of the most brilliant orators at labor assemblies and at Histadrut conferences and councils. Back in the Kinneret days, he became acquainted with the poet Rachel and patronized her work. It was then, too, that he met Berl Katznelson, who was to become his mentor in the labor movement and in the party. Even in those early days, the kibbutz movement found a place in Shazar's rich soul. He saw in the kibbutz a marvelous establishment of socialist and Zionist values in their day-to-day realization. Meeting Shazar on kibbutzim, it would occur to me that he must have seen in this socioeconomic creation a kind of Hasidic continuity and rediscovery in our generation.

I met Shazar when I first arrived in Eretz Israel at the end of 1932. I had already heard much about him at home in Pinsk, both in the youth movement and in the Zionist Federation. Zalman Rubashov, whose speeches sent sparks flying, was well known throughout the Jewish communities. I was to become more closely acquainted when we were both members of the Histadrut Executive, and later of the Zionist Executive. Shazar was head of the Department of Education and Culture in the Diaspora, and at times, also acted as chairman of the executive. He devoted special attention to Mosad Bialik and to the Zionist Library Publishing House, and he did much to present the spiritual heritage of our people to the young generation in a new form, and by suitable means. At that time I used to visit his home. We would talk for hours about the dangers to the Jewish people of assimilation, and about the need to establish a network of Jewish schools as a sure bulwark against assimilation and intermarriage.

Shazar visited distant communities and encouraged the people involved with Hebrew education and culture. He also established friendly ties with Yiddish writers and educators, mainly in Latin America. Because of the dire lack of Hebrew teachers, he established the Institute for Teachers in the Diaspora. It was dedicated to his friend Chaim Greenberg, Zionist philosopher and member of the Zionist Executive. Shazar was well acquainted with American Jewry. He had worked in the United States as a Histadrut emissary, and had seen the decline of Yiddish journalism and literature there. In the Jewish Agency Executive he did much to raise the level of discussion, and we always enjoyed his contributions to the debates. His remarks were sound and profound. Even when one differed from him it was with respect.

When I was head of Youth Aliyah, Shazar save me great encouragement. He knew the Jews of Germany well, for he had studied there. He clearly remembered the beginnings of the organization when Recha Freier gathered around her young boys and girls who had been dismissed from German schools, and prepared them for their aliyah to Eretz Israel and their absorption in kibbutzim. Shazar took an interest in all of Youth Aliyah's educational activities and in its rehabilitation work, both with children who had survived the Holocaust and with those who had immigrated from Arab countries. During his presidency we held conferences at the presidential residence, and found that he knew most of the educators who participated.

Zalman Shazar was one of the most learned men in contemporary Israel. He acquired his vast knowledge at the Baron Ginzberg "Institute" in Petrograd, at German universities, from independent study, and from his deep penetration into Jewish and Hebrew literature. He had an extraordinary memory—like the proverbial plastered cistern that does not lose a drop. He remembered everything—hence his easy access to Jewish sources. His speeches at gatherings of writers, rabbis and historians, educators, and Zionist thinkers were always of such exceptional interest that his audiences were spellbound.

Shazar had a special talent for sketching personality portraits. His appraisals were wonderful creations. His book *Or Ishim* (Personalities), in which he drew portraits of his teachers, colleagues, and friends, is a brilliant achievement in monographic literature. It can compete with Nahum Sokolow's *Ishim*. Shazar also wrote memoirs. *Kokhvei Boker*

(Morning Stars) is a work that merits study. It describes his milieu, his family, Jewish life in his hometown, and other periods of his life.

Shazar was greatly influenced by David Ben-Gurion, who won him over completely with his vision of political sovereignty. Shazar respected and admired Ben-Gurion, and held him in great affection. As for Ben-Zvi, from the days of Ber Borokhov Shazar had regarded him as his mentor. When Ben-Zvi was president, the three of us used to pray at the "Hanassi" Synagogue in the Rahavia suburb of Jerusalem, and there I observed how high was the esteem in which Shazar held Ben-Zvi. When, after Ben-Zvi's death, Shazar was elected President of the State, he maintained the tradition, set by his predecessor, of a presidential residence open to the Jewish people of the Diaspora and to Jews from the Diaspora living in Israel: they used to hold counsel together at the residence. When Yom Kippur was over, people would come to the residence to sing and celebrate, among them Hasidim and musicians. This was a tradition from Second Temple times, when the high priest would make a feast for his close friends after he had entered and left the Holy of Holies in peace, and had completed his tasks as emissary of the people of Israel before their Creator on the great holy day. Like Ben-Zvi, Shazar would spend the entire day of Yom Kippur at the synagogue in prayer and supplication. I felt that he regarded himself as an emissary of the entire people of Israel as he prayed for peace and security.

The two presidents had much in common. They were both scholars, both labor leaders, both founders of the Poalei Zion movement, and both leaders and builders of the Histadrut, whose basic principles they helped formulate. Both were steeped in the culture of Israel; both were closely involved with the various communities of which the people of Israel are composed; and both were accepted by the nation as seeking its unity and its highest spiritual values. Yitschak Ben-Zvi expressed himself with reserve and was a cool-tempered man. Even when he wished to react forcefully, he did so after reflection and in a level-headed manner. Shazar, by contrast, was easily roused, lyrical, and emotional in his literary expression.

In his last will Shazar expressed the wish that on his death there be no eulogies; he had eulogized too many people in his lifetime. And indeed, Shazar's eulogies were works of art; like the preacher-eulogizers of the past, he would bring the personality of the deceased to life so skillfully that his listeners were moved to tears. Many of the eulogies were later reworked into monographs and published in books and newspapers. The personalities in his book *Or Ishim* seem to be carved in stone, yet are alive.

Shazar was a humanist, versed not only in his people's culture but also in that of the Western world. While still in Russia he studied the Russian authors who have won an eternal place in world culture. In Germany, he acquired his knowledge of the great German philosophers, writers, dramatists and poets. And he familiarized himself with the writers of England and the United States, too. He always had an honorable place at international gatherings of intellectuals and men of letters, and took a prominent part in them. He was a fine translator into Hebrew, an exemplary editor, a decision maker in matters of Judaism, Zionism, and socialism, and a man accepted by circles far removed from each other. He had an exceptional talent for gathering around him men who believed in his good intentions and were influenced by his radiant personality.

Shazar was privileged to serve as the first minister of education and culture of the State of Israel. He was indeed worthy of the honor, for he was an expert in educational affairs. He was one of the educators of his generation, able to give expression to the wealth of Hebrew culture at all levels. I often wondered whether Shazar was not sacrificing his knowledge and talents to his public activities. But the truth was that he enjoyed public life for it enabled him to fuse the eternal and the contemporary. It was not in his character to concentrate only on the past. He was among those who left their mark on Israel in our time and he had a gift for bringing together worlds that were far apart. Everyone regarded him as a member of their camp, and no one was prepared to do without him. It is not easy to write about Zalman Shazar. One does not lightly compete with his own talent for describing people.

Engraved in my memory are interesting episodes from my meetings and conversations with Shazar when I was a member of the Histadrut Executive during World War II. At that time he used to go out for rifle practice so that he would be able to shoot if the Nazis invaded. I remember, too, the period when we worked together at the Jewish Agency and our discussions at that time, then the days in the Knesset, the Ministry of Education, and finally, the presidency.

Shazar's literary work, which he managed to republish at the end of his life, is varied and interesting, and those who read it cannot fail to be influenced by it. But even that body of work does not give full expression to the personality of this lover of Israel, this vibrant conversationalist, this smiling, pleasant man who influenced all those who surrounded him or came in contact with him. Zalman Shazar died at a ripe old age, an outstanding president of the people and state of Israel. Much will yet be written about him.

Israel was blessed to have had in its first three presidents men who left their mark on two generations, laid the foundations of the state, and molded its life-style for the coming generations. Shazar was a great admirer of Chaim Weizmann, and marveled at the splendor of his personality. They were both born in small towns, went out into the world, and fought their people's battles in order to bring Israel to a secure haven. They both sprang from the same roots, and their devotion to their people was obvious in their conversations and discussions, in their personal encounters, and in their conduct of vital missions. Weizmann, Ben-Zvi, and Shazar symbolize the period of national awakening, the struggle for independence and the first twenty-five years of Israel's statehood.

The death of Zalman Shazar brought to a close one chapter in the history of the presidency of Israel. He was one of the last of the great men to go to his eternal rest.

Yitschak Greenbaum

After a full life, Yitschak Greenbaum died as he was nearing the ripe old age of ninety-one. Two years before his death he told me that he did not wish to die as his father had, old and senile. Greenbaum's wish was realized: he was fully rational when he died. After living for twelve years at Kibbutz Gan Shmuel near his son and his family, Greenbaum had moved to Tel Aviv to be among his followers and admirers.

Today we can look back to Greenbaum's first steps, and place his achievments and those of his generation in their historical perspective. The leaders of the state, friends and admirers, celebrated his ninetieth birthday with him. I noted then that we were marking that important date in Greenbaum's life as the great history of Polish Jewry was coming to an end; even the handful of Jews who had remained in Poland, and in recent years had been the victims of anti-Semitic Communism, were leaving their homes. They could no longer breathe freely in that stifling atmosphere; they could no longer live a continuous nightmare.

Greenbaum passed away as Polish Jewry died out. It was a tragic symbol; and yet it was of great significance from the Jewish—and perhaps even the general—point of view that these two dates coincided. Greenbaum's lifetime covered a period of splendor and heroism, of war and struggle, of achievement—and of destruction and annihilation.

In 1950, Greenbaum wrote in the preface to his book *Hador Bamivchan* (The Generation Put to the Test): "There is no happier generation than mine, a generation that began life in Poland at the beginning of the century and was privileged to reach the present time; and there is no generation unhappier than mine, a generation that brought such an enormous sacrifice in blood during the first fifty years of that century, a period of progress and achievement, of suffering and destruction. In all the generations of our people from the day it went into exile there has been none like it."

These lines summarize Greenbaum's feelings twenty years before his death, after he had had the privilege of witnessing the renewal of Jewish sovereignty.

Yitschak Greenbaum was born in Warsaw on November 24, 1879. He was educated in Plonsk and Plotsk and completed his law degree at the Faculty of Law in Warsaw. Most of his life was spent in the Polish capital: it was the center of his struggles and the place where his great leadership abilities flourished. Other periods of his life were to be spent in Vilna, Saint Petersburg, Paris, Jerusalem, Tel Aviv and Gan Shmuel. Greenbaum grew up among the Jewish masses in Poland; he lived their problems and dreamed their dreams; his pulse beat to the rhythm of those masses, who were counted in the millions. He stood at their head, fought their battles and was their acknowledged and respected leader. As a high school pupil at the gynasium in Plonsk he had been attracted to Zionism. For him, the renaissance movement and the redemption of the people were the essence of his life.

Let us recall some of the struggles Greenbaum fought during his long life.

The Two Fronts of the Renaissance Movement

Greenbaum was among those who paved the way for practical Zionism. On the one hand he worked for the construction of the Yishuv in Eretz Israel, for the immigration of pioneers and the conquest of the land by labor; on the other hand, he was the most consistent fighter in the struggle for equal rights for the Jews in the Diaspora. He was one of the most active delegates to the Helsingfors Conference, and among those who faithfully implemented its doctrine in Poland.

He considered the construction of the National Home—the striving for a Jewish State—as the main goal, but at the same time he was constantly involved in the day-to-day problems of the Jewish masses in the Diaspora. He took the lead in the struggle for the rights of national minorities and against anti-Semitism, worked to strengthen the communities, to build schools, and to educate the children in a spirit of Jewish nationalism. At the same time he fought to reinforce Zionism, and the spirit of national renaissance, for as long as the Jewish masses remained in the Diaspora.

When he returned to Poland after World War I, he was elected a delegate to the Sejm and appointed head of the elected Jewish representatives to the Polish Parliament. He fought his people's battle, stiffened the backbone of the masses, and saved a considerable part of the young generation from assimilation, whether to Communism or to Polish nationalism. In the course of these struggles he endeared himself to Polish Jewry; indeed, they placed him on a pedestal. During that period he did much to restore the Polish Jewish community, which had been severly affected by World War I.

But he never forgot the essential: the rebuilding in the historic homeland of the Jewish people. He considered the Balfour Declaration the beginning of the redemption, and within the framework of his struggles for the rights of the Jews in Poland he assumed an active role in the creation of a network of Jewish schools, acted on behalf of the national funds, encouraged the Hehalutz and other Zionist youth movements, and strengthened immigration to Eretz Israel.

He pursued these activities in independent Poland until his immigration to Palestine in 1933. At that time anti-Semitism and totalitarianism were growing in Poland, stifling almost every possibility of continuing the struggle for Jewish national minority rights there.

At the end of World War II Yitschak Greenbaum came to the most tragic conclusions about what had to be done in the Diaspora: Polish Jewry was no longer; it had been annihilated. He had reached his conclusions at a time when hundreds of thousands of Jews were repatriated to Poland from Soviet Russia, walking about like shadows in the ruins of the Jewish communities:

> Every assistance must be given to the survivors, but no effort must be made to renew the diaspora or restore its ruins. All our efforts must be directed toward throwing off the yoke of the diaspora and concentrating the people in its free homeland. . . . There is no place for human life in the cemeteries. As Poland rises from the ruins, the remains of its Jewish community see no place for themselves within it, and do not feel themselves partners with the Polish people in the work of reconstruction. . . . The history of the Jewish people in Poland is at an end. So history has decreed, and there is no appeal.

What tragedy is expressed in these lines! Those who remember the glory of Polish Jewry when Yitschak Greenbaum lead the masses, then three-million strong, will be moved to tears by his words. They were written by a man who had drunk the poisoned cup to the dregs; his words echo Lamentations.

The National Minorities Bloc

Greenbaum's fight for Jewish rights in Poland was enhanced by one of his most daring political acts, one that gave rise to much controversy: establishment of the National Minorities Bloc, which he organized with the other national minorities prior to the elections to the Sejm, the Polish Parliament. He built a complete doctrine around the rights of national minorities and, after World War I, was one of the leaders of the movement in Europe. In the wake of the Versailles Treaty new states were set up within which were national minorities, whose special rights were safeguarded in the peace treaties. Those minorities had common interests. For the most part they were territorial minorities who lived on their own land and had their own languages and cultures. Not so the Jewish minority, which was scattered among different countries.

Greenbaum claimed that the rights of the scattered minority must be safeguarded in the same way as were the rights of the national territorial minorities. He developed the concept that Poland was a pluralistic state composed of many nationalities, and that it had to ensure the welfare not only of the Polish people but also of all the minorities within it. It must allow them national-cultural autonomy, guarantee them equal rights, and develop within them a sense of complete participation in the life of the state. He brought the Jews into partnership with the other national minorities, establishing the common front that aroused the admiration—and fear—of the Polish people.

The situation of the Jews in Central Poland was slightly different from that of their brethren in the eastern border villages and in Galicia, where they lived among either White Russians or Poles and Ukrainians. The eastern Jews' situation was extremely delicate, and led to a sharp debate over the Bloc and the justice of its course. The National Minorities Bloc did not last long but it is worth recalling, for it demonstrated the great daring of a Jewish nationalist leader.

Radical Zionism—Al Hamishmar

Greenbaum was a popular Zionist leader all his life. The socialist roots of his Zionism found original expression in a manifesto appealing to Jewish workers to join the "Revolutionary Movement of the Jewish People."

"Zionism awakens the Jewish people to life and to work. But we will not be able to begin a new life until all the minorities and opinions which dominate our people's attitude to life and work, to honor and human feeling undergo a radical change." Thus wrote Greenbaum in 1903, calling upon the Jewish workers to mobilize for the liberation of our people. He demanded a change in the values guiding the building of the Yishuv. This approach lead him to a firm partnership with the settlers, the workers, the builders of kibbutzim and moshavim—all those who were revolutionizing national values in Eretz Israel.

His Zionism was rich in social and cultural content. It stood for social and cultural renewal in terms of Jewish nationalism, advocating the theory of the nationalist Jew conquering his land by his labor, his creativity, and his blood. It was thus only natural that he always fought for the true democratic substance of Zionism. He strove for the complete fusion of nationalist, social, and cultural values—which, in fact, was the aim of radical Zionism, one of whose leaders and creators he was.

He fought against the expansion of the Jewish Agency, fearing that it would blur the popular and democratic character of the Zionist movement. He came out against the pettiness and short-sightedness of the Zionists "bosses" who wanted to rouse the Jewish middle class in Poland against the members of Hechalutz and the kibbutz builders.

With a group of friends he organized the Al Hamishmar (On Guard) group, calling for a struggle for democratic Zionist values and the liberating substance of the movement. At its inception it was a minority within the General Zionist organization in Poland, but after a few years Al Hamishmar grew to be the majority. It educated Polish Zionism in revolutionary Zionist values and pushed for alliance with the labor movement in Palestine. At that time Greenbaum met Jabotinsky: both of them were engaged in the struggle against Weizmann's collaboration with the mandatory government. But communication between the Radicals and the Revisionists was never established because of their differing approaches to social values and to the labor movement in Eretz Israel.

Difficulties of Integration into the General Zionist Camp

Greenbaum was a classic General Zionist in the broad sense of the term. He considered the General Zionist movement to be the Jewish renaissance movement, with its wealth of social, cultural, and revolutionary content. In fact, his radical Zionism was the expression of his General Zionism. In his view, General Zionism was a movement from which the socialist and religious Zionists had broken away, leaving those who did not identify with only one sector or class of the people.

When Zionism began to crystallize it was not easy for Greenbaum to merge with the General Zionist camp and to find his place within it. The World Confederation of General Zionists was not established until 1935—after the split that took place at the World Conference of General Zionists at Cracow between the right, class-conscious wing that wished to separate from the Histadrut and establish its own workers' organization, and the various groups that made up the Progressive Zionist wing. United within it were Zionists loyal to Weizmann, the Progressive Zionists in Eretz Israel, and members of the Zionist Workers and the Young

Zionist. It was also joined by the Radical Zionists, including Greenbaum and his friends, who were integrated within the confederation.

In his youth Greenbaum had belonged to the Democratic Zionist faction, the first nucleus of the Progressive Zionist Synthesis movement, which fought for the combining of political, spiritual, cultural and practical Zionism.

After his election to the Zionist executive at the Prague Congress in 1933, Greenbaum settled in Eretz Israel. I then wrote in *Ha'aretz* that the time had come for Weizmann and Greenbaum, together with their colleagues who had established the Democratic Zionist faction, to revive the movement in Eretz-Israel. Dr. Moshe Glickson, then editor-in-chief of *Ha'aretz*, supported the idea. And, indeed, efforts were made to unite the Progressive and Democratic Zionists, the Radical Zionists, including Greenbaum, the Zionists of German origin led by Kurt Blumenfeld and Felix Rosenbluth, and the members of the Zionist Youth and the Zionist Workers into a single force that would renew the grandeur of Progressive General Zionism.

The combination was not easy to achieve, for the people concerned had been leaders of different schools of thought in the countries in which they had lived, and they were not prepared to accept a new authority or corporate leadership. The union was made all the more difficult after Greenbaum gave in to his follower, Moshe Kleinbaum (Sneh), who united the Union of General Zionists and the General Zionist Alliance, almost liquidating the progressive wing of General Zionism as a result.

Greenbaum's position was weak at the time. The Zionist Workers did not join. The Zionists of German origin also stayed out, and established Aliyah Chadasha (the New Aliyah). If the Radical Zionists led by Greenbaum, the German Zionists, the Democratic and Progressive Zionists in Eretz Israel and the workers and pioneers of the Zionist Youth and the Zionist Workers had united in the early thirties into one organization, they would by now have become a strong and influential camp within the state.

Only the Progressive General Zionist Party, and later the Independent Liberal Party, continued that course in Israel. But the great force crumbled. This put the leaders who failed to foresee the future in a tragic position.

His Attitude to the Zionist Youth Movement

Greenbaum's relations with the Zionist Youth (Hanoar Hatzioni) began in an atmosphere of skepticism and suspicion. When the Zionist Youth was established in Poland, it was based on a belief in General

Zionism as a renaissance and revolutionary movement abounding in ideas and ambitions and capable of providing an answer to the hopes for redemption of the young Jewish generation. Greenbaum was not among the first to help and encourage it. At first he was skeptical, fearing that this was merely a disguised attempt by right-wing, classs-conscious Zionists to draw Jewish and Zionist youth away from complete pioneering fulfillment. In 1928 he published an article in *Derech Hashomer Haleumi* (The Way of the National Guardsman) in which he tried to convince the movement that it should be an educational organization only, not a youth movement that would go on to implement its principles in Eretz Israel. When Greenbaum was asked why he had suggested this, he replied openly, as was his wont, that he greatly feared that after the pioneers and graduates of the movement immigrated, they would try to establish a separate, antisocialist workers' federation in Palestine.

To his credit it should be recalled that he did not maintain this stand for long. When the Zionist Youth pioneers immigrated, built kibbutzim, joined the General Federation of Labor—the Histadrut—established their own group within it, stood watch (and were arrested) in the defense of Jewish labor, and participated in every pioneer action, Greenbaum was the first to support them. He declared that the pioneers of the Zionist Youth and the Zionist Workers had belied his suspicions, and that their efforts to renew General Zionism constituted a daring, successful experiment.

Real friendship developed between the Zionist Youth and the Zionist Workers and Greenbaum. But there was not a complete identification between them and misunderstandings sometimes arose; it would seem that the skepticism that had accompanied the birth of our movement had not disappeared completely. Greenbaum did remain sympathetic to our labor movement and to the Histadrut as we fought within that camp in defense of our course and our opinions—a struggle that was to justy itself.

Thus there were ups and downs in our relationship with Greenbaum. In the end, after the establishment of the state, our ways parted. A certain kinship remained, but not an identity of views. It may well be that the generation gap was partly responsible, since our fundamental Zionist beliefs were identical.

The Struggle for the Secularization of Jewish Life

Greenbaum was a staunch fighter for the secularization of Jewish life. He was consistent and uncompromising. In this he continued the struggle of the Enlightment, which sought to throw off religious constraints and rabbinical authority. In his view, Zionism was a rebellion against the authority of the rabbis and of the Orthodox. He demanded the separation of religion and state, of the renaissance movement—Zionism—and religion.

However, in the Jewish Agency Executive he reached a complete understanding with the religious element. His good relations with Rabbi Yehuda Leib Maimon are well known, and sometimes he even found the golden mean in his relations with the Aguda. The agreement with the religious parties was based on the assumption that they would not interfere in the life of the Zionist movement and the state and would live as they pleased, on condition that they did not attempt to force their will on the majority of Israeli citizens.

Greenbaum's fight for secularization had its roots in the Polish Jewish scene. The anti-Zionist rabbis and teachers were against taking matters into their own hands and not waiting for the Messiah, which in their view was what Zionism was doing. The religious elements compromised with the Polish authorities and cooperated with them after having been granted authority over the Jewish communities, whereas the Zionists fought for the rights of the national minority, for internal democracy in the community and in the life of the people, and for national social revival.

Greenbaum continued his struggle for decades, first within the Zionist movement and later within the state. He was extreme in regarding the religious authority as a danger to the state. Even his closest colleagues did not accept his approach to religion and the religious elements. Nor did the members of the Zionist Youth and the Zionist movement. Dr. Moshe Glickson's call for synthesis appealed to them more. The truth is that the religious parties in Israel made Greenbaum's struggle easy for him and strengthened him in his opinions. Fears of a confrontation between the majority of Israel's citizens and the religious parties led to postponement of debate on a constitution. Greenbaum continued his struggle consistently and uncompromisingly, arousing the admiration both of his opponents and of those who were in partial agreement with him for his firm stand.

In Favor of a Jewish State in Eretz Israel

As head of the Radical Zionists, Greenbaum for years opposed collaboration with the mandatory government. The symbol of collaboration was Dr. Chaim Weizmann. For Greenbaum, Weizmann's compromises were too far-reaching. Following publication of the Passfield White Paper,

Weizmann resigned in protest, and a committee was set up to negotiate with Ramsay MacDonald; the Radicals, with Greenbaum at their head, then stood by Weizmann.

After the decision was taken to establish the expanded Jewish Agency—a decision which Greenbaum fought bitterly—the Radicals also decided to join. Their opposition was statesmanlike and responsible, an attitude expressed after publication of the Peel Commission's report, which for the first time proposed the establishment of a Jewish state in part of Palestine.

Greenbaum then extended a helping hand to Weizmann, stood firmly behind him, and joined the campaign in favor of the plan. From then on he fought consistently for the proposed Jewish state in Palestine.

At that time a stormy debate was raging within the Zionist Movement as to whether we should demand the whole of Palestine as a Jewish state, on the assumption that eventually we would have to compromise, or frankly propose partition as the sole solution. Greenbaum was against the tactical approach, favoring maximum candor on the question. At congresses, and at meetings of the Zionist Actions Committee before and during World War II, he fought unflinchingly for a state in part of Palestine. He argued that we should learn from the Maccabees, who contented themselves with a small state to begin with in the hope that they would expand in the future.

On the day independence was declared at the museum in Tel Aviv, Greenbaum was in Jerusalem, and so was unable to participate in the festive occasion. During the siege and the battle for the capital, he assumed responsibility there in his capacity as one of Israel's leaders. He had the privilege of being a member of the provisional government and the country's first minister of the interior. The vision of this veteran fighter and leader had been fulfilled; the period of statehood had begun, and with it new battles, many disappointments, and much happiness.

Birth Pangs of the State

When Greenbaum was offered the post of minister of the interior in the provisional government he demanded exclusion of the police department from that ministry. In most countries the police force is one of the main elements of the Ministry of the Interior. Many people could not understand—and do not understand to this day—Greenbaum's approach to this question. He argued that since the country would be in a state of emergency, internal security affairs would be in the hands of the minister of defense and the army. Ministerial responsibility would, therefore, devolve in practice upon the minister of defense. There is question as to whether Greenbaum's attitude was correct. It seemed—and seems—to many of us that if the Police Department, which has a very high standard in Israel, were part of the Ministry of the Interior, everyone would be better off.

During his tenure as minister of the interior, Greenbaum laid the foundations of a fine tradition. His friend and colleague from his youth, A. M. Hartglass, was appointed director-general of the ministry while Greenbaum was still besieged in Jerusalem. The fruitful collaboration between the two men produced positive results. The first democratic elections in the State of Israel were held in a spirit of respect, integrity, and responsibility, and were a festive occasion for the entire population. But the days to come were to bring not only satisfaction and happiness but also failures and disappointments. Greenbaum ran on his own list in the elections to the parliament-in-the-making, the first Knesset, but was not elected. It was a bitter tragedy—he, the veteran parliamentarian who had represented his people for many years in the Polish Parliament, was not elected, while members of Agudat Israel, who had been among the greatest opponents of Zionism and the renaissance movement in Poland, were elected and even joined the government.

Other disappointments followed. Greenbaum saw that the pioneering spirit was weakening and that the people were no longer prepared for sacrifice and suffering after so many years of struggle. "Will we not respond to the national redemption as others responded to the social redemption?" he asked in his conclusive article in 1950. In the articles he published thereafter he expressed his bitterness and disappointment. He had believed that the alliance that had been established decades earlier between him and the heads of the labor movement in Israel would not be dismembered, even after his election defeat. But he was wrong, and was disappointed once again. The last twenty years of his life, following his retirement from Israel's political arena, were similarly strewn with disappointments:

> The State we have succeeded in establishing is merely the beginning of that redemption which we set out to achieve through our efforts and sacrifices in construction and creation, war and defense. Like every liberation, renaissance and reconstruction movement, our redemption can only be achieved in stages; and we have not yet passed the first stage. But the State increases our force, does away with difficulties and obstacles which, had the State not existed, we would have had no hope of overcoming. It creates those possibilities we had imagined, and which are now a reality. Do not say that it is a means to a higher end. It is the aim of the period in which we live.

Here, too, we see Greenbaum at his greatest, a Zionist of no mean stature, making his own and his generation's historical reckoning. The bitterness, the skepticism, and the disappointments vanish, and he appears to us once again as one of the victors, one of those who led the people in this generation and, perhaps, did not dream that in their day the state would come into existence and they would be among its founders. He was optimistic: "The suffering will yet increase and the sacrifices will become more numerous, but the State we have established will not be a transitory episode in the life of our people. Thanks to our heroic efforts it will exist forever. How happy is my generation that witnessed its beginnings, saw the beginning of redemption, the beginning of the Messianic days; . . . there is no end to the act of creation in nature and in the life of peoples."

There is a basis for the happiness expressed in these lines. Greenbaum, a man who fought his people's fight for redemption and liberation, deserved satisfaction for his achievements and victories; in the final analysis, the victories were certainly more numerous than the failures. Polish Jewry is no more and will never be revived, but the State of Israel does exist.

A Fighter—and a Master with Disciples

Yitschak Greenbaum was one of the outstanding figures of his generation, a man fashioned from the stuff leaders are made of. He was a solid, independent fighter who left his imprint on his generation and his epoch. He fought the battles of his people, most of whom followed him, but he had many opponents. He possessed the characteristics of a rabbi-master of his disciples. He, who fought the anti-Zionist rabbis, liked the concept of "Rebbe" (master), and would treat his students, supporters, and friends as his disciples. He made decisions on Jewish, Zionist, political, religious and cultural affairs, and the Zionist camp around him often resembled a great Hasidic court.

The famous Jewish writer Y. L. Peretz was Greenbaum's rebbe, which is how Greenbaum referred to him in his book *P'nei Hador* (Face of the Generation). Peretz had a very great influence on Greenbaum. He revealed to Greenbaum the light and beauty of Hasidism. Greenbaum, who was far removed from religious Judaism and the Hasidic courts, suddenly discovered this splendid world. Here we evoke the memory of Greenbaum as a great rebbe in the Zionist movement and among the Jewish people.

Following the elections to the first Knesset, Greenbaum's public activity narrowed but his journalistic and literary life commenced. He continued with it energetically, consistently, and with great enthusiasm.

Greenbaum was a political Zionist, a faithful follower of Herzl. At the same time, he considered himself a disciple of Ahad Ha'am. For him, political and cultural activity had always been intertwined harmoniously. In Poland, when he headed the struggle for the rights of Jewish schools, he demanded recognition of the Hebrew and Yiddish languages; at the same time he was also among the heads of the Tarbut (culture) organization and one of the promoters of Hebrew primary, secondary, and teachers' training schools.

As a member of the Zionist Executive in Jerusalem, he devoted time and energy to Mosad Bialik; one of its founders and consolidators, he was its chairman from its creation in 1935 until his retirement from the Jewish Agency Executive. Greenbaum was a political activist, writer, historian, and journalist all at once. A versatile personality, he was thus an integral Zionist in the full sense of the concept.

Yitschak Greenbaum was always a member of the Democratic Zionist camp. At all times he spoke out against displays of any tendency to domination. His opposition to the expansion of the Jewish Agency also stemmed from his fears for Zionist democracy. Indeed, he had belonged to the small but important fraction that had demanded from Herzl the democratization of the World Zionist Organization and its cultural activity.

As head of the Al Hamishmar group in Poland he fought to turn Zionism into a popular movement that would attract Jewish youth, students, and the "little man." When he headed the radical group within the World Zionist Organization, fighting its battles at Zionist congresses together with Nachum Goldmann and other prominent personalities, his struggle was directed largely against compromise with the mandatory government, against the expansion of the Jewish Agency, and in favor of an alliance with the pioneering and labor element in the movement and in Eretz Israel.

There was a time when the views of the Radicals and the Revisionists were seen to converge, as in the struggle against Weizmann. But they never concluded an alliance. The Radicals fought well, but after the battle accepted the rule of the majority. They considered themselves partners and allies of the rest of the movement and responsible for the unity of the Zionist organization—the state-in-the-making. Not so the Revisionists, who withdrew and sought to break up the World Zionist Organization as well as the Histadrut, the General Federation of Labor.

At the tragic Prague Zionist Congress in 1933, a narrow coalition was formed based on the Zionist Workers movement, the Progressive Zionists A, the Radicals, and the Zionist Youth. This coalition was to bring Weizmann back to the presidency at the Lucerne congress in 1935. It was later expanded through cooption to the Zionist Executive of the General Zionists and Mizrachi. At the same Prague congress during which Greenbaum became a member of the Zionist Executive, the strength and influence of the labor parties increased, as did that of the Progressives and Radicals. The alliance, which held for fifteen years, eventually brought about the establishment of an independent Jewish state in Eretz Israel.

Bitter Words—Only Part of the Picture

In the introduction to *P'nei Hador*, which was published in 1958 by the Zionist Library in Jerusalem, Greenbaum wrote:

In this collection [of tributes to teachers, colleagues and friends], I have dealt only with the people of Poland and Russia and the period of my life during which I reached the peak of my activity and influence. After that came the Palestinian period and with it, stagnation and even decline. When I am mentioned, people usually refer to me as "the leader of Polish Jewry," remaining silent about my activity in Eretz Israel. This is a bitter judgement of my participation in the work of the Zionist Executive over a seventeen-year period of struggle and creation and later, for a short time, in the Provisional Government. That is my fate within the World Zionist Organization in which the situation in Eretz Israel is the decisive factor.

These bitter words, the conclusion of a most tragic soul-searching, are unjust, and do not reflect the total picture. Had it not been for the same Zionist Executive, which rested on the alliance between Greenbaum and the leaders of the labor movement in Eretz Israel, who knows whether in 1948 we would have achieved Jewish independence?

From 1933 until 1948 the Zionist Executive, headed by David Ben-Gurion, prepared the Yishuv in Palestine for independence. Those were years of immigration and economic consolidation, years of preparation and of the formation of the national and sovereign apparatus, years of struggle against the White Paper, years of great rescue operations. And Greenbaum, as one of the most prominent Zionist leaders of the period, was a full partner in those enterprises.

At first he headed the Department of Immigration and Labor. Later when it was split into two, he remained head of the Labor Department. At the same time he made a significant contribution to the consolidation of Jewish labor in the villages: he had homes constructed for the workers, established funds for auxiliary farms, and had camps built for the kibbutzim. He took an interest not only in the worker but also in the orange grower who worked himself as a Jewish laborer; he encouraged the National Farmers and established the Agricultural Fund under the direction of Shmuel Zakif Zuchovitzky.

Those were the years of the great struggle for Jewish labor. The victory of the principle of Jewish labor was the victory of Zionism. Greenbaum was not content with mere words in support of Jewish labor. As head of the Labor Department, he made a great, constructive contribution to the successful outcome of that struggle. Further, he devoted himself to the establishment of proper labor relations and provided for an arbitrator to mediate between employers and employees. His faithful assistant, Joseph Rabinowitz, was the moving spirit in the campaign for Jewish labor, while Avraham Wertheim seconded him in the area of labor relations.

At that period, the general employment offices for the distribution of work were set up, and the separate offices run by individual parties and organizations were abolished. This was an' important step in the depoliticization of employment procedures. As the first chairman of the General Labor Exchanges Center, I well remember the festive occasion that marked the opening of the exchanges. They were established by Greenbaum and the Histadrut in collaboration with all the other workers' organizations. Greenbaum tried to take the sting out of the relations between the workers and the Histadrut, between the employers and the various workers' organizations.

During World War II, when unemployment was widespread and the Labor Redemption Fund was established by the Histadrut in collaboration with the National Council and the Jewish Agency, Greenbaum was responsible for the establishment of a Citizen's Redemption Fund to assist small businessmen and unemployed artisans. There were many who spoke loftily on behalf of the middle class, but Greenbaum, in a spirit of Zionist loyalty, tried to do something concrete for them.

He did much for "illegal" immigration, working to maintain harmony between the various pioneering elements involved in its organization. He was partly responsible for the agreement on the structure of the Haganah command, which was headed at that time by his follower, Dr. Moshe Sneh (Kleinbaum). On the outbreak of World War II and during the period of the Holocaust, Greenbaum headed the United Rescue Committee. He devoted himself fervently to the rescue of the Jews of Europe. In cooperation with the political department of the Jewish Agency, important defense and rescue operations were carried out. He was in contact with American Jewry and with all the Jewish and non-Jewish organizations who could be coopted to the task, and he demanded vigorous rescue action.

At the same time, in his capacity as chairman of the Rescue Committee, Greenbaum sent cables to President Roosevelt, Marshal Stalin, and Winston Churchill, demanding categorically that they order the bombing of the extermination camps and gas chambers. He saw European Jewry being led to the slaughter, and with all his heart and soul sought to do everything possible to save it.

Just as he maintained Jewish and Zionist unity in the Rescue Committee, as a member of the Zionist Executive he did his utmost to prevent bloodshed between the Haganah and the Etzel and Lechi organizations. Very little of the fierce struggle within the Zionist Executive and the Actions Committee became public knowledge.

Greenbaum sensed that we were approaching the decisive period in the struggle for our independence (it would be waged once the British evacuated the country), and he wanted to preserve the unity of the Yishuv and a united Jewish front. He did all in his power to prevent bloodshed between Jew and Jew.

When the Zionist Executive established the People's Council and the Provisional Council of State, Greenbaum became a member of the latter. He remained in Jerusalem and, as a member of the Provisional Council assumed responsibility, together with E. Dobkin and me, for continuation of Jewish Agency activity during the siege of Jerusalem.

Those were difficult days for Greenbaum. He was a member of the government but because of the siege he could not attend its meetings. He preserved the status of the Zionist Executive, and kept it functioning at a minimum: most of the staff had been called up to man our defense positions.

During that period Greenbaum's son fell in the defense of Ramat Rachel, but Greenbaum continued heroically, and with quiet courage, to come every day from his apartment to the offices of the national institutions, drawing around him the members of the Provisional Council, the Zionist Executive, and the National Council administration who had remained in Jerusalem during the siege. Only during the cease-fire did he move to Tel Aviv to assume his post as the first minister of the interior of the State of Israel.

A Man Who Withstood Trials, a Man of Action

Greenbaum lived in Jerusalem for fifteen years, from his immigration in 1933 until the establishment of the state in 1948. For the next ten years he lived in Tel Aviv, and then moved to kibbutz Gan Shmuel in the

Shomron to be near his son Binyamin and his family. In the Shomron, not far from Gan Shmuel, Alonei Yitschak, the youth village named after Greenbaum, was established by Yechiel Charif and his colleagues. This is one of the most beautiful and flourishing youth villages in the country. Since its establishment in 1949 it has educated thousands of citizens who today hold important positions in Israel and in all walks of life. Greenbaum was greatly attached to Alonei Yitschak.

At Gan Shmuel, Greenbaum continued with his literary activity and led a quiet life. He witnessed the development and prosperity of the State of Israel, its wars, and its victories. Greenbaum was interred in the Gan Shmuel cemetery alongside his wife, who had died many years earlier.

Greenbaum's followers and admirers, all those who had the privilege of drawing inspiration from his powerful personality, members of the kibbutz, and the people of Alonei Yitschak—all will bear in their hearts the memory of Yitschak Greenbaum. Around his memory a legend will be woven, its threads paralleling the stages of the struggle for the state and its establishment. There is no doubt that Yitschak Greenbaum was one of the founders of the independent State of Israel. He labored to prepare the ground and the conditions for its establishment during his decades of activity in the World Zionist Organization abroad, particularly in Poland, and later, in the Yishuv and on the Zionist Executive of which he was a prominent member for the fifteen fateful and decisive years which preceded the declaration of the state.

Yitschak Greenbaum was one of the great men of action who stood at the head of the Jewish people from the beginning of this century. He had a deep, fundamental sense of history. His image will remain forever in the annals of the Jewish people and of its renewed sovereignty in Israel.

A generation could be educated on Greenbaum's character. The values he believed in and symbolized were a wonderful, lofty synthesis of the best Jewish and human values. He was a proud nationalist. He believed that the State of Israel would be superior to other states, would learn from the mistakes of other peoples, and—in cooperation with the Jewish people in the Diaspora—would ensure the continuity and eternity of Jewish history.

Moshe Glickson

The eve of Shavuoth in 1979 was the fortieth anniversary of the death of Dr. Moshe Glickson, the Hebrew writer and philosopher, mentor and spiritual leader of liberal General Zionism. He was a symbol and model, and his personality, his qualities as an educator, molded the life of individuals—and of the Yishuv as it crystallized into a political and cultural entity in Eretz Israel during the period of British mandatory rule. Glickson was in essence a moralist. Moral principles were the basis of his Zionist and social outlook, and served as the motivating force behind his public actions. He never advocated public or political action that lacked the moral dimension. For him, Jewish and humanitarian ethics were the essence of social and individual life, of the life of peoples and states.

Moshe Glickson was a combination of qualities: he was of the spiritual elite and also a man of the people. He won people by his simple ways and he expressed himself courteously and logically. His colleagues and his followers, and even his opponents, looked forward each day to his editorials in *Ha'aretz;* they derived inspiration from the richness of his thought and from his profound analyses of contemporary problems. He taught and acted on the principles of philosophy, judging in their light every event, great and small, in our national life. He never proposed rigid solutions to complicated problems out of a sense of exaggerated self-confidence, or declared that these and only these were the best of all possible solutions. Glickson would examine each problem from all angles, as befitted a skeptical philosopher, before drawing any conclusion. He never sought popularity or general agreement; his thought was original and generally ran counter to routine, accepted theses. He was not unduly concerned by the widely held view that he was a typical compromiser, always looking for the golden mean to smooth out difficulties. The truth is that he at no time compromised on basics and on truths in which he believed; instead he compromised on secondary issues that, in his view, were not really worth a fight. He did fight courageously over matters of belief and social problems, and detested routine and accepted ideas. He protested openly against the powerful and the violent and did not hesitate to take issue even with his teachers or to take up the cudgels against important public figures. He was known to detest intrigue, and he would come out forcefully in defense of the national interest in accordance with the aspirations and principles of political redemption and cultural-spiritual renaissance. Many years before the establishment of the independent State of Israel, Glickson taught us to consider ourselves a reformed society, capable of enforcing a political, social, and cultural regime that corresponded to Jewish principles and Zionist aspirations. He insisted that we behave under the mandatory government as though we were living in an independent state of our own.

As a faithful disciple of Herzl, Glickson strove for the establishment of a Jewish state in Eretz Israel. Following a clear political line, which determined that our fight for independence was just and essential, Glickson took his place among the leaders of the struggle against the mandatory government at a time when the British were trying to go back on obligations undertaken in the Balfour Declaration, and, in fact, were pursuing a policy designed to throttle the growth and development of the homeland. Even though he was very close to Dr. Chaim Weizmann, the president of the Zionist Organization, Glickson did not recoil from any action in the fight against British politicians and officials who were enemies of our national renaissance. As for Weizmann, Glickson agreed with his attitude toward the pioneering and labor movements, and with his conception of a constructive, practical Zionism that would rebuild the country. Such was not the case when it came to Britain: on more than one occasion Glickson differed from Weizmann. Glickson considered the White Paper that barred the immigration of Jews and placed obstacles in the way of land purchase and settlement a betrayal of international moral principles. Glickson claimed that Great Britain was merely the repository of Eretz Israel, having assumed the obligation to implement the mandate. To the extent that Britain repudiated the policy of the Balfour Declaration it reduced its right to rule in Eretz Izrael.

In the struggle over the form and social pattern that the Yishuv was to assume, Glickson fought both within the Yishuv and within the General Zionist movement, of which he was one of the leaders, in true partnership with the labor movement and the pioneering camp. He had a positive attitude toward the new ways of life that were developing among the workers where moral, social, and Zionist principles were fulfilled in everyday life. However, although he endorsed this partnership and its struggle for a single General Federation of Labor, Glickson forcefully rejected the largely Marxist-inspired class policy of the trade union camp. He considered Marxism a negative—and one of the most dangerous—social theories, and called upon the Israeli labor movement to follow the independent path of Judaism and Zionism. One of the greatest articles he ever wrote was a polemic against Marx and Marxism. Glickson fought for the regulation of labor relations at the national level; for a just distribution of work; for a reformed regime that would prevent social upheavals and would consolidate a Jewish society inspired by the principles of justice evoked by the prophets of Israel and by Jewish thought through the ages. Moshe Glickson was essentially a humanist, and his main struggle was against the enslavement of man by any kind of totalitarian regime. He wanted our society to advance toward political independence through unremitting effort, and to express in its way of life the ideals of Judaism and of humanitarian liberalism. His entire being was permeated by this aspiration. He demanded that socialist Zionism not sharpen the contrasts in our society by aping the ideas and goals of foreign labor movements—goals that did not correspond to the spirit of our people.

Glickson considered himself a disciple of both Herzl and Ahad Ha'am. His ambition was that the spiritual center that would be implanted in Zion, and whose influence would radiate to the entire Jewish people, would be located within an independent political framework. He did not believe that a Jewish spiritual center alone would be able to bring about a Jewish renaissance unless political independence had first been achieved. Thus, he regarded the education of the young generation the basis of our future society, and for that reason he took an interest in our prestatehood school system, fighting against the politicization of education and for a uniform school system that would act as a melting pot for the ingathering of exiles and would mold us into a homogeneous people. Glickson considered the general school the appropriate basis for a uniform school system although he did not withhold criticism of the general school itself. There is no doubt that the national education system that was established in the independent State of Israel was founded on the principle that Glickson had advocated many years previously.

Just as he called for the regulation of labor relations and the reform of education, he also insisted that no sector of our economy subjugate the individual or deny him his freedom and independence; the worker, like any other citizen, should be free to live according to his beliefs, of his own free will. As a religious man, Glickson was upset by the way our festivals had lost their significance, and he demanded the restoration of the lofty spirit of the sabbath and festivals. His articles on the sabbath and the festivals are among the choicest in our literature. Today, as a center is being established for the fostering of Jewish consciousness in the national school system, let us remember the man who called for this decades ago. Today, as tension reigns between the religious camp and other sections of the population in independent Israel, we would do well to seek inspiration from Moshe Glickson's theory of dialogue to achieve national unity. Glickson was a religious man, but he opposed all forms of religious coercion and preached tolerance and mutual respect among the different sectors of the Yishuv.

He was unhappy about the introduction of politics into religious life, for he rightly feared that it would damage the essence of the Jewish religion. Instead of bringing those who were far from religion closer to a pure and honest religious life, politics would lead to the estrangement of the young generation from an understanding of eternal religious values. Glickson called for the abandonment of both intellectual skepticism and Marxist atheism, for in our times a synthesis is required, a melding of the positive emanations of the creativity of generations. Addressing himself to religious Jewry, he said that it must struggle for the basic content of the Jewish religion and not for the shell that had grown around it in the Diaspora.

In his conception of Judaism, Glickson was a faithful disciple of Maimonides. But he was also greatly influenced by the philosophy of Hermann Cohen, under whom he studied at Marburg University. Glickson agreed with Cohen's view of the close relation between religious principles and social justice:

> The demand for inner union between the theoretical and the moral consciousness came from Judaism. The Jew prays: "And unite our heart that we may serve Thy Name"—hence the great value which Judaism attaches to religious learning. Thus, too, social differences could not be sharply pronounced among Jews. Knowledge of Torah made the rich and poor equal. This moral concept penetrated the entire social system and made of the image of social justice a law that could not be broken. These demands found their highest expression in the commandments pertaining to the Sabbath. "Thou shalt not do any manner of work, thou . . . nor they manservant nor they maidservant. So has the Lord Thy God ordered thee to do on the Sabbath day."
>
> And consider: if the basic concept embodied in the Sabbath is social freedom, Judaism follows with its declaration of moral freedom in its entirety. The verse "You are the children of the Lord Your God" (social equality) can be understood in all the depth of its faith only if we add to it the phrase "and you choose life" (moral freedom and moral responsibility). The inner connection between moral freedom and political and social freedom is revealed in the Messianic idea, the crowning glory of the Israelite ethic. The prophetic vision of the Day

of Judgement is the essence of morality. There is no redemption for the individual only. Moral redemption will be brought about only by society as a whole. Only the future of humanity is the guarantor of the moral existence of the individual.

These principles enunciated by Hermann Cohen did not deter Glickson from criticizing his teacher. He wrote:

> Cohen's absolute idealism does not perceive the living man, the man who suffers, falls and rises, loves and hates and fights for his very survival; it cannot perceive him, for the living man is sometimes a living contradiction to the "concept of humanity," and he has no place in the sublime and perfect accomplishment of the actions with and by himself. Absolute universalism rejects individualism which is not subjugated to it and to its laws; rejects both the struggles and the creativity which are part of individualism. Cohen's philosophy does not know of this creativity, just as it knows nothing of struggle and evolution in the world and in life. It knows only of the development of concepts outside time, but is unaware of the living evolution in time, of the development of separate objects into new ways of life, into new varieties of life. The denial of personal individualism in Hermann Cohen's theory also applies to popular individualism—hence the sorry sight of Cohen, a great philosopher and a great Jew, holding aloft the banner of Judaism, and regarding the law of Israel as the pinnacle of ethical culture, but at the same time denying the existence and national future of the people of Israel. . . .

In his criticism of Cohen, Glickson comes to the following caustic conclusion: "We, who do not depend only on some idea for the existence of our nation; we who desire a life of individualism, a life of creation—we cannot follow Hermann Cohen in his ultimate demands. For that reason, Hermann Cohen has not become a guide to his people."

Glickson was able to accept from his mentors what was basic and fundamental in their philosophies, but his spiritual stature gave him the right and the ability to criticize his teachers when they denied the aspiration to national and political renaissance, and to the return of our people to its spiritual source.

The Synthesis

In his concept of the problems of society and its evolution, Glickson chose the path of synthesis between the rights of the individual and the rights of society. He believed that the new Jew involved with the land of his people and nourished by its roots will produce a fine composite of the individual and the general, of the personal basis—the basis of freedom and will—and of the popular basis—the basis of nature and instincts—which is the mother of all great human creation.

Creation is synthesis, the synthesis of fecundation, even if it is a long road and must take time. This synthesis is first of all the synthesis of the individual and society, of the personality and the nation . . . the soul which creates within it anarchy or the transitoriness of the individual who is not part of society. . . .

These conflicts which give life and the combat of life to the soul, are better for us than absolute unity in a void. Indeed, the human soul cannot be without conflict and war. . . .

Harmony does not mean peace but reconciliation; not peace between the conflicting elements as each one relinquishes something of its own in order not to provoke its opponent, but a mutual reconciliation between them, the perfection and elevation of them both. That is the harmony of the conflicting elements themselves. Their expression is their correction. Their projection and clarification constitute their elevation and their combination. Both elements arise, mature, become clear, and in the process combine in a supreme union, a union of creation, one complementing the other and one serving the other. The creative individual needs the nation to bear him along on its course, and he offers it his soul, his essence, his creation; the nation needs the creative individual to mark it, to give form to its matter and to substantiate its essence. . . . Our national mission is first and foremost a moral mission, and it is therefore an all-embracing human mission. [And Glickson asks] Is it possible that a nation arising today to build for itself a new world will not beware of the old failures and will build on the rickety foundations which became a source of catastrophe and danger to other societies?

Reform of the social order in new living conditions in accordance with our national spirit is the essence of our national and human mission. We must beware of two things: of the social error which is rocking the institutions of Europe, and of its reform in the spirit of materialistic socialism and the war between man and man. There is no redemption but the redemption of will and freedom, the redemption of action and moral responsibility . . . . The socialist movement sinned towards man in both of these and therefore failed in the great historical experiment . . . Marx's theory of socialism deprived man of his freedom and moral responsibility, bound him in a complicated tangle of iron laws, of reasons and actions and pretexts which subject him to a rule which has no limits, and turn him into a small cog in the huge world machine. Thus it has weakened his moral will and exhausted his strength to oppose the evil in the world . . . hence its second great sin: it sought the remedy to humanity's failures not in a moral resurgence, in the victory of the spirit and the theory of man, but in fratricidal warfare, in polemics between classes who contend with one another. And so it increased the confusion and the sorrow of man; the crisis which the socialist movement is traversing should be a warning to us. Just as we must shy away from the socialist failure must we shun the "reform" by subjugating spirit to matter and indulging in war between man and man. . . .

This article serves as an expression of Glickson's national and social philosophy, and he concludes thus: "Three aims/ideals which have emerged in the decisive life of our nation—the ideals of society, of the enterprise and of the moral mission—are leaving their imprint on the life of the generation and creating the renewed nationalism which will restore the foundations of our national life."

Glickson's Concept of Nationalism and Socialism

Glickson's concept of nationalism and socialism explains why, after he arrived in Eretz Israel in the thirties, he saw in the Zionist Youth the savior of General Zionism. They represented his Zionist-philosophic synthesis; they were nationalist Jews who sought the political and cultural redemption of the people in its homeland; they were working people, builders of villages, and sought the renewal of the Jew in a reformed society in his homeland. They strove for a better, brighter world that would provide the highest expression of the synthesis between society and the individual; they came physically to realize their vision, and they wanted to serve as an example to the tens of thousands of Jewish youth whose pioneers and first standard-bearers they were. They aspired to reform society but not by Marxist means, and they opposed with all of their being the historic materialism that subjugated spirit to matter; they brought new hope to General Zionism, which instead of forming the backbone of national rebuilding in the homeland had degenerated into the representative of a small class of people, detached from the world that was in the making and from the creative process. Glickson encouraged the young men who reached Petah Tikva at that time and pitched their tent in the Kraminski garden (where the Beilinson hospital now stands). Here the first Zionist Youth conference was held and a new period began in working General Zionism—a Zionism of achievement, a Zionism that struggled and created and, as Berl Katznelson said, "bears the standard of labor and pioneering fulfilment in the General Zionist camp and at the same time raises the standard of supra-class General Zionism within the Labour Movement, in the Histadrut." Glickson was the guide of these young men who established the Zionist Worker's Movement. He realized that his philosophy had acquired followers, men of vision and faith who would fulfill it—the pioneers of the Zionist workers movement.

If there exists a liberal party with a vision of social liberalism, if we have an active Independent Liberal Labor movement within the Histadrut, and if we have become an important factor in the life of the independent state, it is in no small measure due to the covenant formed in the early thirties between the intellectual and philosopher Moshe Glickson, who was our leader and guide, and the great camp of the revivers of General Zionism. In the wake of the regeneration of General Zionism, the ranks of the Zionist Youth and its pioneers also took on a new lease of life, and those who immigrated to Eretz Israel en masse became a constructive fighting and creative force. It was they who brought about the decisive change in General Zionism in Eretz Israel and in the world, altering its path and its historical development.

And so, forty years after the death of Moshe Glickson, we commune with him, with his personality as an educator who left his imprint on us all, his innate honesty, and his love for his people and for every single individual within it. Prodigious changes have taken place during those forty years: we became an independent state, responsible for our own destiny. But as a movement we must even today study and familiarize ourselves with Moshe Glickson's teachings; they stood the test of time, and for many years to come will inspire us with faith and strengthen within us those same ideals that are as vital to the State of Israel and its society today as they were then. The two volumes of Glickson's works that have been issued are a treasure for all the independent people of Israel, but first and foremost for us and for our entire movement.

Among Glickson's published works are his memoirs, *Derech Hakotzim* (The Thorny Path), which he completed before becoming editor of the Hebrew daily paper in Moscow, *Ha'Am* (The People). He also edited two collections, *Olameinu* (Our World) and *Masuot* (Beacons), and contributed frequently to the monthly *Ma'avarot* (Transitions), to *Hapoel Hatsair* (The Young Worker), and to other Hebrew weeklies and monthlies. But he acquired his position and influence during the period of over fifteen years when he was chief editor of the daily *Ha'aretz* (The Land), from 1922, shortly after the British government had accepted the mandate over Eretz Israel, until two years prior to the outbreak of World War II.

In his leading articles, which bore the general title "From Day to Day," he expressed his opinion on political, social, cultural and Zionist issues. Every day the readers of *Ha'aretz*, as well as those of other newspapers—sympathizers and opponents alike—read the leader signed "M.G.," and found in it decisions and discussions on questions affecting the Yishuv.

Glickson fought the mandate through his newspaper, attacking the decrees, the failures, and the disappointments that it brought to the Yishuv in Eretz Israel. He fought for his opinions on spiritual and social affairs, and sometimes on economic issues. He was certainly not a compromiser and concession maker on matters in which he believed, issues that appeared to him to constitute the fundamental basis for the construction of the Yishuv, the Zionist movement, and society. Moshe Glickson was an independent personality whose only judge was his own conscience, yet he respected the opinions of others. He searched constantly for a middle way on issues that to him seemed amenable to compromise, in order to preserve the unity of the Yishuv and the people. But on fundamental issues he stood firm against the many, even when he was alone in the struggle and had his faith as his only ally. Glickson was one of the best publicists that the Jewish people had during the period of its liberation and struggle for the rebuilding of its ancient homeland. He was a high priest in that small community, known and accepted by all. His extensive knowledge of Judaism on the one hand, and of the social sciences and philosophy on the other, fitted him for that high position.

As a student of the yeshiva and of Western universities, he absorbed both Jewish law and literature, and acquired a rich general education. He translated philosophical works—M. Wiendelband's three volumes—and was qualified to lecture on philosophy. He also wrote about Maimonides, Spinoza, and other Jewish and non-Jewish philosophers with great erudition. He often complained that he was wasting his energies, talents, and knowledge on public affairs, and on the day-to-day work of a publicist. There is no doubt that he could have won an honorable place for himself in Hebrew literature, and could have left mature works for the benefit of his own and coming generations.

In his fine tribute to Moshe Beilinson, one of the editors of *Davar* (The Word), three days after Beilinson's death, Glickson wrote:

> His journalistic work was a sacrifice from the start. No intelligent, talented, broadly-educated man takes up journalism unless he has a prodigal, indulgent character, and does not seek his own pleasure and benefit. Journalism is a difficult job; our sacrifice has no recompense and no limit. It would have been easier for a man such as he to make a niche for himself in literature, to do his own work, to create and to win for himself a place in "the world to come" rather than to invest his energy in day-to-day affairs, a mad scramble after the chaotic round of days, without a trace remaining to show for his great efforts. Does the

public realize that it is far earier to write books, and even good books, than to write articles every single day on the burning, clamoring issues of the hour? Beilinson was one of those prodigal, indulgent people. The two or three volumes that he left do not reflect the wealth and treasure of his soul and the tolerance of his spirit, qualities which the journalist Beilinson invested in his articles. There are very very few journalists and publicists among us of the stature of Beilinson, men of his knowledge and his journalist's character. And that is the secret of his educative influence on his readers.

This extract from Glickson's tribute to Beilinson has an autobiographical quality about it; Glickson was thinking no less about himself than about Beilinson. Glickson never abandoned his mission as publicist, because he realized that the daily newspaper was a forum that enabled him to mold the character of the people, and that his articles constituted a political, social, and cultural weapon that he could employ for the general good. Glickson did not leave many books, but he is considered to be one of the central figures in Zionist history and in the annals of the Yishuv—one of the greatest educators of his generation. His spiritual inheritance is made up of only four books, one pamphlet on Ahad Ha'am, and one on Maimonides, which was published as a supplement in *Ha'Aretz.Ishim ba-Madda u-va Sifrut* (Personalities in Science and Literature) appeared in 1940–1941; *Ishim ba-Ziyyonut* (Zionist Personalities) appeared in 1940. *Im Chilufei Mishmarot* (With the Changing of the Guard) appeared in two volumes and was published by, and at the initiative of, the secretariat of Zionist Youth (Hanoar Hazioni). The first volume contains an anthology of articles on social, labor and educational questions, and on the fundamental problems of Zionism. The second volume is composed of articles on Jewish festivals, the Sabbath, Marxism, and political and spiritual issues. Both volumes, which appeared in 1965 under the auspices of the Glickson Publication Committee, are dedicated to personalities in contemporary Zionism and in the scientific and literary world. There is no doubt that many more articles could be chosen from among the thousands Glickson wrote, and published in several more volumes. Glickson left not only articles, he also left the heritage of his life in Zionism. Progressive Zionism in Israel can justifiably be allowed to consider itself the heir of his ideas and his public activity.

Glickson was a Zionist leader who never claimed the crown of leadership. He considered himself a servant of the people, a counselor, a formulator of opinions, a guide, a colleague, and a friend. But those who believed in the way of Zionism that he preached regarded him as their mentor and master.

The Democratic Zionists who struggled against the class and rightist tendencies of General Zionism saw him as the head of their group. He represented integral Russian Zionism—the outcome of the synthesis between Herzl's political Zionism and Ahad Ha'am's spiritual Zionism. It was to those two fundamental elements that Glickson added the constructive Zionism of Weizmann, and he considered himself the disciple of all three leaders—from whom he accepted only the essentials.

It was that Zionist synthesis which Glickson preached all his life; in the success of the synthesis he saw the success of the Yishuv and of the Zionist movement, and of the construction of the homeland. Glickson was one of the outstanding unifying forces of the movement and the Yishuv. He wrote profusely about disintegration, secretarianism, gratuitous hatred, and the struggle within the Yishuv. He saw great social and national assets in the United Workers Movement and in the single workers' federation, the Histadrut, and for that reason he fiercely opposed all attempts to break the Histadrut. But at the same time he sharply criticized Histadrut opposition to the settlement of labor conflicts by compulsory arbitration.

When the German Zionists immigrated to Eretz Israel in the thirties, Glickson knew how to approach them and find a way to their hearts. When the first members of Zionist Youth arrived, also in the early thirties, Glickson was among the first to help and encourage them. He participated in the first Zionist Youth Conference, and published an editorial in which he gave prominence to this positive pioneering element within General Zionism. From then on an alliance was formed between the teacher and his pioneering settler-students, and it has persisted to this day.

Within the General Zionist federation, which was united at that time, Glickson, together with Ben-Zion Mossinson, Eliyahu Berlin, Chaim Harari, Michael Olienkov, L. Y. Rokach, S. Rapaport, Arieh Bichovski, Z. Shoham, and members of the Zionist Youth and Zionist workers groups fought for a supra-class, popular, integral Zionism. The members of the Zionist Worker, part of the New Aliyah, and the General Zionists of Glickson's school constitute the Independent Liberal Party, and all of them continue on his path, inspired by the same social and Zionist doctrines.

Glickson and the Zionist Youth

The innovation in the creation of Zionist Youth was cooperation in the creative enterprise. When Jewish villages which supported the idea of

General Zionism were established, and raised that banner not only within the Yishuv but also within the Histadrut, Glickson did not stand idly by. He was one of the leading militants against foreign labor in the Jewish economy, for he was well aware that every Jewish worker added political, economic, and defensive power to the Yishuv. He fought uncompromisingly for the principle of Jewish labor, and took part in keeping watch beside the orange groves. As one of the leaders of Democratic Zionism, he fought for obedience to the representative organization of the Yishuv. He also spoke out in favor of its demcratic constitution, which was to become the first sovereign element of the Yishuv. (Glickson's friend Eliyahu Berlin was among its drafters.) In the municipalities, too, and especially in Tel Aviv, Glickson fought for democracy. For him, democracy was not just the right of the majority to decide; it must also defend the minority, civil rights, and above all, the human being. Glickson's democracy was interwoven with liberal elements and was based on humanitarianism and justice. Thus, he admired the working settlement movement and the new forms of life that grew up in Eretz Israel. Nonetheless, he argued that the new must be built on the foundations of the old—the sources, the Jewish essence. Here too he sought the synthesis, and when he saw that attempts were being made to build the new while uprooting the old, his whole being rebelled.

Glickson was a religious, observant Jew, but he nevertheless sought compromise—a synthesis between the old and the new among those who no longer believed in religion. He wanted the young generation in Eretz Israel to be nourished at Jewish sources and, as it grew, to introduce its own innovations, but he simply could not conceive of there being a chasm between the glorious past of our people and its cultural creations, and what was emerging in settlement and culture in the homeland today. In his excellent essays on the holy days and festivals he gave expression to these ideas. They are among his finest works. Particularly now, when the Ministry of Education is seeking to introduce greater Jewish consciousness into the national school system, Glickson's essays on the sabbath and festivals of Israel can serve as excellent material for both teacher and pupil.

Glickson was also involved in the economic aspects of his newspaper. He did not overlook the advertisement columns, and he did not read only the articles and reports. He tried to make sure that his paper would be free of all defects, coarse expressions, or cheap attacks. He was a man of enormous charm, always ready to do favors. He was blessed with precious qualities of the soul: love of Israel and respect for man, created in the image of his creator.

He shunned honors and position in the party and other organizations, insisting that his time for study, learning, and writing not be taken up with these affairs. He remained ever faithful to his beliefs, and he was as concerned with form as he was with substance. A pleasing form and a cordial style were as dear to him as substance and belief.

On the day he died, his students, members of the Lamakor Kibbutz in Herzliya, established a settlement in Samaria. This was after the publication of the British White Paper that contained the decrees prohibiting Jews to acquire land. The settlement was set up on land belonging to PICA (the Palestine Colonization Association) and the settlers were building the tower and stockade as the festival of Shavuoth, the festival of the first fruits and of the giving of the Law, approached. While they were still at work, a parcel was thrown to them from an airplane, and in it was a newspaper. From it they learned of the death of Moshe Glickson, the mentor and leader of the movement. All work stopped immediately, and those present gathered together to commune with his memory. It was then decided to call the settlement Kfar Glickson.

The Two Volumes

Not infrequently Glickson would digress from a conversation and ask whether he had not made a mistake in his choice of career by becoming a publicist. Was not his place at the university or in the literary world? I was present at some of these conversations, in particular when I came to suggest to him that he publish two volumes of his ideological articles on the problems of Zionism and the Yishuv.

He was perplexed by my suggestion, asking how a choice would be made from among the thousands of articles he had written. After I had sketched out for him the outline of the books as envisaged by members of the Zionist Youth secretariat, he agreed—although he had wanted a third volume that would have contained his political articles, particularly the series "Ba'Shaar" (in the Breach), which attacked the mandatory government for the betrayal of its alliance with the people of Israel.

Those political articles were important to Glickson. In the main, they dealt with the mandatory government's betrayal from a moral point of view. He did not accept the dissociation of statesmanship from morality; he rebelled against politicians who despised moral values. In his view the outcome of such an approach would bring the world and its people to destruction. Those were the years in which fascism was blossoming, nazism was on the rise, and liquidations were taking place in Soviet Russia. He suffered deeply and wrote: "Do we really desire to bring that corruption from Europe to us? Will we not learn from the mistakes that

Europe has made, contaminating itself in various directions and in various ways? Will we not comport ourselves here within the Yishuv, even though we have neither state nor government, as though we were already under independent Zionist rule, and we had to fulfill moral-political and social principles amongst us?"

In this struggle was inherent, perhaps, the beginning of the War of Independence. Zionist journalism made a great contribution to the formation of public opinion. It strengthened the Yishuv and raised its stature. Those were difficult days for the Yishuv, and fierce discussions raged over the question of "havlagah"—self-restraint. Glickson, who supported self-restraint, regarded it primarily as a moral issue. He protested with all his being against our sanctioning the murder of Arabs because there were Arabs who had murdered Jews. I remember the article he wrote in *Ha'aretz* on the day that the first person comdemned to death by the British government in Eretz Israel, Ben Yosef, was executed. The article shook my entire being.

As it was with his mentor Ahad Ha'am, so it was with Glickson; Ahad Ha'am wrote articles and reacted to events, and those articles are his literary heritage. The same was true for Glickson. Glickson saw no contradiction between Herzl's political Zionism and Ahad Ha'am's spiritual Zionism, but just as he differed from Weizmann on his attitude toward Britain, so he differed from Ahad Ha'am, and believed that a spiritual center would grow and develop properly only within a political framework. As he wrote: "These contradictions complement one another, and should not be regarded as standing in opposition to one another."

Glickson had a profound social awareness. He greatly feared the corruption of European society and the deep contradictions that had formed within it. I remember a conversation with him on events that had taken place in the Weimar Republic when the German Communists helped bring the Nazis to power. He was deeply apprehensive of developments and therefor protested with all his might against divisions within the people and in the Yishuv. He criticized Marxism for two reasons: first, because it freed man of moral responsibility and turned him into a cog in a machine; second, because it split the people and led to war between one section of the population and the other. He had another account to settle with Marxism, too. Marx's attitude to Judaism, and the self-hatred that was revealed in it. His monograph on Marxism is one of the finest on that subject in Hebrew literature. Glickson sought social justice—a better, a reformed society—and for that reason regarded Marxism as a catastrophe.

Glickson also had difficult debates with Berl Katznelson. Moshe

Glickson, the ideologist of General Zionism, faced Berl Katznelson, the ideologist of the Socialist workers movement. Glickson marveled at the pioneering and settlement creation that symbolized the elevation of man, and approved of the effort to create better relations in society, but he asked: "How can that society live in a secular atmosphere?" He did not believe that it was possible artificially, through social events and the artificial organization of festivals, to provide an alternative to the great moral, national and human ideals inherent in our traditional festivals.

He did not, for example, ask the kibbutzim and moshavim to fulfill the sabbath laws according to the *Shuchan Aruch*, but he did ask them to observe the sanctity of the sabbath as the sublime creation of the people of Israel. Today, decades after he wrote his articles on the sabbath, the Ministry of Education has awakened to the need to establish a center for Jewish consciousness in the school system. This center is still in the embryonic stage; what will it be like when completed? One cannot force teachers to behave as Jewish consciousness demands if their lives, physical and spiritual, are not in consonance with it.

A collection of essays were published in the sixties by the Zionist Youth, *Chinuch le' Emuna U' Lemasoret* (Education in Faith and Tradition) and dedicated in memory of our friend Dov Shiber, former director of the Nitzanim youth village. It embodies these principles and is drawn from the same pure faith with which Dr. Glickson inspired us all. Glickson's doctrine of Judaism and Zionism has stood the test of time and it is still valid today.

A miracle happened for Glickson and for us: we met. Glickson was delighted when students of the Zionist Youth came to him. Nathan Bistritsky recently told me that a number of years after the meeting with us, Glickson said to him, "I am no longer barren, insofar as the movement and the public are concerned: I have heirs."

Pinchas Rosen

Pinchas Rosen (Felix Rosenbluth) was born in 1887 of a religious family. His father, Shmuel Rosenbluth, came to Germany from Hungary in 1871. He studied at the Pressburg Yeshiva and intended to continue his studies at the rabbinical seminary in Berlin. However, when he was seventeen years old, his elder brother, Isidor, who had left Hungary some years earlier, persuaded him to become an apprentice in the offices of the large metal factory owned by the Hirsch family. The factory was in Messingwerk, a townlet of three hundred inhabitants some forty-five kilometers from Berlin. There Shmuel Rosenbluth lived for nearly forty years and there he raised his family. When he was about thirty, the Hirsch family invited Shmuel to their home town of Halberstadt and introduced him to their children's governess, Fanny Pulvermacher, who came from Berlin. Her family was originally from the province of Posen, which had belonged to Poland before the partition.

The memoirs of Pinchas Rosen's brother, Martin Michael Rosenbluth, contain a wealth of information about Shmuel Rosenbluth's family, and the childhood and youth of his sons. Martin was the eldest son, a year older than Felix. He relates that his maternal great-grandfather, Rabbi Shaul Pulvermacher, lived in Gnesen in the province of Posen in Poland with his wife, Freida. They ran a wholesale textile business and had twenty-one children. Freide—Pinchas Rosen's mother—was also called Freida in Yiddish, but the name was changed to Fanny. Mrs. Rosenbluth used to tell her children much about the interesting family she came from.

The marriage of Shmuel Rosenbluth to Fanny-Frieda Pulvermacher took place in Berlin in 1884. They were a middle-class couple and their living was assured. They had seven children—five boys and two girls. Since the family was religious, all the children prayed and studied Bible, Mishna, and even Talmud. The celebration of the sabbath and of the Jewish festivals left an indelible mark on the young Rosenbluths. As for the Bar Mitzva, it was not just a family affair: it was a public event. In Messingwerk there were a number of Jewish families, among whom a spirit of friendship and cooperation developed. The children grew up together, and the adults maintained the Jewish community in the best traditions of German Jewry of the time. However, Kurt Blumenfeld's description of the Rosenbluth family as ultra-Orthodox seems to have been exaggerated.

Felix Rosenbluth, then, had a thoroughly Jewish upbringing. He learned Hebrew as a child, and also studied Rashi. However, his parents made sure that all of the children would be given a German education and would have a thorough knowledge of German language, literature, and culture. So many hours a day were set aside for the study of the Bible and the Jewish holy books, and so many were devoted to reading German poetry and prose. There was no contradiction in this system of education. As religious Jews the Rosenbluth children had to study and become familiar with their Jewish sources in order to maintain their Judaism; as loyal German citizens whose future was in Germany, they had to be thoroughly conversant with German culture and with the customs of the German people. They also studied European literature in German translation, and their parents saw to it that they acquired a knowledge of other European languages as well.

On summer Saturdays, the Rosenbluth children used to walk quite a distance to their secondary school, where they were exempt from writing on the sabbath. In winter they would stay over Friday night with a family who lived near the school so as not to have to walk the long way from home in the cold and frost. Thus, they fulfilled both the easy and the more difficult commandments. Life in the Rosenbluth family ran on blissfully and smoothly. More about Felix Rosenbluth's early years can be found in Martin Micheal Rosenbluth's memoirs, mentioned above. Martin and Felix were great friends. They also looked very much alike, and people often mistook them for one another.

Zionism reached Messingwerk two or three years after the first Zionist Congress of 1897. Theodor Herzl's speech had marked the turning point. Even before that, European Jewry, including the German Jews, had been shocked by the Dreyfus trial in Paris. Other signs of anti-Semitism had also sprouted—even in Germany. But it was Herzl who wrought the change in the ideas and opinions of the Jews of Europe, in particular among the youth. His meetings with Emperor Wilhelm II as well as his other activities spawned legends that circulated among the Jews. When Lazarus Barth came to Messingwerk to preach Zionism, Felix was one of the first to be won over to the idea and to the new movement. His parents later joined the Mizrahi movement, and the rest of the family was to follow suit. Lazarus Barth had great influence on religious Jewish circles in Germany. This was a period of great awakening among the younger generation of German Jews. Indeed, one of the main centers of world Zionist activity was in Germany.

The ninth Zionist Congress was held in Hamburg in 1909. David Wolffsohn was then president of the World Zionist Organization and was under heavy attack from the opposition, led by Menachem Ussishkin, Yechiel Tchlenow, and Chaim Weizmann. Dr. Arthur Hantke was active alongside Wolffsohn. The smaller Zionist Actions Committee was composed of David Wolffsohn, Professor Otto Warburg and Jacobus Kahn.

At the tenth Zionist Congress in Basle in 1911, Wolffsohn's opponents gained the upper hand, and he resigned. Professor Otto Warburg was elected president of the Zionist Organization, and the smaller Zionist Actions Committee consisted of Nahum Sokolow, Shmaryahu Levin, Victor Jocobson and two German Zionist leaders, Warburg and Arthur Hantke.

In 1910, Felix Rosenbluth's brother Martin had been invited by David Wolffsohn to act as secretary to the president; that was the beginning of his Zionist career, which was to last for fifty years. In the same year, the Rosenbluth family moved from Messingwerk to Berlin. Felix was one of the most active members of the German Zionist organization. He and his colleagues, primarily Kurt Blumenfeld, transformed the German Zionist Federation into one of the principal constituents of the World Zionist Organization.

Felix Rosenbluth studied law in Berlin and in Freiburg. As his studies progressed, his Zionist activity expanded. When the seventh Zionist Congress was held in 1905, Felix came for the first time from Freiburg to Basle to participate in the congress as an usher. He was greatly influenced by "The Zionists of Zion" who fiercely opposed the Uganda project. His Zionism was always consistent. He conceived of it as a route leading directly to its goal. For him, Zionism was constructive: its basis was practical work in Eretz Israel, its soul the Hebrew language and culture. It's first goal was aliyah to Eretz Israel and personal identification. These were the principles that guided Felix Rosenbluth's life. Even after the establishment of the state, when he discussed with Ben-Gurion the need for the continued existence and activity of the World Zionist Organization, he argued in favor of the thesis that Zionism implied aliyah, claiming that without this principle it had no future.

During the period of his Jewish and Zionist activity in Germany, Felix probably never imagined that in the early twenties, after the Balfour Declaration, he would be called upon by Dr. Chaim Weizmann to become a member of the World Zionist Executive. The fifteen years between the first Zionist Congress he attended and his appointment to the executive were fateful years both for German Zionism and for the World Zionist Organization.

Felix Rosenbluth belonged to the faction of German Zionism that had come to the conclusion that the Jews of Germany, although citizens of the German state, were not Germans. In 1912, the Conference of German Zionists held at Posen resolved that, in accordance with Theodor Zlocisti's proposal, every Zionist must consider Eretz Israel the aim of his life. Rosenbluth was among those who fought for implementation of this resolution. During the language conflict in Eretz Israel he came out squarely in favor of Hebrew and against German as the language of instruction in the Hilfsverein schools. For Rosenbluth, loyalty to the basic tenets of Zionism was the practical expression of the renaissance of the people and its reorganization for the rebuilding of Eretz Israel. His struggle and his activities in support of these ideas were to bring him to the head of the German Zionist Federation.

Felix's friends knew that he could be relied upon, and that he was worthy of leading them. His earnestness, his honesty, and his devotion earned him support and appreciation. German Jewry had become an important prop for Weizmann after the Balfour Declaration. The German Zionists did not adopt the Helsingfors Program, which advocated a struggle to obtain national rights in the Diaspora, nor did they believe in Zionism on two fronts, one in Eretz Israel and the other in the Diaspora. German Zionism was centered on Palestine and had only one goal: the construction and development of Jewish settlements in Eretz Israel. This principle united Chaim Weizmann, Felix Rosenbluth, Arthur Hantke, Kurt Blumenfeld and many other German Zionist personalities.

After years of service as head of the German Zionist Federation, Rosenbluth was called upon in 1925 to head the Organization Department of the World Zionist Executive in London, where he remained until he immigrated to Eretz Israel. At that time London was becoming the center for the regeneration of the Zionist movement, now in need of reinforcement and expansion. It was vitally important to reconstruct the national bodies of the World Zionist Organization, to guarantee the democratic character of the Zionist movement, and to transform it into a central force among the people. Felix Rosenbluth brought with him to London the benefit of his experience of public life in German Zionism.

Rosenbluth's service on the executive in London is one of the landmarks in his career. However, faithful to his beliefs, Felix had been thinking of aliyah for a long time. In 1923 he had visited Eretz Israel, and had remained there for two years (from September 1923 to September 1925), to learn the language and acquaint himself with conditions. His sister Malli, together with her husband, Dr. Felix Danziger, founded a hospital in Jerusalem in 1923. Six years later they transferred it to Tel Aviv, where it is still functioning. His brother, Dr. Leo, was living in Rishon le-Zion, where he practiced medicine. At his death he was surrounded by the affection and esteem of the inhabitants of the pioneer town and in particular of the mothers, whose children he had cared for with such devotion. That same year, 1924, the Rosenbluth parents came to visit Malli, Leo, and Felix in Eretz Israel. In 1931 Felix decided to immigrate, putting into practice the Zionist principle for which he had fought for so many years. He brought with him a wealth of experience from his years as a Zionist in the Diaspora—a brilliant past, rich in achievement, which was to serve him well as he took his first steps in the Land of Promise.

Felix Rosenbluth began life in Eretz Israel as a lawyer in the office of Dr. Moshe Zemora, a prominent lawyer who, after the establishment of the state, was appointed president of the Supreme Court. A few years after Felix Rosenbluth had settled in Eretz Israel, the terrible tragedy of German Jewry began to unfold. For years prior to this period, he and his friends in the German Zionist leadership had been warning against the complacency of the leaders of German Jewry who believed that the Jews had a future in Germany.

Even after the Nazis came to power, not all Jews believed that the time had come to abandon Germany, but the anti-Jewish measures that the Nazi regime began to implement shook German Jewry to its foundations. Felix Rosenbluth considered it an obligation to help his colleagues and friends, the Jews and Zionists of Germany, who decided to immigrate to Eretz Israel and make their homes there. The Union of German Immigrants was established at that time, and Rosenbluth was one of its central figures. The Union of German Immigrants accomplished more than any other immigrant organization. It set up an apparatus for the absorption of the immigrants into economic, social, public, and professional life. During that same period, 1935 to 1945, Rosenbluth was a member of the Tel Aviv City Council, and within that forum he voiced his opinions on local issues as well as on matters of concern to the entire Yishuv. It was only natural that during that period Felix should belong to the General Zionist Movement, whose spokesman was Moshe Glickson. When Kurt Blumenfeld organized "Hakidma"—which included most of the German Zionist immigrants—Felix Rosenbluth did not see any contradiction between membership in the General Zionist movement and affiliation to Hakidma; in fact, he belonged to them both.

In the early forties, Felix Rosenbluth and George Landauer, along with many other German Zionist leaders who had immigrated, came to the conclusion that maintaining the Union of German Immigrants as a means of immigrant absorption was not enough; it was time to penetrate the institutions of the Yishuv and of the Zionist Movement. To do that, a public poitical organization was needed. They created the New Aliyah, and Felix Rosenbluth presided over it from 1947 to 1948. The great success scored by the New Aliyah in the elections to the National Assembly became the central event. The New Aliyah fought for cooperation between the Yishuv and the mandatory government, and struggled openly against the "dissidents." It was a progressive Zionist organization that held to social values and represented the moderate wing of political Zionism. It united within it both the middle class and labor elements of the German immigrants and primarily the working intelligentsia. It also had its own group within the Histadrut: the New Working Aliyah. Its outstanding achievement was the involvement of the new German olim in the highest institutions of the Yishuv, and in local councils. In this way, the new element was woven into the fabric of Zionist settlement.

Meanwhile, the political struggle of the Yishuv against the mandatory government was intensifying because of Britain's repudiation of the principles of the mandate and of the Balfour Declaration. As Nazi domination spread, it became imperative to save an increasing number of Jews from Europe; and as collaboration with the mandatory government grew increasingly difficult, agitation within the New Aliyah grew. A debate raged over the question of direction. The World War II era forced everyone to take a clear stand and to chose the path he wished to follow. Felix Rosenbluth headed the group that supported partition—the establishment of a Jewish state in part of Eretz Israel. On this issue he was loyal to Chaim Weizmann. He of course wanted the plan to be carried out without precipitating a crisis in relations between the Yishuv and the British government. I well remember his appearances at the meetings of the Inner Zionist Council in Jerusalem when he opposed the Zionist Executive's policy, later formulated in the Biltmore Program. He also disagreed on more than one occasion with the "combat" operations, and he was particularly revolted by terrorism. However, any effort to describe him as having objected to the establishment of the Jewish state does him great injustice and denies historical fact.

Within the New Aliyah Rosenbluth fought for the establishment of the state against Landauer, who did not believe in political independence and feared that the struggle the Yishuv was waging would bring it to a disastrous end. The differences of opinion between the two groups eventually led to disintegration of the New Aliyah. It was the eve of the establishment of the state. The Zionist Workers movement was trying to unite all the progressive Zionist elements in the country into a new political force. Its past attempts to do so had failed, but in 1948, just before the establishment of the state, the possibilities were better. And indeed, the Rosenbluth wing of the New Aliyah united with the Zionist Workers and the progressive faction of the General Zionists to form the Progressive Party. Felix Rosenbluth did not hesitate, therefore, to dismantle the New Aliyah organization and to join up with like-minded elements in the new Progressive Party. The three elements that constituted the new party complemented one another.

Dr. Nahum Goldmann was among the personalities who brought the three partners together under the "bridal canopy." They declared the establishment of the Progressive Party at the founding convention held at the Habima theatre. Felix Rosenbluth was the central figure of the new party. He was accepted not only by the members of German origin but also by many in the Yishuv and in the Zionist movement. He already had a brilliant record: in Germany, in London, and in Eretz Israel between 1931 and 1948. He had a fine reputation as a conscientious lawyer and both his personal qualities and his rich public and political experience fitted him to fulfill the greatest role of his life as the first minister of justice of the State of Israel. He was one of the signatories of the Declaration of Independence, and one of the founders of independent Israel. From the establishment of the state he served in the government of Israel for nearly thirteen years—the entire period during which the Progressive Party existed—with the exception of one year, when his party was in the opposition. He built Israel's legal system and was accepted by all parties as minister of justice: they knew that he fulfilled his functions with complete impartiality. His speeches in the Knesset carried great moral weight, and he was one of the most prominent and influential ministers in the government. The people had faith in Israel's judges; they knew that the judiciary was independent and that it was one of the foundations of the new Israeli democracy.

As minister of justice, Pinchas Rosen née Felix Rosenbluth was at the peak of his public Zionist career. He was not only minister of justice; he was also "Minister of the Knesset." His friendly relations with Joseph Sprinzak, Speaker of the Knesset and architect of Israeli parliamentarianism, assisted him in promoting cooperation between the executive and the legislature. He and his deputies represented the government to the Speaker and regularly attended Knesset sessions. He frequently replied to questions on behalf of the government, not only those relating to his own ministry. However, being a member of the cabinet implies much more than only ministerial responsibility, however important the ministry may be. Vital decisions are made by the cabinet. Between David Ben-Gurion, the first prime minister, and Pinchas Rosen, the first minister of justice, friendly relations developed over the years even though their opinions frequently differed. The friendship and cooperation between them continued until the Lavon affair.

Difficult decisions had undoubtedly been taken during the years that Pinchas Rosen served in the cabinet—decisions concerning the War of Independence, the Sinai campaign, and other difficult issues. But it was the Lavon affair that led to the parting of the ways between Ben-Gurion and Rosen. Rosen was chairman of the "Committee of Seven" that decided that Minister of Defense Pinchas Lavon did not give the order that launched the misconceived operation in Egypt. Ben-Gurion disagreed with their handling of the matter and the committee's findings. He resigned. Pinchas Rosen, as a friend and colleague of Ben-Gurion, made supreme efforts to prevent the prime minister from taking this step.

The state, the Knesset, and the cabinet were deeply shocked by the affair. Its handling in the Foreign Affairs and Security Committee, and the facts that were published concerning the committee's deliberations, shocked public opinion. Rosen believed that the path he had chosen—appointment of the Committee of Seven—was the best way to contain the affair. But Ben-Gurion did not accept the committee's judgment and did not heed the advice of Rosen and his many other friends—so a fierce political struggle developed.

The 1961 elections were approaching. The Progressive Party came to the conclusion that the crisis which had overtaken our young democracy in the wake of the Lavon affair made it imperative to create a larger liberal-progressive force. Pinchas Rosen had wanted for some time to create such a force, and he supported Nahum Goldmann's bid to unite the Progressive and the General Zionist parties. The issue was brought up for decision at the Progressive Party's conference in Netanya in 1954. I was among those who worked, at that time, against the proposed union. The General Zionists were then a large group in the Knesset—more than four times the size of the Progressive Party— and there was, therefore, no prospect of the united party representing progressive social liberalism.

In 1961 however, the picture was different: the General Zionists then had only eight seats in the Knesset, while the Progressives had six. It was therefore possible to envisage a party based on parity between the two elements that would create it. The troubles that had beset the General Zionist Party previously, the setbacks it had suffered, and its sharp drop from the second largest parliamentary group to a mere eight members, led to some real soul-searching among its leaders. For months they negotiated with Herut, and when they came to us after these talks had failed, our first question was whether this meant a volte-face on their part. We asked whether they would be prepared to accept a union between our two parties only, and to assure us that no initiative would be taken at a later date to unite with Herut. (For the Progressive Party, union with Herut was out of the question.) We were given that assurance, but subsequently it was not honored.

In 1961, then, the time was ripe to establish a progressive, liberal, center force whose role would be to counterbalance rule by the Poalei Eretz Israel Party (Mapai), and in time, perhaps, become an alternative to it. The new United Liberal Party's list was headed by Rosen: he was then at the peak of his popularity as champion of the struggle for moral democratic principles. The bulk of public opinion was on his side. There is no doubt that the crisis in his relations with Ben-Gurion was one of the most difficult periods in Rosen's life and public career. The crisis was to last for several years, and I am not sure that the wound ever healed. From time to time attempts were made to reconcile the two men, but there seemed to be no way of bridging the gap between their respective stands on the way in which the Lavon affair had been handled. After the elections the United Liberal Party remained in the opposition, so Rosen's ministerial appointment came to an end. During his years in the opposition, Rosen, as head of the parliamentary group, did his best to uphold in the Knesset the legal, moral, constitutional, and political values in which he had always believed.

The transition from the cabinet to the Knesset opposition changed nothing in Pinchas Rosen's behavior. He enjoyed a privileged status within the party, and he knew that his opinion carried great weight. Personal relations within the United Liberal Party were excellent; its leaders had confidence in one another. It was obvious that our General Zionist Party partners were very disappointed that they had not entered the government. Both for the development of the Liberal Party, and in the national interest, it was undesirable for the cabinet to be one-sided and unbalanced in its social structure and political tendencies. Levi Eshkol, who formed the government for Ben-Gurion, gave in to the demand of Achdut Ha-Avodah, which agreed to join the government only if the Liberals were kept out. Since Eshkol nurtured hopes of uniting Achdut Ha-Avodah and Mapai, the agreement that he had already completed with the Liberal Party was, at the last minute, not put into effect. Our partners, the General Zionists, who had hoped to enter the government through their partnership with the Progressive Party, began to seek arguments to back up the assumption that the Liberal Party had no future. We, the ex-Progressives, did the opposite: we demanded patience, explaining that the Liberal Party's time would come: the slow increase that had appeared in the 1961 elections—seventeen seats for the united party as against fourteen held previously by its two groups before unification—was only the first step toward a large liberal center. It would have to grow step-by-step, win the voters' confidence, and seek no new partners, for additional elements could well destroy the united party that had been established.

But Rosen's efforts, and our own, were of no avail. In 1964, the ex–General Zionist leaders began to whistle a new tune: they claimed that no alternative to Mapai was possible without a union with Herut. Thus all our attempts to explain that Herut was not a liberal party and that a partnership between them and ourselves was impossible, our respective political aims were not identical, and our respective approaches to the fundamental problems of the state were dissimilar came to naught. In the end, we demanded that the gentleman's agreement that had been made when the united party was founded be respected. Rosen was particularly sensitive over this issue, and he warned the General Zionists against their hasty step, and against repudiating their 1961 undertaking.

Rosen made a supreme effort to save the united party. He was apprehensive about the ex-Progressive camp going it alone in the elections because the entire "independent" press was preaching at us, day in and day out, to join the Likud bloc. We were prepared to promise that we would accept the majority decision in the united party for coalition or for opposition and in the event of our remaining in the opposition we were prepared to reach some form of collaboration with Herut. However, we insisted on running for the elections independently under our own banner and with our own platform. But those who no longer believed in the future of social liberalism and who sought their salvation with Herut did not heed Rosen's warnings. Nor, apparently, did they know us well enough: they thought we would give in to the pressure of the press and public opinion—a campaign they had organized to that end.

For Rosen, as for us all, it was a rude shock. At the personnel level, too, things were not easy. Some of our leading members were ill. And we did not possess either the means or the apparatus to start all over again. We could either disavow ourselves and disappear from Israel's political map, or we could take the step that our conscience dictated: part company from those with whom we had hoped to build a liberal center, and raise the banner of humane, democratic liberalism alone, even if it meant swimming against the strong current of psychosis that had been whipped up in public opinion.

Rosen was in a more difficult situation than the rest of us. He was, in fact, thinking of retiring from political life in the Knesset, and he told the party so. He did not want to head the list in 1965. But when the split came, and we established the Independent Liberal Party, it was clear that Rosen would resume his political activity and would head the Independent Liberal Party list. The period immediately preceding the establishment of the party was one of the most difficult Rosen had known. Some members, prophets of doom who were influenced by the press, claimed that we would win only two seats in the Knesset. Rosen asked himself and his colleagues if that was how his long career in Zionism and in the state was to end. He found encouragement among supporters who rallied around us, but was disappointed by those who abandoned the Progressive camp. However, in his public appearances he was extremely restrained. The separation from the General Zionists, now called the Liberal Party, was without personal recrimination, but there is no doubt that it left a sense of bitterness.

The electoral campaign was fierce. Rosen went into action with all his vigor, and did not refuse a single task imposed upon him during the combat; it was, perhaps, one of the most difficult he had waged in public life. He came to party headquarters every day and made many personal contacts in order to convince the waverers who had developed cold feet. The elections came, and proved that fidelity to one's principles pays. The result was a great surprise: the Independent Liberal Party won about the same percentage as the Progressive Party had won in the past, despite the fact that it had fought the elections under extremely difficult conditions; that it had had to reorganize its branches, and that it did not appear to have the necessary financial means and organizational apparatus. Gahal, on the other hand, took a beating, and the vision of the alternative, which had pushed the general Zionists into establishing Gahal with Herut, vanished. Rosen returned to the Knesset at the head of a five-member group and was very active in the coalition negotiations that led to our partnership with the Labor Party, the National Religious Party, and Mapai in the leadership of the state. Rosen was particularly sensitive about the promises he had made to his electors. And indeed, we remained faithful to our principles and our promises.

The public knew and appreciated this. We entered the cabinet as partners of the liberal public, and despite the fact that we were a small party, we were promised that our principles would, as far as possible, be maintained. We also obtained influential posts in two economic ministries (Tourism and Development).

Rosen was active on Knesset committees and scrupulously fulfilled his obligations as a member of the Knesset. We were all full of admiration for him; we listened to his advice, and we knew that his opinion carried great weight not only with us, but with the entire Knesset as well.

The unanimous respect in which Pinchas Rosen was held was clearly expressed on his eightieth birthday when the entire government united to congratulate him. The opposition parties, leading personalities and institutions did likewise, and he was surrounded by affection and esteem. The Zionist Executive confirmed in principle our proposal to establish a new settlement that would bear his name. Rosen was against any of the celebrations that were usually held to mark the attainment of four score years. He did not agree to the formation of an anniversary committee, and refused to listen to speeches about himself. He did not wish his birthday to be turned into a public event. But as a faithful Zionist he gladly accepted the suggestion to name a new settlement after him. He also agreed that the Israel Philharmonic Orchestra, over whose destinies he had presided for many years, should give a special concert in his honor under the patronage of the president of the State. He was always overcome by music, and he did much for the Israel Philharmonic Orchestra.

Rosen remained faithful to himself. One might say of him that his life was like a tree that neither bent nor broke. He was an unswerving Zionist and democrat, a humanist in all his being, and a progressive liberal who represented the best values of European and Jewish culture. His disillusionment with Germany was enormous, and he refused to visit that country after the war. He never forgave the German people, and although for political reasons he was in favor of the establishment of diplomatic relations with Germany, he was extremely restrained in his relations with it. The degeneration of the German people under Nazi rule and the genocide it perpetrated on the Jewish people led to a deep spiritual rift in Rosen's attitude to the land of his birth. He was therefore all the more disappointed by the Jews who returned there. He opposed fundraising for Israel and other Zionist activities in Germany, and did not accept the idea of reestablishing Jewish communities on German soil. For him, German Jewry had come to an end. He was not prepared to sanction any renewal of it. This attitude was characteristic of Pinchas Rosen. All his life he had rebelled against double standards of morality.

In 1968, after three years of service in the Knesset, Pinchas Rosen retired. His departure was accompanied by editorials of appreciation and gratitude. Unanimous appreciation was expressed for his contribution to the establishment and consolidation of Israel's independent judiciary, and for his services to Israeli parliamentarianism, the symbol of our sovereignty and our democracy. The party institutions asked him to remain in the Knesset until the end of the parliamentary term, but he refused. He wanted to make way for young Nissim Eliad to enter the House. He continued as president of the Independent Liberal Party, and he participated regularly in the meetings of the party leadership. Until 1974 he also continued to hold the position of governor of the World Zionist Organization and of the Jewish Settlement Fund at the Bank Leumi Le'Israel. Rosen was acutely aware of political and social problems. He refused to head the Independent Liberal Party list in the Knesset elections once he had retired from the House. On Rosen's eighty-fifth birthday, Ben-Gurion proposed a reconciliation. Rosen asked Ben-Gurion to promise him that if he intended to criticize the Committee of Seven, he would level his criticism at its president, and not at Levi Eshkol. Ben-Gurion refused to give such a promise, and relations between the two men remained cool. Rosen refused to publish a selection of the speeches and lectures he had delivered in the Knesset and in Zionist institutions. He said that they had been written under his guidance by a team of advisers and assistants, and that he did not wish to indulge in the coquetry of publishing *Complete Works of . . .* as others had done. Nor did he write memoirs, as did his brother Martin.

Pinchas Rosen's personality and his action over many decades, first in the Zionist Movement and then as one of the founding fathers of the state, have left their mark, and will undoubtedly serve as an example to many others in the future.

To mark Pinchas Rosen's eighty-fifth birthday, a Chair of Constitutional Law was inaugurated in his name at the Tel Aviv University. On that festive occasion I made the following remarks on behalf of the Independent Liberal Party:

On one of my visits to the Queen Mother of Belgium, Elizabeth, she said to me with great feeling, "Justice and music are in your blood." She was referring, of course, to the Jewish people who gave to the world not only prophets, and men who fought for justice and social values, but also composers and musical geniuses. Queen Elizabeth herself had met many of the latter: they had been her guests and she had attended their concerts or invited them to play at her palace. On that occasion I replied to the Queen, "There is one in Israel who represents both those values. He is the minister of justice and the president of the Israel Philharmonic Orchestra, and a great music lover." When I told her of Pinchas Rosen's personality, his life and his career, the queen requested me to convey to him her warm greetings. And I did so.

Mr. Rosen does not like exaggerations and neither do I, but I believe I was speaking the truth because for many people in the State of Israel he is the symbol of justice and honesty. As Israel's first minister of justice, he laid solid foundations for Israel's independent judiciary. The people have confidence in our legal institutions and in Israel itself as a law-abiding state, which is among the most reformed in the world.

Pinchas Rosen is blessed with responsible judgment in national affairs. He is a man of political moderation—not moderation as a compromise but a moderation that springs from the responsible attitude that statesmen must know how much power they dispose of, and what the limits of the permissible are. But he knows how to fight, how to stand his ground on the essential and not yield on issues vital to the existence of the people and the state. Pinchas Rosen has a talent for fighting for moderation and reason. He has an aversion to puffery and boastfulness, and is a man of common sense. He represents a polite, cultured way of life and respects other people and their opinions out of fidelity to the principle of tolerance and mutual attentiveness.

His liberalism is humane. His belief in democracy is unconditional and is unaffected by whether he is in the majority or the minority. He was born in a religious family—hence his basically Jewish outlook and his respect for the nation's traditions. But he opposes religious coercion. He possesses the gift of remaining loyal to his colleagues. He takes an interest in the individual, and respects decisions and conclusions even if he does not agree with them. He listens to and examines every reason and opinion, and only rarely, and then on vital issues, does he express himself in order to influence the decision to be taken.

Pinchas Rosen is loyal to the Zionism of Chaim Weizmann. He was a Zionist from his youth, and for over forty years he served the Zionist Organization as a leader of German Zionism, as the Zionist Organization's attorney, and as a member of the executive. He is faithful to the Zionism of constructive settlement in town and village, and this brought him closer to the pioneer and labor movements. At the same time, he has complete faith in private enterprise, upholding the right of the individual to practice it and fighting for a balance of influence between the various elements in the economy and in society. He had the privilege of being one of the founders of the State of Israel, and he did much to ensure that our state would be a progressive democracy representing the highest human and national ideals of the people of Israel and of western civilization. Many were those who learned from him and were influenced by his radiant personality, and we are happy to congratulate him today, as the Chair for Constitutional Law at the Hebrew University takes his name. No name could be more suitable for the chair than that of Pinchas Rosen, Israel's first minister of justice. The students who study here will seek inspiration from his personality and his career.

All those who helped in the establishment of the Pinchas Rosen Chair regard it as a privilege: the university, the government, the

Jewish Agency, the Bank Le'umi and the Dan Hotel Company. This ceremony takes place on the eve of Pinchas Rosen's eighty-fifth birthday. The Independent Liberal Party is proud of its president and leader, and joins with him and his family in celebrating his birthday.

Levi Eshkol

I was a member of the Histadrut Executive secretariat during World War II when I met Levi Eshkol. He was then a member of Kibbutz Degania B, secretary of the Tel Aviv Workers' Council, director of the Mekorot company and one of its promoters, and a member of the Haganah command.

Our personal ties grew closer when we were both members of the Jewish Agency Executive. I was head of Youth Aliyah and Eshkol was head of the Settlement Department. When Eliezer Kaplan was appointed Israel's first Minister of Finance in the Provisional Council of State and the first provisional government, Eskol replaced him as treasurer of the Jewish Agency and retained his Settlement Department post as well. I was then co-treasurer of the agency, and close cooperation was established between the two of us. During that period I came to know Eshkol well and became familiar with his ideas and his fields of interest. In certain areas Eshkol did a great deal, applying the theories of his teachers in the labor movement. A whole series of enterprises are linked directly to his name, his action and his vision.

Mekorot, for example, the national water authority, was in large measure Eshkol's own creation—the realization of his vision. Pinchas Sapir, who worked with Eshkol closely for many years, later assumed his position as director of Mekorot, promoting the water supply network plans and the drilling for additional water supplies throughout the country. Eshkol's major achievement, however, was the planning and realization of mass settlement after the proclamation of the state.

Many Arab villages had been abandoned; plantations were beginning to wither and rot. Eshkol could not come to terms with the fact that on the one hand thousands of unemployed Jews were languishing in the ma'abarot, while on the other, enormous possibilities existed for settlement and for the establishment of new Jewish villages in localities that the Arabs had deserted as they fled their homes during the War of

Independence. Eshkol tackled the problem, together with a team of devoted workers at the Settlement Department, giving the Jewish Agency Executive no respite until it gave the green light for the planning of hundreds of new villages throughout the country and authorized the transfer of the immigrants, people with neither skill nor agricultural training, to the abandoned lands and villages. The new settlers were told: "Here you will bring forth bread from the land." Skepticism reigned in many circles about the success of the enterprises, for the immigrants were, by nature, more attracted to city life.

Among them were immigrants from the Arab countries and North Africa, some from the primitive townlets and villages of the Atlas mountains, and the question was whether we would succeed in rooting them in the land. Eshkol called upon Ben-Gurion and the settlement movement to help him draw leaders from the veteran kibbutzim and moshavim, and transfer them to the new localities where they would live with the immigrants and teach them agriculture and the organization way of life in a Jewish village. Despite the difficulties there were many recruits, mostly from the second generation. The nuclei of the new villages began to take shape, and their various sections became productive. Naturally, large budgets and much agricultural equipment were required. To finance the operation, the Jewish Agency floated loans in the United States, some of them in the form of machinery and material. Eshol ran the entire operation, working with unparalleled devotion.

It was a huge enterprise. Naturally enough, the moshav proved the most suitable way of life for these adult immigrants who were not suited to kibbutz living and were also apprehensive about just what was meant by "cooperation." The mass settlement enterprise succeeded beyond all expectations, and Eshkol was always proud of those villages that were established on broad stretches of the newly independent Israel. The first housing units were concrete and wooden huts, but as the villages were consolidated and families grew, rooms were added and new houses were built to replace the temporary dwellings.

Levi Eshkol, a member of Kibbutz Degania B and of the pioneering and settlement movement, lived the problems of the Jewish village in every fiber of his being. Whenever problems of settlement or water resources arose during cabinet meetings, both before and after the Six-Day War, I would whisper to my neighbor at the cabinet table that the moment Eshkol embarked on a discussion of water, land, and settlement, all other items on the agenda would be postponed. Eshkol was obviously fond of these subjects; they reminded him of the past. I well remember the debate on settlement in the Jordan Valley. Eshkol returned from those areas and told the cabinet: "There is good land there;

we must find a way to bring water to it." That new settlement enterprise reminded him of his early days in the Jordan Valley when he and his colleagues established Kibbutz Degania B. The discussions on the Gaza strip and Rafiach settlements also delighted him. He lived those problems in all their gravity, showing deep insight and enthusiasm.

It was pleasant working with Levi Eshkol. He was a man of wit, humor, and good fellowship. He was able to cooperate even with political opponents. He made a good impression on leaders of other countries who saw in him the man of the soil, the embodiment of the new Jewish creativity. Everyone knew that during the years he was responsible for the state treasury—from the death of Eliezer Kaplan until he became prime minister—Eshkol did much to consolidate the Ministry of Finance and to build up Israel's economy. In fact, it was he who laid important foundations for the creation of the government companies and the development of new areas of the country. Eliezer Kaplan had not been able to expand and consolidate the economic branches of government activity, both because of his illness and because of a severe lack of financial resources. Eshkol was an economist; he had a broad vision of settlement and development. He loved to challenge the desert and develop new areas, search for mineral resources, and raise Jewish and non-Jewish capital for immigrant absorption and for the fulfillment of the state's great tasks.

His tenure as prime minister was difficult for him from the personal standpoint; first, because of the divisions within his party and the strained relations that developed between him and his mentor, David Ben-Gurion; second, because of the struggle between the Alignment—which he had established by bringing together Mapai and Achdut Ha-Avodah—and Rafi, headed by Ben-Gurion, along with Moshe Dayan, Shimon Peres, and many others whom Eshkol considered his colleagues, disciples, and heirs. He was forced into sharp conflict with them, not only on public issues but also on the personal level. The complications surrounding the Lavon affair; Ben-Gurion's accusations against Eshkol as the central figure who influenced Pinchas Rosen's Committee of Seven to reach the conclusions it did; the deep, unbridgeable breach that opened up between Eshkol and Ben-Gurion; the stormy debates in the press and public opinion—all these caused him great mental strain and hindered him in the fulfillment of his functions as prime minister. Even though Eshkol and his colleagues triumphed in the elections against Ben-Gurion and Rafi, the struggle continued and the tension mounted. It was a period of intense governmental preoccupation with foreign affairs and security on the one hand, and economic issues on the other. Just before the Six-Day War, when the skies over Israel were darkening, it was impossible to heal the breach between Ben-Gurion and Eshkol.

As a general rule, Eshkol showed generosity toward his political opponents. He agreed to bring the remains of Ze'ev Jabotinsky for reburial in Israel, in accordance with a government decision, fulfilling the last will of the Revisionist leader.

On the eve of the Six-Day War, when Israel faced great danger, Eshkol had the privilege of forming and heading a government of national unity for the first time in Israel's history. Despite the many cabinet debates, in which the broadest spectrum of opinion and outlook was represented, Eshkol did his utmost to maintain good relations with political opponents and to inspire the cabinet with a cordial and friendly spirit. Those were great days for Eshkol: the victory, the liberation of the Old City of Jerusalem; the historic visit to the Western Wall after nineteen years during which all contact with the hallowed site had been barred; the liberation of the Golan Heights, whence for nineteen years the Syrians had bombarded our agricultural villages; the stationing of the Israeli Army at Suez and Sharm-el-Sheikh, on the Straits of Tiran, and on the banks of the Jordan River. They were great, epochal days. Whoever had the privilege of having been a member of the cabinet at that time will never forget those days. Important discussions began with the great powers and also at the United Nations on the possibilities of peace with our neighboring countries. Then came the breach with the Communist bloc headed by Soviet Russia—a sharp contrast to the huge wave of enthusiasm that had just swept over the entire Jewish Diaspora.

Eshkol's special talent for winning the confidence of the world's great policymakers stood him in good stead, first and foremost in his relations with the president of the United States, Lyndon Johnson. For the first time, the doors of the White House were open to Prime Minister Levi Eshkol. There was no need to invent a pretext—such as the granting of an honorary doctorate—for his going to the United States. That first visit not only produced practical results but also led to an extraordinary relationship of mutual confidence, which in time was to bear important fruit. It became clear that the confidence Levi Eshkol had placed in Lyndon Johnson was justified, particularly during the waiting period that preceded the Six-Day War. Levi Eshkol did not doubt the Israel Defense Forces' ability to win, but he and the cabinet did not want to lose the fruits of victory after the war. They therefore decided to wait a few days to prevent our political isolation. And indeed, those few days preserved the confidence of Johnson and Eshkol in each other. Johnson was convinced that Eshkol and his government had exhausted every possibility before they embarked on the Six-Day War, especially after Johnson himself had proved unable to open the Straits of Tiran after Nasser had closed them; it was a task that only the IDF was able to accomplish.

The military victory was due entirely to our fighters and we paid the full price, but the political victories were not ours alone. Our partners were our loyal friends, with Lyndon Johnson at their head. When our troops stood at the Suez Canal, at the Jordan River, and on Mount Hermon, it was due in no small measure to the fact that the president of the United States agreed with us that this time we must achieve real peace and that the IDF must not budge from its positions until that peace was achieved. This policy was maintained by President Nixon, who consolidated and deepened it, working in a spirit of confidence and friendship with the then prime minister, Golda Meir. This proves the importance of keeping one's friends. Even when one struggles with them—as we did more than once with the United States government after the Six-Day War—that struggle must be conducted with a sense of responsibility, with understanding, and with care to retain friends even when one cannot accept their opinions and advice.

Levi Eshkol visited Lyndon Johnson for the second time at his Texas ranch, where he received an exceptionally warm welcome. That visit had very important results; the consent of the president to sell us Phantom and Skyhawk airplanes, and his agreement that the United States would become Israel's major arms supplier.

The last month of Eshkol's life was full of powerful emotions, both of sadness and joy. He received two letters from the president of the United States: in the first one, the president informed him that he had approved the signing of the contract to sell Israel fifty Phantom fighter planes—this during the period of the French arms embargo and the interruption of the sale of Mirage war planes to Israel in the wake of DeGaulle's decision. The second, and last letter from Johnson before he left office, was in payment of a debt to Eshkol: a promise to promote water desalination in Israel in accordance with the president's proposal to Congress within the budget framework. Although the desalination plant has not been installed in Israel to this day, Eshkol was extremely moved by the possibility. At the cabinet meeting during which Eshkol informed us of the letters, I sent a note to him saying, "It seems that Degania B and Texas speak the same language. The confidence between you two has produced two great things for Israel: Phantom fighter planes and the prospect of a desalination plant." Eshkol thanked me sincerely. I remembered Yosef Sprinzak's oft-quoted remark: "We pay compliments to a man when he is no longer capable of hearing them. We praise him after his death. Perhaps we could pay at least some of the compliments when the person concerned is still able to appreciate them?"

Among the last things Eshkol did was to convene two conferences. The first was devoted to Israel's economic development and was attended by all those who had the necessary means and experience to invest in Israel and become partners in the development of our economy. It was a most impressive assembly. I remember Eshkol rightly saying: "We have attained a new dimension." Since then, the governments of Israel have continued to hold economic conferences and to maintain the apparatus that was established by the first assembly. The second conference, the last of Eshkol's life, was devoted entirely to the Jewish Diaspora, particularly the problems of youth education and reinforcement of the ties between Israel and world Jewry.

Levi Eshkol not only had the privilege of establishing national unity in Israel in great and fateful times; he also built Jewish unity between Israel and the Diaspora. In his lifetime he accomplished great things as a pioneer, labor leader, builder of the national water authority, man of settlement, minister of defense, prime minister, and unifier of the Jews in Israel, and of Israel and the Jewish people.

Levi Eshkol earned his eternal place in the history of the people and the state.

Moshe Sharett

I first met Moshe Sharett at the eighteenth Zionist Congress, held in Prague in 1933. The congress was convened after the murder of Chaim Arlosoroff, the gifted young head of the political department of the Zionist Organization. During the congress the coalition executive composed of the labor movement, the Progressive General Zionists, and the Radical Zionists was set up; Moshe Sharett was elected to the Jewish Agency Executive and appointed head of its political department. He was thirty-nine at the time—the youngest member of the executive. He did not reach this position out of the blue: since his youth, he had been extensively involved in the party and in politics. Moshe Sharett was born in 1894 in Kharson, Russia, of a "Bilu" family, which bore the imprint of the personality of his father, Jacob Shertok. Jacob had been born in Pinsk, my own hometown, and while I was still a boy I heard talk in Young Zionist circles of the Bilu Jacob Shertok, born 1862, who had immigrated to Eretz Israel in 1881 at the time of the "Negev storms"—the term used to describe the pogroms that broke out in southern Russia—and of the birth of the Bilu movement. His first stop in Eretz Israel was Mikve Israel. A year later he joined up with a group of Zionist Bilu students who had immigrated from Russia about the same time. A few years later, Jacob Shertok returned to Russia for a short time, but the visit was prolonged for many years.

In 1906 Jacob Shertok immigrated once more, this time accompanied by his wife and sons. After a short stay in Jaffa he moved to a remote Arab village between Jerusalem and Shechem (Nablus). Moshe's father was not only a pioneer and a Bilu, he was also a Hebrew writer and translator. The Shertok home was imbued with a Jewish, Zionist atmosphere even when the family was still living outside Eretz Israel.

Moshe was twelve when he immigrated, and the two-year period during which the family remained in the Arab village left its mark on him for the rest of his life. It was here that he learned Arabic and acquired an intimate knowledge of the Arab way of life. This knowledge was to stand him in good stead many years later in the course of his political career. From the Arab village the family moved to Tel Aviv, the young city that had just been founded; indeed, the Shertok family was one of the first to settle in the city-on-the-sands. Moshe attended the Herzliya Gymnasium and was in the first graduating class. He continued his studies in Istanbul, capital of the Ottoman Empire, of which Eretz Israel was then a part. There he met Yitschak Ben-Zvi, David Ben-Gurion, David Remez, and other sons of the Yishuv who were also studying at the university in the Turkish capital.

With the outbreak of World War I, Moshe Shertok returned to Palestine. In 1916, he joined the Turkish Army, where he carried out important assignments. During his military service he acquired firsthand knowledge of the problems besetting the waning Ottoman Empire. Istanbul, its capital, was an important political nerve center. Among other things, Moshe also learned French, the language used by the ruling classes and the intelligentsia of the Middle Eastern countries. In time he became a highly talented polyglot. When the war was over, he linked his fate to the Labor Party and was active in its ranks. Even earlier, while still at the Gymnasium, he had had contacts with the Hagana and members of the pioneer movement; the pioneering ideals of the Second Aliyah had made headway among the secondary school pupils.

After the British conquest of Palestine and the establishment of the mandate, Moshe traveled to London with the intention of completing his studies, which had been interrupted in Istanbul by the war. Between 1920 and 1924 he studied at the London School of Economics and Political Science. He was greatly influenced by his teachers, the most distinguished of whom were Fabians and members of the British Labor Party. He was very active in Poalei Zion circles, which accepted him as a representative of the Labor movement in Eretz Israel.

On his return to Palestine in 1925, he joined the staff of *Davar*, the Labor Party newspaper which that year began to appear under the chief editorship of Berl Katznelson. When *Davar* started to publish a weekly English edition, Moshe naturally became its acting chief editor.

He had a penchant for lecturing to young people on political subjects. This affection for the young generation remained with him all his life, and during the trips on Zionist and political business which he undertook on behalf of the Zionist Movement or the state, he spent his free time working with the young Jewish generation and the Zionist youth movements. He was one of the few within the movement who were fully conscious of the great value of the youth movement and of the rising generation. The debates and conversations that developed after his lectures to the young people always delighted him. That was the only reason he assumed responsibility for Beit Berl after he left the government. Beit Berl was the major institute for the ideological education of the young members of his party, the Poalei Eretz Israel (Mapai).

His great interest in and extensive knowledge of Jewish and world literature, his special spiritual feeling for poetry (to which he devoted his leisure time), and his devotion to the Hebrew language, which he enriched with a wealth of idioms and expressions, led to his appointment as head of Am Oved, Histadrut's publishing house, during the last years of his life. Among his other qualities he was a highly talented draftsman of statements and speeches. He suffered virtual physical pain from sloppy Hebrew expression. On more than one occasion he lost his temper, corrected speakers, and made audible remarks about their language. If he did not do so on the spot, he would send them handwritten notes pointing out their mistakes.

Without doubt, the many memoranda and letters he wrote or delivered orally during his three decades of intense poliltical activity were linguistic and stylistic masterpieces. But his concern for fine style was not a superficial one; it was deeply rooted in him, an integral part of his way of life, a fundamental element of his public career, of his relationships with people, and of his many public appearances. He was uncommonly sensitive to style in human relations. Written and oral expression worthy of the name were not for him a matter of elegant or correct use of language, but an integral part of human contact. He was always properly dressed, simply and without ostentation. His whole appearance inspired respect. He was clean-handed and pure-hearted, and behaved with refinement both toward those who were close to him and toward those far from his own circle. This was the Moshe Sharett way of life. He was concerned not only with substance and standards, but also with tone and phraseology, which to him were an integral part of the substance. Only rarely did he lose his calm. At the many conferences and gatherings of the World Zionist Organization, the Histadrut, and the party, Moshe Sharett's wording was not always accepted, although everyone respected and praised it. I would say that he was influenced in no small measure by the style of the English gentleman. He adopted from it the elements that suited him and were in keeping with our way of life.

When I made Moshe Sharett's closer acquaintance—he was then a member of the Zionist and Jewish Agency executives and head of the political department—I discovered a man who, in his appearance and speech, tried to concentrate his entire being on persuading his audience, going into far too much detail in his effort to succeed. He still bore the mark of the teacher endeavoring to transmit everything he knew to his pupils, with all requisite thoroughness—trying to leave no possible doubt of the justice of his words and assumptions. Moshe Sharett had, in fact, been a schoolteacher in his youth, and it had left its imprint on him. When he began his political career in the upper echelons of the Zionist movement in Jerusalem, he was already outstanding for his extensive higher education and his command of both western and eastern languages. Naturally, he knew Russian, the language spoken by his parents and family, and even in Hebrew, the language of his national culture, he was uncommonly well versed. His three decades of activity, first as a member of the Zionist Executive, later, as a member of Israel's first cabinet, and finally as Chairman of the Zionist Executive and the Jewish Agency (the honorary post he held until the day of his death)—all those years constitute a succession of tremendous, comprehensive achievements rarely accomplished in one man's lifetime. During that entire period he was at the center of events.

A few months after his election to the Zionist Executive in 1936 the Arab riots broke out, continuing without interruption until 1939. During that period a unit of Jewish guards was set up, and a tough continuous political battle was waged in Jerusalem and London. In that struggle, Moshe Sharett was President Chaim Weizmann's right-hand man. Moshe belonged to the Weizmann school of Zionism, those who followed a moderate, constructive line, who sought to exploit everyday acts to add power to the Yishuv, and to reinforce positions for the decisive political confrontation that was to come.

Those who believe that Moshe Sharett was a compromiser are absolutely wrong. The truth is that he always knew where the limit of concession lay, what was vital and what was secondary, and what should be given priority. The White Paper and the mandatory decrees were issued, Tower and Stockade settlements were set up, and the Hagana was reinforced. The political department of the Jewish Agency was the center of all the discussion and action relevant to these enterprises. Memoranda had to be drawn up for the British government, the high commissioner in Jerusalem, the League of Nations, and other governments; it was Moshe who prepared the drafts and drew up the documents.

World War II came, with its evil and sorrow, the Holocaust and the rescue efforts, the constant recruitment of the men of the Yishuv to the Jewish units on the one hand and the British Army units on the other. Moshe Sharett strove to establish a Jewish military force that would fight the Nazis. With his fine political sense he realized the importance of such a force both in the present and for the future. It would not only acquire military knowledge and experience—things which in themselves require study and preparation—it would also earn us credit for our share in the great historic struggle against the murderers of our people. Moshe never for a moment forgot that the time would come when the decisive struggle for our independence would begin. He recruited the Jewish units for the British Army, fought for their rights with the military authorities, and did all he could to ensure their independence and their Jewish character. The struggle was crowned with success, and Moshe was finally able to raise the banner of the Jewish Brigade within the British Army. All his life Sharett never forgot the great moment when his aspirations were fulfilled. This achievement is comparable only with the other momentous event in his life, when he had the privilege of raising the flag of the independent Jewish state among the flags of the United Nations at Lake Success, following Israeli acceptance as a member of the international body.

There was a profound connection between the two events: in 1946 Sharett was arrested on "Black Sabbath" together with other members of the Jewish Agency, and imprisoned for two months in Latrun. His nonofficial political activity did not stop for a single day. On his release, preparations began for the United Nations commissions of enquiry on Palestine, and in particular, the Special Committee. It was essential to scrupulously prepare every detail so that the justice of our cause would be properly presented. This required vast knowledge and a talent for formulation and expression. Moshe had already had some experience, for he had appeared before the Peel Commission prior to the World War II (this was the commission that recommended the establishment of a Jewish state in part of Palestine), and before the later Anglo-American Commission. But only very few intimate associates knew the efforts Sharett invested, or that he spent days and nights trying without respite to win supporters for our cause. Even before the establishment of the state he built up the Israeli Foreign Office apparatus within the framework of the political department of the Jewish Agency.

Following the United Nations Committee's report recommending the establishment of a Jewish state in part of Palestine, the struggle shifted to the General Assembly in New York. Special headquarters were set up, headed by Dr. Abba Hillel Silver. Moshe transferred his activity to the United States in order to be with the members of the executive in New York. A vigorous plan was drawn up to obtain the necessary two-thirds votes of United Nations member states.

Those were not easy years for Sharett. At the Zionist Congress held after the war and the Holocaust in December 1946, Dr. Chaim Weizmann was not elected president of the World Zionist Organization, and the breach between the World Zionist Organization and the British Labor government was now an established fact. Moshe was immersed in the tragedy of the Jewish people, one-third of whom had been liquidated by the Nazis. He met the survivors and saw the remnant of Europe's great Jewry. He wanted to express the rage in the hearts of the survivors against those who had closed the gates of Palestine to the Jewish refugees. And he succeeded, expressing himself in his own particular style—vigorous and aggressive, yet cultured and restrained. Those who claimed that the agony of the murder of six million of our brethren did not find full expression in Sharett's words and actions were wrong. Who more than he was seized with burning anger at the sight of the cruelties inflicted upon us on the one hand by the Germans, and on the other hand by the British government as it plotted against us and refused to allow the Yishuv to absorb the survivors? The illegal immigrant ships and public opinion (which was seething over the so-called illegal immigration organization at the ports of departure and on the coasts of Palestine) kept him busy day and night. Sharett worked as a member of the political department, of the Haganah, and of the illegal immigration network. The tragedy grew sevenfold in his eyes as he saw Jews maltreated, their rescue prevented, their ships sunk—all under the rule of the British Labour government. The foreign minister of Britain was Ernest Bevin, a hard-hearted and alienated man, and, as foreign minister, Moshe Sharett had to fight him. They were both members of socialist parties and of the Socialist International. Moshe Sharett, who had been in contact with British socialists since his student days in London, was affected the most because he had believed, even more than Ben-Gurion, in the solidarity of the international working class.

The crucial days of decision came, and the independent State of Israel was established. On 14 May 1948 David Ben-Gurion read in public Israel's Declaration of Independence, of which Moshe Sharett had been one of the leading draftsmen. He then devoted himself to the consolidation of the Foreign Office and to the forging of young Israel's diplomacy. For eight years—from 1948 to 1956—Moshe Sharett served as Israel's first foreign minister. They were both turbulent and delightful years: the armstice agreements, the period of Arab infiltration and the reactions that came in their wake, years of unrest on the borders and of stormy Knesset and cabinet debates on the young state's policy among the nations of the world. From January 1954 to October 1955, Moshe Sharett was also prime minister of Israel, retaining at the same time the Foreign Affairs portfolio. This was the period during which David Ben-Gurion retired to kibbutz S'de Boker. It was a time of grave security problems: the borders were in turmoil, political relations with the great powers had reached a decisive point, and disputes had arisen over the division of competence between the military and political authorities. It was also the beginning of the Lavon affair, which was to raise a storm for many years to come—indeed, it has not yet subsided. During those years diplomatic relations were established with scores of nations throughout the world, the IDF's potential grew, and the struggle to acquire arms went on. Prior to the establishment of the state, Ben-Gurion and Moshe Sharett often represented opposing positions on Zionist policy. There were periods of very close collaboration between them and periods of sharp differences. At the end of 1955 Moshe Sharett was forced to resign from the premiership and in June 1956 from his cabinet post as foreign minister: the breach between him and Ben-Gurion over Israel's political line had by then reached its peak. For Moshe Sharett, a long difficult time of pain and depression followed. He had been deeply hurt, but he restrained himself and remained silent. Nor did he alter his style of speech or his way of life. He accepted the verdict in silence as behoved a man of noble spirit.

Sharett agreed to accept the administration of Beit Berl and the Am Oved publishing house; he continued to participate actively in the Knesset election campaigns on behalf of Mapai until Nachum Goldmann, president of the World Zionist Organization, persuaded him to accept the chairmanship of the Jewish Agency. During the lull between his resignation from the cabinet and his entry into the Zionist establishment, he undertook a goodwill mission on behalf of the state to Asian countries and to many Jewish communities throughout the world. At the Jewish Agency, to which he returned after an absence of ten years, he resumed his activity with his characteristic fervor. To his credit, it should be mentioned that even while he was a member of the cabinet he had opposed Ben-Gurion's approach to the Zionist Organization. In the party and the cabinet he always defended the need to maintain a strong World Zionist Organization as a loyal partner to the state in responsibility for the fate of the Jewish people. Nor did he support the identification of aliyah with Zionism, even though he did all he could to encourage immigration.

Moshe Sharett did much to raise the prestige of the World Zionist Organization and to strengthen its institutions, adapting them to the tasks involved in the large-scale rescue of the Jewish communities of North Africa and Eastern Europe. He was indefatigable, traveling widely, participating in Zionist conventions and refusing no invitation from the Zionist Organization or the United Jewish Appeal. Moshe Sharett concentrated entirely on Zionist activity, doing much to increase the Zionist establishment's influence among the Jewish people. With that, he devoted himself heart and soul to the achievement of world Jewish unity. A fine spirit of collaboration and friendship reigned between him and Nachum Goldmann. They held similar outlooks, although differences arose between them from time to time on fundamental Zionist issues. It should be stressed that these differences were always expressed in a friendly manner. Moshe Sharett felt that he was surrounded by the affection and esteem of the mass of the Jewish people in the Diaspora and in the Zionist movement.

Within the Zionist Executive, too, he built up exemplary friendships. I was very close to him at this time. I sensed his special regard for Youth Aliyah—he was familiar with its saga from its inception. In difficult moments he would lend a helping hand, and I discovered that I could rely on him. He would often remind me that our families were from the same town—Pinsk—and that we therefore had something else in common. Throughout the years, I always felt that he had confidence in me. We met at various stages of our activity—in the thirties, when I was a member of the Zionist Executive and he was a member of the Jewish Agency Executive, and during World War II, when I was a member of the Zionist Actions Committee and he was invested with the authority to make political decisions and was one of the leading lecturers at our meetings. When the state was established, I was the first chairman of the Foreign Relations Committee of the Provisional State Council, while Moshe Sharett was the first foreign minister. This brought us into close daily contact. However, there were interruptions in this contact: I was caught in the siege of Jerusalem, and Sharett, because of his position, had moved to Tel Aviv and Ramat Gan. In the last years of his life we used to meet in the Jewish Agency building almost every day. He seemed to me to be a scion of real Jewish aristocracy, who combined within himself the best traditions and values of his people's culture. I was greatly influenced by his personality: he was a man of enormous charm, gifted with knowledge, with political, public, and party experience, and with the ability to inspire those around him.

Moshe Sharett's last year was the most difficult, and the most fraught with suffering, of his entire life. He fought against the malignant disease that took hold of him until the very last, not interrupting his normal activity for a moment. When his illness reached the point where he could neither walk nor sit, he would convene the members of the Zionist Executive at his home and conduct meetings from a special wheelchair. He became weak and was terrifyingly thin in body, but his mind and spirit were clear right up to the last.

When he passed away, the people paid him their respects and displayed their esteem for him. His memory was evoked with affection and emotion by the masses of the House of Israel, in the state and in the Diaspora. The people sensed that with his passing a son of Israel had disappeared—one who had left his imprint on the history of his people in times of crucial change, and had accompanied it along the road from life in exile to a life of political independence.

Berl Katznelson

"I am one of those people who are crazy about unity . . . I am a sworn unifier." Berl's desire for unity came from the heart; he was a lover of Israel who attracted people far from his way of thought and turned them into disciples and close colleagues. Berl loved the Jewish masses; he sought to bring as many people as possible to Eretz Israel and to draw around him a large number of pioneers and intellectuals. We would see him walking gloomily about, immersed in thought. He refused to accept reality and constantly asked questions, although he was well aware of the inhibitions, internal and external, delaying redemption. He was one of the few among us who had made a reckoning of our Jewish and human world, saying: "We did not enjoy any sympathy, and we were forced to draw from within ourselves and only from within ourselves, awareness of the importance of our stand and struggle. We drained the cup of bitterness to the dregs." Who amongst us would have dared to utter such bitter words?

Berl did not follow the clear orientations to east or west: "We did not choose isolation, but there are those who impose it upon us. We will emerge from it only if we learn to bear it, and from within it to claim our place in the world as equal among equals." What accusations and slander were heaped upon this opinion, absolute truth as it is—the epitome of the Jewish experience in our generation, and indeed in all generations! Only a man whose being was immersed in his people's past, who had absorbed its sorrow and suffering and had learned from the facts of life without illusions—only such a man could defend that opinion and fight for its acceptance as the heritage of the Jewish and Zionist world. Berl did not give up after the experiences and disappointments of his predecessors. "I was with the handful of people who understood that we would not dwell here in isolation. We created practical and spiritual ties between the worker in Eretz Israel and the international workers' movement. But we did not ignore its weaknesses, its errors and even its transgressions. We did not accept them; we fought them." Are there many people among us who dare to state that simple truth? Katznelson was far from being dogmatic; he rebelled against all accepted thought and reexamined every idea to see whether it was fulfilled in real life and studied and examined it to see whether it had petrified or still preserved its vitality. His place was among the sages of Israel who respected their people's traditions, its sabbath and festivals, and appreciated its national and cultural creativity. But he belonged no less to the creators, the vanguard of the conquerors and the daring, who were educating a new man and a new society.

Berl Katznelson was head and shoulders above all his colleagues, but there was not the slightest trace of arrogance about him. There was never a barrier between him and any sector of the people, young or old, of one opinion or another. The sense of personal tragedy that marked his last years was due to the attempts made to erect such a barrier between him and his followers. He moved among us as one of the sages of past generations, full of humility, shunning pomp and ceremony, suffering the poverty of the people, discreetly accomplishing good deeds, influencing the generation and elevating it toward its goal. It was in this light that we saw Berl Katznelson through the years. We met him, were influenced by him, found in him wisdom and counsel, and regarded him as the living conscience of the Jewish labor movement.

"I was with you in Petah Tikva fourteen years ago. You and *Akiva* were the first portents of working pioneers raised in General Zionism. I was greatly interested in coming to you and having a close look at the new force that was joining the pioneering camp. You may have suspected that I came to stir up trouble. I did not seek to change your views. . . ." Berl declared at the ceremony that marked the unification of the "A" and "B" Zionist Youth groups at Magdiel. These words indicate his great interest in us during all our years of creative work in Eretz Israel. And just as Berl always took an interest in the growth and development of our movement, so did the movement welcome every meeting with him. No important event took place in our movement in Eretz Israel from which Berl was absent. We had many debates and discussions, but he always accepted them in good spirit. Very few people in the Jewish labor movement were able to grasp the ideas that our movement developed as it realized the concept of General Zionism and infused pioneering content into its theory. Berl was one of the few, and he encouraged and strengthened us, both for the sake of the unity of the labor movement, and because he considered us creative pioneers of a particular social view—General Zionist—within the ideological spectrum of the class struggle. He was sympathetic to our movement and we did not fail to perceive this. Dr. Moshe Glickson, who discussed with Berl our movement and its aims and development, revealed that secret to us. Thus, Berl's statement that "he did not seek to change our views" was superfluous. (He was referring, of course, to our General Zionist views.) We knew that perfectly well. He wanted to see us strike root in the Histadrut: "My hope is that not only will you find this house solid, strong and loyal, but that you will also pave the road for others; that others will envy you, and you will constitute, within the Histadrut, faithful testimony to the fact that all imaginary conceptions, all the quasi-nationalist conceptions which they held about the Histadrut, are erroneous, and that the workers in Eretz Israel, whatever their style, whatever their formula, and whatever the fine nuances they support, whether rightly or wrongly, can live together, maintain and create together the values which are those of the national renaissance in our time." Berl spoke these words from his heart—and they went to the hearts of his listeners. Indeed, we always considered ourselves as symbolizing the unity of the workers and the universality of the Histadrut, and we fought for that status even during times of spiritual crisis.

Berl knew that our path in the Histadrut was not strewn with roses and that we were not treated with particular favor. He sat for long hours and listened to the discussion on our place in the Histadrut. I remember that some of the leaders of the Histadrut took part in that debate. Berl knew that it was a fateful meeting and that it would determine our future. He knew, too, that his word could be very influential. For precisely that reason he refused to take the floor and asked only to listen. His reaction to the hostile attitude of the Histadrut officials toward our members, to the series of deprivations and pressures to which we were subjected, and to the lack of encouragement for the young branch in the labor movement, was expressed at meetings of his own party. We knew that Berl had not been indifferent to our arguments; he had demanded that the Histadrut abolish all discrimination. In this he revealed militancy, even though he kept as far away as possible from practical Histadrut affairs. He accepted our invitations only to listen to our views and hear the questions that weighed on us.

"I do not wish to enter into discussions with you on the theoretical issues which divide us, but to involve myself with you in the practical, creative affairs which are common to us. The latter are more numerous and take higher precedence than the former," he once said to us. In his mind's eye Berl Katznelson envisaged the handful of members of Zionist Youth becoming a large group in the Histadrut, in the kibbutz and the moshav, the cooperative village and settlement, the youth village, the factory, the academic world, the conquest of labor, and in defense.

Since he was a man of broad horizons, without jealousy, and since he knew that behind our movement stood a pioneering youth movement several thousand strong whose aim was pioneering fulfillment, he told us at the unification convention at Ra'anana:

> My hope is to see you involved and rooted in a life of work, and that your number will multiply. . . . Your convention constitutes an opportunity for pioneering youth raised in General Zionism, to prevent it from dissipating its forces and enable it to link up with what was achieved before it came into being without effacing itself or blurring its identity. This opportunity to work within the labor world as members with equal rights and obligations, without abandoning your ideological or party image, is granted to you within the Histadrut not because you bargained for these provisions, but because they are the basis of the Histadrut's existence, and the reason it was created: to reconcile the contradictions between the different orientations among the working and pioneer immigrations, the contrasting ideologies, the differences in "race" and "origin." The Histadrut does not come into conflict with its members over their views and outlook. Its structure allows each group within it to lead an independent ideological and political life and to defend its own views and interests without losing its ties to the labor world as a whole, or its ability to influence the course of events and the character of our society. [Berl added,] In order to leave no room for error about my outlook, I would stress this: All my life I have aspired to complete unity within the Zionist Labor Movement, not only in the accepted Histadrut sense, but in a much more profound, dynamic sense: the ideological, political, spiritual and social sense. But I do not impose it on others. In my view, we must seek to abolish all barriers between the workers, but for as long as there exist among us differences of opinion, style, and attitude, we have no right to ignore them. Our primary Zionist and labor obligation is to work conscientiously toward gathering them all together under one roof in order to crystallize and put into action all that is common to us, and in order that the internal controversies between members be carried on among friends, not among enemies."

Berl regarded the Zionist Youth faction (later the "Working Zionist") in the Histadrut as an important labor and Zionist issue. He said:

> Not only the good of the workers (which is also a Zionist concern), but also concern of the state of Zionism in the Yishuv and for the Zionist character of the Jewish workers should, on the face of it, make the full participation of all Zionist workers in the Histadrut imperative. Whichever way one looks at the Histadrut, there is no one in the Yishuv who does not recognize it as a formidable economic, settle-

ment, political and cultural driving force. There is not a Zionist, not even the fiercest opponent, who does not realize that the Histadrut constitutes a powerful national and international force. . . . And that is your group's merit: you bear high the standard of General Zionism within the Histadrut, and you bear within General Zionism the standard of the one, universal Histadrut. . . . You seek to build yourselves within the Histadrut as a substantial public force. But in order to build yourselves in the Histadrut, you must build the Histadrut and collaborate in its creation. At the moment you are only one of the "minorities" in the Histadrut, a young minority. I hope that you will bring thousands of pioneering youth to the country and that you will become a constructive force in the Histadrut and in Zionism. And I caution you not to allow to spread among you a minority spirit devoid of the creative impulse which only makes claims on others. Educate your members and your potential members to consider themselves responsible for the Histadrut, partners in its creation and construction; educate them not only to demand and take, but also to give and do. Educate them to a passion for Histadrut construction, to perfect citizenship, with all its rights and obligations. . . . Your future in the Histadrut does not depend on the granting of privileges but on the creative force you display. Look around you and see how many of our youth have remained outside the existing youth federations. What does their Zionism consist of? What is their nationalism? They have practically no contact with the creative pioneering in the country. Flying dust—take it. If others did not find a way to this element and allowed it to dissipate, try your strength and see if you cannot make pioneers out of those youngsters. Even people who are not in your group would congratulate you for that. . . . Blessed will be every wave of immigration that brings with it ambitions, be they clear or undefined, for something better, more faithful, more just, more authentic.

Berl concluded his powerful speech at the founding convention of our Histadrut faction: "The ancient prophet said, 'Let not the wise man boast of his wisdom.' Let us say, 'Let not the socialist boast of his socialism, and the General Zionist of his General Zionism.' Let good deeds prove the justness of our claims."

We were well aware of the deep uneasiness that overcame him during his last years. "Happy is the man who can say 'Comfort ye.' Whoever says 'Comfort ye' can surely already see the dawn. But I am still at the stage of 'may the darkness depart,'" he wrote in one of his articles. He witnessed the destruction of the people, and published the testimony of its murder and annihilation. No one listened as he did to the reports of the emissaries from the fields of death. All that time the Yishuv was shrouded in apathy. There were futile discussions; no one wanted to learn from our national catastrophe:

> I am not asking others, the audience. I am asking myself: Are we capable of adapting our way of life, or at least our way of thought, to the warnings that are succeeding one another? And I do not address myself to those who block their ears and seal their hearts. I am speaking to ourselves. Are we not afflicted by some paralysis of the senses, as though we had been deprived of our intuition of danger? We discuss, we live, we contend with one another, but it all revolves mainly around what will happen after the war. I am not against those who ask "What of tomorrow?" I am against those who are fleeing from today.

He also drew his own conclusions about the present. He demanded more unity in the pioneering movement and its organizational framework, protesting harshly against those who were ready to abandon it. The Am Oved (Working People) publishing house became an original national enterprise whose aim was to strengthen the worker's love of his people, its history, and its national creativity. Berl's plans were far-reaching. He wanted to reveal the light of Judaism to the Jewish workers who were living in a generation of estrangement from it, flooded as the country was by foreign literature. He strove with all his spiritual might for the unity of the people, with political and national Zionism serving as the guiding light. He considered illegal immigration as the sanctification of aliyah, for which Jews had sacrificed themselves through the generations. He regarded new settlement as a great political act of frontier extension. In the work of the Keren Kayemeth, and in its success, he found a perfect combination of national and social ideas. His appreciation of Beilinson was in fact a tribute revealing his own reflections. In it, he stresses the national role of every labor movement: To serve as the bearer of the national renaissance, and of the aspiration to become a working society. Indeed, there was no one at the Zionist congresses who succeeded as he did in expressing the feeling of the active sector of the nation.

Berl died. Many of those he had raised and educated rebelled against his teaching. Opponents to him arose from among his closest colleagues. It was a terrible blow after thirty-five long years of devoted work for the common cause.

Berl Katznelson was a political, Herzlian Zionist. He formulated his Zionist theory in 1936 thus: "Our movement is, by the nature of its creation, the Jewish State movement. No matter how much we learned and inherited from Ahad Ha'Am, it was not the vision of a spiritual center for the people that brought us to the pioneering life, but the vision of the transplation of the people to Eretz Israel, the vision of a new Exodus from Egypt." A few years earlier, in 1929, he had written: "Political Zionism in its true sense—the ingathering of the exiles, popular immigration and political independence—is the soul of our movement. It is the trunk out of which grew all our human and social dreams."

The fundamental Zionist theory of Herzl, the leader and visionary, influenced Berl throughout his life. Herzl was a constant source of inspiration to him. Berl's own words confirm this:

> For Herzl, Eretz Israel was a refuge for the majority of the Jewish people, for all those in Judaism who would need Eretz Israel. . . . Herzl foresaw the change in the world's geographical center. He predicted that the Mediterranean seaboard would revive, and would play an important role in the economy of mankind. Herzl combined an awareness of the Jewish human vision, of the people's suffering and of its hidden resources, with a perception of change in the world order, the development of technology and the spiritual revival, all of which were clear to him; Herzl envisaged a greater Eretz Israel, saw its great value for the world, and considered Eretz Israel as the site of the ingathering of the exiles.

It was to this great Zionism that Berl educated the people, the workers and the youth; in this spirit he issued warnings and made demands upon the Zionist movement lest it tarry in fulfilling its mission. These words should be spoken to the Zionist movement today just as they were decades ago. Did we not witness the sight of Algerian Jewry as it went from one Diaspora to another at a time when a free Jewish state existed? Did not most of the Jews of Cuba scatter to the United States and other dispersions? The South African Zionists are sitting on a volcano and are not budging in the direction of Zion; the Jews of South America are still waiting, and the Jews of Iran—why are they not coming to us?

Is the feeling that our final destination is here, and that the ingathering of the exiles is the principal aim of Zionism, indeed the heritage of the entire Zionist movement, consciously and in practice? Many years ago Berl said: "Zionism totally lacks a sense of time, the feeling that there are things which, if one does not do them today, one will be unable to do tomorrow." Elsewhere he wrote: "The entire history of Zionism is strewn with delays which fill us with shame and disgrace." That was why he demanded, with all his powers of persuasion, "not just a spiritual contact with Herzl's personality and charm, not just open-heartedness toward the genius and the splendor that radiated from his personality;

one must constantly recall his objectives, objectives which from time to time are in danger of becoming blurred. One must recall the Zionism which does not for a moment abandon its aim: to transplant the mass of the people of Israel to its land and renew the Exodus from Egypt." For that reason he stimulated us "to enhance the memory of the man who encompassed the idea in its entirety, and with that power to encompass, and that daring, led us to our redemption, made the blood flow through our veins and commanded us to pioneering creation in every walk of life."

These lines were written in 1925. In 1936, Berl wrote in *Davar* about "Herzl's Army" as follows:

"Herzl Commemoration Day is not just a day of personal commemoration, a day on which to draw courage and comfort from this harbinger of better times. It is also a day of the movement. It awakens in us, the army which followed his vision, the spiritual need to see ourselves through his eyes, to measure the road we have travelled by his yardstick, to examine our will, our character and the quality of our action as he would have examined them. What would he say of our stance if he could see us? Are we proving his vision right, not just in words but by our actions and in our lives, or are we denying him? Are we worthy of his paternity and his sacrifice? Herzl's sharp eye looks down on us all the time in pity and in anger, examining, enquiring, demanding. More than once it has observed us in deep decline, neglectful, discouraged, unconsciously despairing, irresponsibly gay, vainly amusing ourselves, prematurely sounding the trumpets of victory. . . .

In the same year, when the riots broke out, he wrote: "This time Herzl would not be ashamed of the army which followed his vision as it withstands siege and is tempered in fire. Herzl's army did not, and will not, disappoint him. Even if the suffering is not over and the struggle is to become seven-fold heavier, we will emerge from it forged together and united to face the great days that await us." We know how these predictions were fulfilled. Herzl's army withstood and overcame, and Herzl's Jewish state arose, exactly fifty years after he had prophesied it.

Berl Katznelson did more than any other emissary or leader of the Zionist labor movement to educate the people and the youth in Herzl's theory, and to foster in them a real consciousness of Herzl. Berl's greatness lay in the fact that he stood at the center of the labor movement's creative life in Eretz Israel and guided it in its struggles. In his wisdom, he always attributed his ideas to some great authority. I do not ever remember him speaking of himself or of his original ideas. When we listened to his brilliant remarks, expressed with great humility and in a popular tone, we knew that Berl was the father and creator of many bold ideas, projects, and plans, but he always referred to others, to his teachers and predecessors in the Zionist movement, as though they had directed him on his path and in his actions.

The World Zionist movement is obliged to give a moral reckoning and to put its house in order. It is obliged to take cognizance of its central role among the people. Berl Katznelson's theory is there to teach us how to achieve that goal:

> Zionism must revert to what it was in Herzl's times: the exodus from Egypt; not as a propaganda slogan but as a way of life and action. There must be energy for that, and if we do not posess that energy, then Zionism will become just one more of the many Jewish organizations that worry away at Israel's sad fate but have neither the energy to change the situation nor to think Zionism through to the end. . . . We see with our own eyes that the Zionist prophecies of doom have been fulfilled beyond measure. But what happened to Zionism? Its ability to understand and to foresee was not commensurate with the destruction of the Jewish reality. . . . And our movement, if it has retained its inner vitality, must now make desperate efforts to save Zionism. We must once again seek ways to achieve a comprehensive national concentration around Eretz Israel, on mass immigration to this country, and on the national solution.

These words, spoken in 1940, are still relevant today.

Yosef Sprinzak

From my youth and from my days as a member of Zionist Youth I was familiar with the name of Josef Sprinzak, mainly through my reading of the press and literature from Eretz Israel. For me, Sprinzak was the symbol of Hapoel Hatsair—the Young Workers Party—the Zionist nonsocialist labor party par excellence. It was thus only natural that we of the National Guard and the Zionist Youth, builders of a pioneering, nonsocialist youth movement that was constantly involved in debates with the various socialist movements, should have followed closely the path and the statements of the Young Workers Party. We avidly absorbed the words of A. D. Gordon, whose debates with Zionist socialism were for us like a breath of fresh, invigorating air. We read the weekly papers of the Young Workers and drew great encouragement from them. When the emissaries of Hashomer Hatsair—the Young Watchman—preached to us that the "Eretz Israel reality"—a term they used frequently—would impose socialism upon us, the Young Workers Party was for us the "King's witness" that nothing was inevitable. On the contrary, it was glaring proof that socialism often placed Zionist pioneers in a moral dilemma.

The Young Workers members interested us, even though we had not met with them face-to-face, for we regarded their feelings and approach similar to our own. Only after I immigrated to Eretz Israel at the beginning of November 1932 did I meet Yosef Sprinzak personally. He won me over immediately with his warm smile, his captivating charm, his loyal friendship and his willingness to help, listen, and advise.

The Eretz Israel reality did not greet the Zionist Youth pioneers favorably on their arrival. General Zionism in Eretz Israel at the time was for the most part veering to the right, with the exception of the small group of Democratic Zionists. On the other hand, within the Histadrut—which they joined—the Zionist Youth were made fun of. Their appearance provoked contemptuous smiles, and sometimes they were even pitied—these innocents, who were determined to become Jewish workers in Eretz Israel, to fight for Jewish labor in the orange groves, and did not consider themselves socialists, but were linked with the Zionist "bourgeoisie" of the General Zionist federation.

However, there were certain personalities in the labor movement who realized at once what a fine, positive element the pioneers of the new Zionist Youth movement were. Among them were Berl Katznelson, Yosef Sprinzak, and David Ben-Gurion. They used to come to the workers' camp, which was pitched not far from the main Tel Aviv–Petah Tikva road opposite the home of Jacob Krol, one of the observers of the "commandment" of Jewish labor in all its details. But it was only natural that a man like Yosef Sprinzak, who served as the spokesman of the Young Workers, should show a particular interest in the burgeoning of the new movement. Perhaps he regarded it as the continuation of the Tse'irei Zion, Young Zionists from Russia, to which he belonged before his immigration, or of the Tekhiya revival in Warsaw, of which he had been one of the organizers and which was headed by Yitschak Greenbaum.

To Sprinzak, the Gordonia movement was the direct successor of the Young Workers, and it also belonged to the world movement of the Hitachdut, of which he was a founder at the Prague conference in 1920. The connection between the Young Zionists and the General Zionist federation seemed somewhat strange to him. The Young Workers was a Zionist labor movement, but it had never been placed in an interclass framework. Nevertheless, Sprinzak not only took an interest in the beginnings of our pioneering movement; he also learned from his many contacts with international Zionism that the boys and girls of Zionist Youth ran a fine, well-established, widespread youth movement with authentic roots, and that the pioneering ideal was to them a challenge of the first order. Thus, Sprinzak's relationship with the emerging movement was a close and intimate one. He searched for a way to help us take our first steps in the country, and he was far from unsuccessful.

At that time a fierce struggle was going on in the Yishuv between the followers of and the opponents to the Histadrut. The Revisionist movement, together with the middle-class camp of General Zionism, wanted to break up the labor federation, which served as the bastion of the labor movement and Weizmann's Zionism. Sprinzak was well aware of our numerous connections with the General Zionist camp throughout the world. He and Berl Katznelson kept in regular contact with us, and we told them of the ideological struggle we were waging within world General Zionism in favor of the idea of a single federation of labor. I well remember our meetings with them prior to the world conference of General Zionists in Cracow in 1935. At the heart of the discussions lay the question of whether to preserve the unity of the Histadrut or to establish a separate General Zionist workers' organization. Over this issue the Cracow conference split. I took part in that conference as the emissary of Zionist Youth from Eretz Israel. With me was Poldo Reiss from kibbutz Kfar Hamaccabi, who represented the Young Maccabi pioneers. We both aimed to fight for the unity of the workers within one federation, with each Zionist trend enjoying the possibility of waging an ideological fight within the Histadrut framework.

Following the Cracow conference and the nineteenth Zionist Congress—which was held in Lucerne the same year—we decided to establish officially the General Zionist workers' group within the Histadrut, and to that end we convened a founding convention in Ra'anana at the end of November.

The convention turned into a great event for the Yishuv. Eliezer Yaffe, one of the leaders of the Young Worker, founding father of the moshav movement and an opponent of union between the Young Workers and Achdut Ha'Avoda (the Unity of Labor), was a delegate. After the convention he presented me with the first financial contribution we received—toward publication of the first issue of the Zionist Worker's paper. It came from Tnuva, whose Tel Aviv manager he was. Sprinzak and Berl Katznelson were also among the leading personalities to welcome us and to speak at the convention. Sprinzak, who greeted the convention officially on behalf of the Histadrut, said: "We have come here not merely to bring official greetings, but to participate in your efforts to build up for yourselves content, force and competence within the Histadrut. We have come to discover how your desire to maintain this movement is manifested."

Sprinzak's interest in our movement continued unabated. He participated in the negotiations with the leaders of the Histadrut executive on the integration of our movement into Histadrut institutions. At those meetings it was decided that our colleague, Zvi Michaeli, would take a position at the Histadrut immigration center. He was the first member of our movement to work in a central Histadrut institution, where he assisted in the absorption of our immigrant members.

Sprinzak held the "minorities" portfolio in the secretariat of the Histadrut executive. It comprised the Yemenites, members from the Oriental communities, and the religious workers. We were also counted among this family. He did his utmost to unite the various fractions within the labor camp from the point of view of ideology, community and country of origin, serving as their defender vis-a-vis the Histadrut establishment, which did not always treat them cordially. His door was always open to us, and his smile, the good joke he cracked, habitually served as the introduction to every conversation. Sprinzak had every interest in our success, for it would guarantee a positive decision on Histadrut in the world General Zionist camp. Our success meant the victory of the idea of the Histadrut's universality, proof that both socialist and nonsocialist members could live together within it. When I was elected as the first representative of the Zionist Workers movement to the Histadrut executive—and later to the secretariat, where my task was to supervise the just distribution of work—I found in Josef Sprinzak a "big brother" and friend who was of great support to me. At the time, the Zionist Workers movement was struggling for the release of the worker in Israel from dependence on a party membership card for everything connected with the distribution of work. We fought for general labor exchanges for the workers and for the abolition of the party labor exchanges run by various organizations. We published a pamphlet entitled *The Distribution of Work—How?*, which provoked strong reactions. Sprinzak greatly appreciated our struggle. He regarded my presence on the secretariat as the addition of a new trend to that institution, and to the executive itself.

I owe him much for the affection he showed me, and for the advice that guided my actions in that faraway period. Those years with the Histadrut Executive were important not only for me personally, but also for the movement, which felt itself represented independently in the highest institution of the General Federation of Labor. Those were years of consolidation and integration of the Zionist Workers within the Histadrut. We became a permanent fixture: we ran in the elections, trained a group of Histadrut workers, and established ourselves at the agricultural center where we were represented by our members in the kibbutzim and moshavim. Among our faithful friends at the agricultural center were Neta Harpaz, who acted as patron of our kibbutzim and of our members in the moshavim, and Avraham Hartzfeld, who gave us substantial help in our first settlement enterprises. Later, personal relations developed between me and Sprinzak, for we were neighbors in Tel Aviv. I used to visit him and enjoyed the hospitality that he and his wife, Hannah, extended to me.

I remember a joint visit to our agricultural youth village in Magdiel, whose director was Dr. Shmaryahu Ellenberg, an outstanding educator who had immigrated from Lodz. He was a member of Hitahdut (the Union) and was a personal friend of Sprinzak. A group of children and youth had just arrived from Romania, most of them from Bukovina. Inside their clothing they had sewn the flag of our movement; they saved it by immigrating to Eretz Israel. The meeting with these youngsters was a deeply moving experience and it brought tears to Sprinzak's eyes. At that time he was extremely active not just on the Histadrut Executive but also in world Zionism and on the National Council, whose main concern was the rescue of Jews from Nazi-dominated Europe. The friendship between Sprinzak and our movement in Eretz Israel continued until his death. There was not a conference of the Zionist Workers, or of the Progressive Party, from which Sprinzak was absent. He was always happy to greet our conventions and councils. He spoke at the convention that united the agricultural workers who were members of the General Zionist workers' organization with the Zionist Workers. In 1943, at the third Zionist Workers convention, Sprinzak said:

> You have overcome various spiritual inhibitions. You did not give in; you shook off your hesitations, your feelings of anger and protest, and united your forces, and won the place you deserve in the Histadrut. . . . Those who follow progressive General Zionism, which produced such outstanding personalities; those who follow Glickson, choosing the slogan "National freedom, social justice, and the revival of Jewish culture," those people cannot harbor spiritual inhibitions about belonging to the General Federation of Labor. . . .
>
> You have discovered that there is room in the Histadrut for a positive creative struggle. . . . I have no intention of saying that you have discovered in the Histadrut a world that is wholly good . . . but that the Histadrut is not so bad, and that whatever is bad can be set right. . . .
>
> All of us have a part in this maturing of the Histadrut, all of us! All those who are loyal to the labor movement. And your experience has proved to many that there is room in the Histadrut for every Jewish worker who lends his hands to building, to the improvement of living conditions, to the realization of the desire of generations for the creation of a productive life, the redemption of the people and of the land.

Since those were the days of the Holocaust, and the news from Europe had depressed us all, Sprinzak added: "We are assembled at a time when we cannot yet define in human language the ghastly reality of these days. Who knows what dates the enemy has fixed for the annihilation. Who knows what will yet befall our people; what living limbs will yet be severed from our body. These days demand much from us: we must cry out, demand, strive and seek for ways and means of reaching those being led to the slaughter, and forge ways to rescue them. We must devote to that action every feeling and every human effort."

This supreme command ruled us all. We did everything that was humanly possible; we carried out rescue work and awakened the conscience of the world. But all that together was so very little, so we worked to strengthen what already existed in the Yishuv and in Zionism so that afterward they would serve as a haven for those who remained alive and a base from which to launch the struggle for the future of the people, and for Israel's independence in its land.

When I moved to the Jewish Agency, following my election as a deputy member of the Zionist and Jewish Agency executives at the first Zionist Congress held after the Holocaust (in Basle, December 1946), I had the opportunity to follow the part Yosef Sprinzak played in the Zionist struggle and in the campaign for the unification of Zionist forces. These were tragic days for Sprinzak, a devoted follower of Weizmann; the crisis we had reached in our relations with the British government affected him deeply. Not only did Britain close its ears to the cries of the Holocaust survivors; it organized the hunt for the illegal immigrant ships and set up the camps on Cyprus. Most painful was the fact that all this happened under the Labor government that came to power in 1945 following Hitler's downfall. It was then that the long, decisive struggle for our future in the homeland began—a struggle that rocked and terrified the entire Yishuv.

Sprinzak feared that the Yishuv might lose its human visage and that what already existed would be destroyed in our fight for justice with the British. It was not easy to maintain those principles during such stormy times. Josef Sprinzak interested himself in the rallying of the Jews in the Diaspora around the Zionist struggle. He met with survivors, and with the remnants of the communities he had known in his youth.

When the state was established, Sprinzak was privileged to be appointed chairman of the Provisional State Council. After the elections to the first Knesset, he became Speaker of the Knesset, a position he held until his death ten years later.

Josef Sprinzak will be rightly remembered in the history of the State of Israel as the father of Israeli parliamentarianism. All his talents and capacities, all his spiritual resources, all his vast experience in human relations (in the Zionist Executive, the Histadrut, the National Council, and various public campaigns) he placed at the service of Israel's legislature. His ambition was that our parliament should be a model; that it should learn from the best parliaments in the world, but also add its own specificity, something of our people's own tradition. He maintained strict objectivity in the fulfillment of his role, and was on friendly terms with all parties and all sections of the House without exception. He always kept the unity of the House in mind when solving problems, and was concerned with the level of discussions, becoming deeply upset by any coarse expression uttered from the rostrum or by any noisy outburst, no matter which side of the House it came from. He determined the procedure of the House and took care that its complete independence from the cabinet was maintained.

During the same period, Sprinzak held the post of chairman of the Zionist General Council. He had been elected to that position in 1946, and he carried out this Zionist mission until his death. He attended meetings of the Zionist Executive, and took advantage of his official visits as Speaker of the Knesset to strengthen the Zionist camp.

As chairman of both parliaments—the state, and the Zionist movement—Sprinzak symbolized the unity between the Diaspora and the people of Israel. He was like a thread running through Zionism and the state. During that period he knew much happiness and spiritual satisfaction, a slight compensation for the terrible days he lived through after his son Aharon David, a pilot and a member of the Palmah, was shot down in the War of Independence.

As Speaker of the Knesset, Sprinzak was privileged to swear in Chaim Weizmann, a man he loved, as president of the State of Israel. Could there have been a happier moment in his public career? Until his death he remained loyal to the Zionist movement. Sprinzak was in the hospital following a heart attack when David Ben-Gurion made his famous declaration that the time had come to dismantle the "blemish" (that is, the Zionist Organization), now that the "house" (that is, the state) had been established. I visited him in the hospital and found him shocked and upset. "What blemish?" he asked, "How can one speak like that and make such comparisons? Is the 'house' complete already, and is the entire people in its home?" I begged him not to upset himself, for it was dangerous for his health, but he did not calm down. A few days after he had recovered somewhat and was taking part in the tenth anniversary celebrations of the Knesset, he suffered another, and fatal, heart attack.

His dynamic life, rich in trials and accomplishments, had come to an end. The people eulogized him as a man they had loved. Sprinzak loved not only the people of Israel, but also every single man of Israel. He was prepared to help wherever and whenever he could, and to take action against injustice and discrimination. He loved the single man, the individual; he sought to prevent suffering and deprivation, and fought every display of small-mindedness in human, party, and personal relations. He overcame the personal defeats he suffered in the party and outside of it.

Sprinzak was a man of good spirit and friendship; he was a humanist, a lover of man in all his being, and his home and his office were always open to all. He was the humanist of the Zionist labor movement, one of its central figures, one of those who played a great part in our achievements and our struggles for freedom and independence. He was one of those who molded the first forms of our life in the state, the man who worked for the unity of the people of Israel with the State of Israel.

Pinchas Sapir

Over forty years ago, when I was a member of Kibbutz Hamefales, near Kfar Saba, I made the acquaintance of Pinchas Koslowsky, then an active member of the local workers' committee. Our usual topic of conversation was the problem of Jewish labor in the surrounding citrus groves.

In those days there was a fierce struggle going on to bring Jewish labor into the Jewish economy. The extent of the immigration authorized by the mandatory government depended on the economy's capacity to absorb the incoming pioneers. The training kibbutzim in eastern Europe were suffering a serious crisis: some of the youngsters had to wait years for their aliyah. The struggle for Jewish labor in Eretz Israel was, therefore, a struggle for increased pioneer aliyah. It was also a struggle for the expansion of the Jewish economy and of the Jewish defense capability. Every Jewish worker was a member of the Haganah, and Jewish labor in the citrus groves that lay a distance from the villages assured those villages greater protection.

Pinchas Koslowsky, who later changed his name to Sapir, was among those who stood watch at the groves where Arab labor was employed. At the entrance to these groves stood a number of other Yishuv leaders of the times, as well as writers, journalists, teachers, and artists who came to manifest their solidarity with the fight for Jewish labor. The British authorities arrested the "watchmen," Sapir among them. Kibbutz Hanoar Hazioni lay on the fringe of the village, not far from the Arab quarter of Kfar Saba, and the employment of kibbutz members in the surrounding orange groves was of prime importance to the security of the area. They worked in Kalmania, in Gan Chaim, and in the groves that bordered the kibbutz camp.

On April 19, 1936 bloody anti-Jewish riots broke out: The Arabs attacked the Yishuv in Eretz Israel. Their financial support came from the Nazis and Fascists who wanted to strike at British positions in the Mediterranean area.

During that period I met with Pinchas Sapir frequently. There was insufficient work in our kibbutz. I discussed with him the problems of Jewish labor, security, and guard duty. I was also looking for a way of developing the kibbutz's small auxiliary farm. Sapir gave of his advice generously and tried his best to help. When he was released from prison, he told me about his experiences behind bars.

When I was a member of the Histadrut Executive, as the first representative of the Zionist Workers, I established the Workers' General Employment Bureau in cooperation with all of the labor organizations and the Jewish Agency. Sapir considered this an important step toward greater unity and cooperation among Israel's workers.

Sapir was then working with the Mekorot Company, together with Levi Eshkol, and he would describe to me his plans for development of the country's water resources, which would make possible the expansion of Jewish settlement. He was a man of broad vision, and he was always helpful—a loyal friend.

With the establishment of the state, Koslowsky was appointed Director General of the Ministry of Defense. At that time I was a member of the Provisional Council of the State and the first chairman of its Foreign Affairs Committee. Although the Provisional Council had a separate committee for defense, headed by D. S. Pincus, there were spheres that were common to the two committees. On one occasion Sapir told me of his difficulties in procuring finance and armaments. Those were his main concerns at that time.

Ben-Gurion greatly appreciated Pinchas Sapir and was full of admiration for his work and ability. He wanted Sapir as a cabinet minister and predicted a great future for him. Pinchas Sapir was appointed minister of commerce and industry when Levi Eshkol was minister of finance.

The friendship between Sapir and Eshkol was deep and boundless. They worked like brothers, with complete coordination and understanding even when they differed over one issue or another. Sapir's service as minister of commerce and industry was fruitful and produced great results. These were the days of the ma'abarot and the mass immigration. The population had to be dispersed throughout the country; employment and a livelihood had to be provided for them. Levi Eshkol was then head of the settlement department of the Jewish Agency, and he established hundreds of settlements in the villages that the Arabs had abandoned when they fled the country. He also set up many villages in new settlement areas.

When Sapir was appointed minister of finance, he became, in fact, the architect of Israel's economy, personally directing its construction and development. The ministerial committee for economic affairs, which he headed, became the state's economic cabinet. He knew everything that was going on in every corner of the economy, in every factory. In the early morning hours he would phone factory managers and inquire about production and export.

I saw him at work during my term as minister of tourism and development. He was a great help in the development of tourism in Israel; he was well aware of the contribution tourism could make to the balance of payments, of its importance in dispersing the population and in developing new areas of the country. I accepted his help gladly. Even when we argued—sometimes vociferously—we did so in a spirit of friendship and mutual esteem that remained unchanged throughout our forty-year association.

Sapir was not only minister of finance; he was also the leading fund raiser among the Jewish people. As financial instruments he used the Development and Independence Loan, the United Jewish Appeal, the Education Fund, and large donations to special social and cultural projects. He knew how to approach wealthy Jews, but he always safeguarded Israel's prestige and his own position as minister of finance. He bargained stubbornly to ensure that Jewish capital in the heads of obscure, far-flung families would not be lost, but would reach the State of Israel.

Pinchas Sapir was actively concerned with the development of Israel's universities, and was no less responsible for them than were the ministers of education and culture. He knew that Israel would have to maintain its cultural and spiritual level if it was to attract able, educated Jews to help develop its society and economy.

He had a boundless capacity for work. When I was in the cabinet, I realized that neither Levi Eshkol nor Golda Meir took a step without asking Pinchas Sapir's advice. For his part, he regarded them as authorities and took their opinions into account when he made decisions. On political matters, he saw eye-to-eye with Levi Eshkol but he often differed from Golda Meir. However, he chose not to take issue with her in public, and only rarely did so in the cabinet.

Sapir had a special talent for bringing together people of widely differing outlooks and for working with all sections of the economy. Just as he collaborated with the leaders of the Histadrut—even when he had tough arguments with Ben Aharon—so he won the confidence of Moshewitz, who headed the coordinating commission of economic organizations.

In his work, Sapir sought the golden mean, but he was not always successful. He made supreme efforts to increase foreign investments, and extended generous help to investors—sometimes more generous than was strictly necessary. He knew that the workers' living standards must be raised to enable a working family to live decently. On the other hand, he warned against a sharp rise in the standard of living to a level we would not be able to maintain. Such a rise would increase our dependence on outside factors and hinder the competitiveness of our products in world markets.

Sapir had confidence in his coworkers and appointed many of them directors of government and public companies. The majority remained loyal to him, although a few took unwarranted advantage of their positions. There were even instances of a decline in ethical standards. When cases of corruption were revealed, Sapir was blamed by a shocked public. Not a few considered him the founder of a regime that bred such phenomena. There was some basis for this criticism, but many people wrongfully attacked him.

Sapir was particularly upset when close friends, who had attained high position thanks to his recommendations, made speeches and declarations to the effect that the time had come to make war on corruption. He would ask, "In my time, was corruption and embezzlement treated leniently?" In his last appearances he had much to say on this subject. He declared that he was prepared to match anyone in the struggle for pure moral standards.

Sapir himself was modest in his ways, and remained attached to Kfar Saba. His home was simple, without ostentation, and his way of life did not change during all the years of his varied activity, both before and after the establishment of the State. He was clean-handed and pure-hearted.

After Sapir's death public figures and journalists—including those who had gone beyond the limits of the permissible in criticizing him—voiced their praise of this man who did so much for the development, advancement and consolidation of the State of Israel.

Sapir was always involved in great struggles, both public and ideological. He enjoyed them. He stood behind Levi Eshkol when Ben-Gurion attacked him. He was extremely critical of the Rafi group, although he maintained good relations with Moshe Dayan. During the Lavon affair Sapir supported Lavon, convinced that he was not guilty. When Ben-Gurion broke his ties with his close friends in Mapai, he still remained on good terms with Sapir.

Sapir knew his strength, and he knew his limitations. Thus, he refused to accept the premiership. As an ardent Zionist, he assumed the post of chairman of the Jewish Agency and the Zionist Organization in order to increase immigration. He saw this as a central mission, together with fund raising. However, it was while he was chairman of the Jewish Agency that the crisis in immigration from Soviet Russia developed, accompanied by a drop in aliyah from the western countries. At that time criticism of him was mounting in Israel as a result of the economic scandals, and Sapir was no longer the same man. He moved among us depressed and disappointed.

Sapir was a central figure in the Labor Party and one of its decision makers. For a time he served as party secretary, and minister without portfolio. He was loyal to the alignment with Mapai, and worked to preserve that partnership. He wanted to prevent a struggle between the Zionist workers' parties and Mapai's political line was close to his own. At the same time he did his utmost to maintain the cooperation between Mapai's "historic partners" in the coalition: the National Religious Party (NRP) and the Independent Liberals. He helped the NRP mostly with the establishment of institutions for religious education, and on more than one occasion rescued their financial and economic organisms. He raised funds for yeshivot, for he never forgot the yeshivot in Poland and their contribution to the existence of Judaism. In this way he won over the leaders of Agudat Israel and Poalei Agudat Israel. He faithfully fulfilled coalition agreements.

Sapir was on particularly friendly terms with the Independent Liberal Party. Dr. Yishayahu Foerder, head of Bank Leumi, was one of his advisers. When an attempt was made to implicate Foerder in the Rassco crisis—he was chairman of that company's board of directors—Sapir brought all his prestige to bear in Foerder's favor. He well knew who was responsible for the Rassco affair. After the death of his friend Foerder, Sapir helped me to establish a liberal college in his name at Kibbutz Tel Yitschak. Similarly, when I approached him to assist in the commemoration of the Zionist Workers movement in Europe by establishing Massuah, a cultural-educational institution whose aim was to deepen the consciousness of the Holocaust among the youth of Israel and the Diaspora, he gave us his full assistance, for he was well aware of the significance of the undertaking. He knew, too, how valuable had been the work of the Zionist Youth when it operated within Hehalutz in Poland. Sapir also helped us maintain Yesodot, the great educational institutions of our movement.

In his last days Sapir worked to repair the injustice that was done to the Independent Liberals, and to their colleagues in the Diaspora, at the last Zionist Congress when they were not coopted to the Zionist Executive. When I asked him, "How is it possible that the movement of Chaim Weizmann, Yitschak Greenbaum and Pinchas Rosen is to be excluded from the supreme Zionist body?" he replied, "Give me time and I'll rectify the matter." Indeed he did: at his initiative, the other coalition partners on the Jewish Agency Executive agreed to coopt a representative of the Independent Liberals and the Independent Zionist movement to the Jewish Agency Executive. I always knew that I could rely on Sapir's word.

Many people regarded Sapir as a hard man, but he was not. He was very sensitive, and was even moved to tears at times. He was particularly affected by meetings with Jews in various countries. He told me how emotional he became at the Bucharest synagogue, and how he had tears in his eyes when he met with Jews during the Six-Day War and after the Yom Kippur War, when he hastened to visit the Jewish communities to raise the funds necessary to continue the fighting and to maintain our ability to stand firm.

Sapir was a many-faceted personality, and a man of outstanding vigor. He has a brilliant record in the history of the Yishuv and the state, and in the realization of the Zionist vision: he created work and a means of livelihood for thousands of immigrants; consolidated the development towns and new settlements; developed educational, cultural, and welfare enterprises; cared for the weak and the old, and laid the foundations of a healthy, dynamic economy.

When his term of office in the cabinet came to an end after years of faithful service, I said a few words in appreciation of his personality and achievements at the last meeting of the ministerial committee for economic affairs that he headed. I was followed by other ministers. After the meeting, Sapir came over to me and said, "I will never forget what you said. I will keep the record of your speech as a souvenir and a mark of friendship." He had tears in his eyes.

Much has been written about Pinchas Sapir and more will be written. He was one of the central figures of the State of Israel in the first twenty-five years of its existence.

Henrietta Szold

In November 1932 Henrietta Szold was preparing to return to the United States, having completed, she thought, her work in Eretz Israel and wishing to spend the rest of her life within her family circle. But the Nazi rise to power in Germany upset her plans. She was called upon to assume a new role: to head Youth Aliyah, to save the lives and the future of German Jewish youth and bring them to Palestine.

Youth Aliyah was the brainchild of another great woman—Recha Freier, the wife of a Berlin rabbi—who had come to the conclusion that the only solution for German Jewish youth was immigration to Eretz Israel, and a new life based on study and agricultural work. The question was, who would take care of the young immigrants on their arrival in Eretz Israel? At the time, a committee for the rescue of German Jews was in formation, and a department for their settlement in Palestine was set up in conjunction with the Jewish Agency. The committee was headed by distinguished Jews and Zionists, among them Dr. Chaim Weizmann, who at that time had been relieved of his official Zionist functions. The best forces in Eretz Israel were drawn to this rescue undertaking, among them Chaim Arlosoroff, head of the Jewish Agency's political department, Dr. Arthur Ruppin, and Dr. George Landauer, who was appointed director of the department for the settlement of German Jews. Leading Zionists in Britain, America and in the Yishuv united around the committee for the rescue of German Jewry.

At that time, some of the finest intellectuals and members of the free professions, economists, businessmen, and young members of the Zionist youth movements began to arrive in Eretz Israel from Germany. As a rule, they understood that there was no future for them in their native land; that the Nazi movement was not a transitory phenomenon but a serious threat to Jews and Jewry. The worrisome question was, who would ensure the absorption of these people, whose importance to the Zionist enterprise could not be questioned? The labor movement in

Palestine, aware of the importance of the issue, sent some of its best people to Germany to direct the departure of the Jewish emigrants. But a suitable personality to direct the absorption of German Jewish youth had not been found.

Henrietta Szold, a member of the National Council Executive and head of its social department, was then seventy-two years old; the time had come for her to rest after decades of public work, but a number of people considered her the ideal person for the job. She was asked to give up the idea of returning to America, and to assume responsibility for the establishment of a Youth Aliyah department, which would serve as the address in Eretz Israel for the youth who were being prepared to leave Germany. She hesitated at first, but then came to see it as a national challenge that she had no right to evade. She traveled to Berlin and was appalled at what was happening to German Jewry. She observed Nazis and their machinations, heard the incitement against the Jews, and learned the thoughts and feelings of parents, youth, and children. Henrietta Szold was skeptical at first; she lacked the means to rehabilitate the underprivileged youth already in Eretz Israel, and did not know where the money for the new project would come from. Nevertheless, she decided to accept the challenge. So began the fourth chapter of her life, the most important and most highly praised of them all. She became a mother to tens of thousands and achieved a degree of personal happiness that she had not known throughout her long life. In 1933, when her sister Bertha came to Eretz Israel, intending to take Henrietta back to America with her, Henrietta Szold took her final decision to accept the Youth Aliyah department, and from then on she devoted to it all her energy and talent. The first six youngsters of Youth Aliyah arrived and were successfully absorbed in the Ben Shemen youth village, headed by Dr. Siegfried Lehman. Henrietta Szold herself had the privilege of welcoming the first youth group members, who arrived in Haifa aboard the *Martha Washington* on February 19, 1943. The youngsters were integrated into kibbutz Ein Harod. The Youth Aliyah period had begun.

In 1935, when we celebrated Henrietta Szold's seventy-fifth birthday, she appeared before the Zionist Congress in Lucerne and reported on Youth Aliyah's first activities. The entire congress was deeply moved, as much by Youth Aliyah itself as by the personality of the speaker. At that congress the famous agreement was signed between Dr. George Landauer, on behalf of Youth Aliyah and the department for the settlement of German Jews of which Youth Aliyah was a part, and Mrs. Rose Jacobs, the national president of Hadassah, making Hadassah in the United States the official agency of Youth Aliyah.

I was getting to know Henrietta Szold and her work for Youth Aliyah, and at the same time I learned about her activity and connections with Brith Shalom and her views on Arab-Jewish relations, which differed from the official line of the Zionist Organization and the Jewish Agency. Henrietta Szold was greatly influenced by Yehuda Leib Magnes, president of the Hebrew University in Jerusalem. Because she held an official position in the Jewish Agency, Miss Szold kept her opinions on the subject pretty much to herself. With her attention concentrated entirely on Youth Aliyah, she considered it preferable not to become involved in political struggles, even though she courageously defended her opinions when the need arose. She was furious at the British mandatory administration for watching in silence when the Arab terrorist bands took over. She had had a taste of riots in Jerusalem immediately upon her arrival in the country in 1920.

She also experienced the 1929 riots, and in 1936 she witnessed the destruction of villages and the injuries inflicted on old people and children. In the thick of the disturbances she was never once deterred from traveling to meet Youth Aliyah children on their arrival at Haifa port. She covered miles, reaching every corner of the country. But her anger smoldered at the neglect shown by the authorities who did nothing to halt the violence, all of which brought her nearer to those who were seeking a solution to the Arab-Jewish question.

Henrietta Szold's first contact with European Jewry was in 1882. There had been riots in Czarist Russia following the assassination of Czar Alexander II, and hundreds of thousands of Jews had begun pouring into the United States. Together with her father, who was a rabbi, Henrietta Szold welcomed the Russian immigrants who reached Baltimore and built a night school for them. The night school for adults was to become a very important institution in the United States for the absorption of immigrants, teaching them English and transforming them into American citizens. In 1934, when for the first time Henrietta Szold met a group of Youth Aliyah children from Germany, the well-known spectacle of the Baltimore days repeated itself. But there were two basic differences: first, the Youth Aliyah immigrants came from a Jewish community whose future had been considered secure until it was suddenly rocked to its foundations; second, she was welcoming them to their ancestral homeland, not to America. In 1882 when the great wave of Jews fleeing Russia broke upon the shores of America, only a small minority, the Bilus, reached Eretz Israel. But that minority of Bilus and the few pioneers with them would succeed in laying the foundations of the Jewish Yishuv which, fifty years later, was able to absorb the masses of Jews that were rescued from Germany. Henrietta Szold was intimately associated with changing the demographic map of the Jewish world in the period between 1882 and 1934. For twenty-five years, from her arrival in Eretz Israel in 1920 until the day of her death at Hadassah Hospital on February 13, 1945, she was one of the central figures in the Yishuv and the Zionist movement.

Henrietta Szold was eighty-five years old when she died. Her long life constitutes a wonderful chapter of contemporary Jewish history. She was a marvelous person who proved what a single woman with a strong personality and a great spirit could accomplish.

Henrietta Szold was born in December 1860, in Baltimore, one month after the election of Abraham Lincoln to the presidency of the United States. She was only four months old when the American Civil War broke out, and she died six months prior to the Hiroshima atomic explosion at the end of World War II. She lived from the Victorian era through the death of Franklin D. Roosevelt.

Henrietta Szold's father, Benjamin Szold, was the rabbi of Ohev Shalom synagogue in Baltimore. Before immigrating to America, he had studied at the famous Chatam-Sofer Yeshiva of Pressburg, complementing this education with secular studies at the universities of Vienna and Breslau. He had a great influence on his daughter and left his imprint on her personality. Her mother, Sophia, née Schaar, was the daughter of a rich Jewish landowner in Hungary. German was spoken at home, and it was in German that Rabbi Szold preached in the synagogue. Henrietta Szold had a religious upbringing, and the Sabbath and festivals were sacred to her. She first went to the religious school run by her father at the Ohev Shalom synagogue. Secular studies were in English, religious instruction in German. When she was eight she was transferred to a general Baltimore primary school, and from there to a girls' school. At age twelve she helped her father read the proofs of the Daily Prayer Book, which he translated into German. She studied Hebrew, Bible and Talmud, and graduated from the girls' school at the age of sixteen.

While she was still very young she published articles and letters in the *Jewish Messenger* in New York under the pseudonym "Shulamit." She was eighteen when her mother and sisters visited the family in Europe, leaving her behind to take care of her father. On another occasion it was the other way around: she and her father went to visit her large maternal and paternal families in Europe. They traveled to Germany, Austria, and Hungary, visiting members of the family and synagogues, and absorbing impressions of Jewish life. Henrietta later wrote many articles describing these visits. The voyage broadened her cultural horizons. Rabbi Szold was a progressive man, and in the debate between the Orthodox and Reform rabbis in the United States, he and his friends tended toward the Conservative movement. Henrietta Szold was absorbed in these discussions, although her public activity was in a different field: she lectured on cultural and social subjects. This activity grew with the foundation of the night school for adults in 1881–82. The school had thirty students when it opened. Astonishingly enough, Henrietta, who revolted at the idea of teaching, became a teacher at this "Russian" school. She loved "her Russians", who attached great significance to their Jewish consciousness—an attitude that had only been strengthened by the persecutions and anti-Semitism to which they had been subjected. Her friends wrote to her constantly of the anti-Semitism in Germany and the rest of Europe, and of the Dreyfus case, which rocked French Jewry to its foundations.

Her father's illness kept her increasingly at his side, and she helped him write various essays, yet her independence was growing steadily. Her faithful friend Dr. Cyrus Adler established the Jewish Publication Society in Philadelphia in order to bring great Jewish works to English-speaking readers in good translation. On his recommendation Henrietta Szold was appointed editorial secretary, and she played a great role in the society. She was completely immersed in her translation work and in the publication of the society's yearbook. At the same time, her activity within the Zionist organization increased. Curiously enough, Herzl and Henrietta Szold were born in the same year and were both of Hungarian Jewish origin. Political Zionism was coming increasingly to the fore, and the reports of Stephen Wise and Richard Gottheil of Columbia University on the Zionist congresses touched Henrietta's heart and fired her imagination.

The turning point of her life came in 1920, after her father's death. The Baltimore period which had spanned four decades—half of her life—was at an end. At that time, Dr. Solomon Schechter was appointed head of the Jewish Theological Seminary of America in New York. Cyrus Adler then asked Henrietta Szold if she would like to become a rabbi, but her answer was a most definite no; she did not consider that her father, even though he had been a progressive Conservative rabbi, would ever have dared to envisage such a possibility. Instead, she accepted the proposition to become a free listener—the only woman—at the seminary. Henrietta Szold then moved with her mother and sister to New York and embarked on the second chapter of her life.

The Szolds lived near the seminary, which served as the center of Jewish leadership in the city. The greatest Jewish personalities used to come to the seminary synagogue when Jewish cultural and social events were held there. Among them were Jacob Schiff, Cyrus Adler, Louis Marshall, and others.

At that time the greatest drama of Henrietta's life took place—a great, unhappy love affair that continued for over five years, from 1903 to 1908. It was unknown for many years, coming to light only in 1961 with the publication of Irving Fineman's *Woman of Valor, The Story of Henrietta Szold*, in the United States. Before her immigration to Eretz Israel prior to World War I she had put her diaries and other papers into a chest, which she left with her sister. It remained untouched until Fineman published extracts in his biography.

Around 1903, Henrietta met and became friendly with one of the most talented professors at the seminary, Louis Ginsberg, who was thirteen years her junior. From her own letters it appears that the professor never regarded the relationship between them as anything more than friendship, while Henrietta was deeply in love with him. So, when the professor declared to her one day that he was about to marry a young woman whom he had met during a visit to his parents, she was deeply shocked. Henrietta's mother decided that travel was the only way to cure her daughter of her disappointment, and they sailed for Europe and Eretz Israel on June 30, 1909.

Henrietta and her mother traveled to Britain, visiting (among others) the Bentwich family. They journeyed to Paris and Vienna, stayed with relatives in Hungary, and from there took the train to Constantinople. From there they sailed for Beirut, continuing by train to Damascus and on to Tiberias.

Their visit to Eretz Israel in 1909 made a great impression on the two women. They toured the villages, towns, and new settlements, and were moved by their encounter with the scenery of the Holy Land. The incidence of disease, notably trachoma and ringworm among the children, shocked them. Henrietta recorded all her experiences and impressions in her diary; they served her as a healing balm.

The two women returned to America in 1910. Their friends and relatives gave them an enthusiastic welcome. Henrietta Szold, who previously had refused to give special attention to women's work, now devoted herself to organizing Hadassah women's groups. On July 14, 1910, she was appointed secretary general of the American Zionist Federation. She turned her attention mainly to education, writing thus in her diary: "My mind harks back to the teaching days. They were happy! After all, there is nothing like association with the next generation either as mother or teacher . . . that is what I most enjoy . . . contact with the optimism and hope and trustfulness of the young."

It would seem that Henrietta Szold had come to the conclusion that if her great love had ended in disappointment and she would not bear her own children, then at least as a teacher or in some similar capacity she could fill the void and build a bridge to the young generation, bearer of the future.

On February 24, 1912, the first meeting of United Hadassah was held at Temple Emmanuel, laying the foundation for the largest women's organization in the history of the Jewish people and of the Zionist movement. Henrietta Szold was appointed president and Gertrude Goldsmith secretary. Professor Israel Friedlander coined Hadassah's famous motto, still in use today: "The healing of the daughter of my people." In 1913 Hadassah for the first time sent two nurses, Rose Kaplan and Rachel Landey, to Eretz Israel to treat trachoma among Jewish children. The two women lived in Meah Shearim, and reported on their treatment of thousands of children suffering from eye diseases. They made contact with the ophthalmologist Dr. Albert Ticho, who gave them his full support. On the outbreak of World War I in 1914, they transferred the clinical work to Dr. Helena Kagan.

At that time Henrietta Szold was a member of the Zionist Executive in the United States. It was an important period in American Zionism. Judge Louis Brandeis was president, and with Henrietta on the executive were Stephen Wise, Shmaryahu Levin, Louis Lipsky, Jacob de Haas, and other prominent personalities. War was raging and American Jewry was concerned for the fate of the Yishuv in Eretz Israel, then subject to Turkish rule and suffering from the machinations of its taskmasters. Henrietta Szold saw no contradiction between her role in the American Zionist leadership and her presidency of Hadassah. She did much to broaden and develop Hadassah as a Zionist women's organization with a dual role—one in the Yishuv in Eretz Israel, the other in the Jewish community in the United States. Within the Yishuv, Hadassah was concerned with social welfare, public health, and education, while within American Jewry its aim was to educate Jewish women, citizens of the United States, to become good and loyal daughters of Israel, devoted to their people, linked with Zionism, and at the same time aware of all that was taking place in American society for the development and progress of the great American democracy. Henrietta Szold's versatile personality was enriched by all she had learned in her childhood and youth, by all the experience she had acquired during her decades of public activity, and by all she had absorbed from European and American culture on the one hand, and Jewish sources on the other. She was then recognized, and rightly so, as the most important Jewish woman in the United States.

In 1916 her mother died. A sudden feeling of loneliness overcame her, but it was mitigated by the increase in Zionist activity on the eve of the Balfour Declaration. On her fifty-seventh birthday, General Allenby conquered Eretz Israel. New horizons opened up for world Zionism in general, and American Zionism in particular. The Hadassah organization confronted a period of trial in its own particular sphere of activity. In 1918 a large medical mission was sent out from the United States to save the Yishuv from the epidemics that were threatening it and to establish health services. The mission, organized by American Zionism, was composed of forty-four men and women—doctors, dentists, male and female nurses and public health workers. The mission carried with it four hundred tons of diverse medical equipment. Henrietta Szold, then secretary of the Education Committee of the United States Zionist Organization, felt that her place was with the Yishuv in Eretz Israel; she had already become attached to it on her earlier visit to the country with her mother. In her heart she knew that the real challenge for her now was Eretz Israel.

On February 21, 1920, Henrietta Szold sailed for London, from there to Naples, and then on to Eretz Israel. Difficulties over the granting of her visa delayed her in Italy, and while she was spending the Passover holiday in Florence news reached her of the riots in Jerusalem and of the defense of Tel Hai. Eventually she reached Palestine and was at once placed at the head of the Hadassah mission. She went on a tour of the country and saw how much there was to be done. Her friend, Dr. Judah Magnes, also came with his family to settle in Palestine at that time. Miss Szold also established friendly relations with many of the finest people of the Yishuv.

She was greatly distressed by the split in American Zionism after the London conference, when Brandeis resigned from the American Zionist leadership. Henrietta Szold was one of Brandeis's devoted admirers yet, for all that, she felt that Weizmann was by and large correct in his approach to the manner in which the Yishuv was to be built and developed so that the Zionist program could be realized. Meanwhile, the financial resources required for maintenance of the medical mission had shrunk. In 1922 Henrietta Szold went to the Zionist Congress in Carlsbad, Czechoslovakia to request funds; in her wide-ranging search she even reached Baron Rothschild. She was bitterly disappointed on more than one occasion. Because of her sister's illness, she went on to the United States, devoting her energies there to the encouragement of Hadassah.

She later returned to Palestine, and in 1927 was elected to the World Zionist Executive and put in charge of the education and health portfolios. The Zionist coffers were empty and there was widespread unemployment in Palestine. Friction arose between the Zionist Executive and various sections of the Yishuv. Henrietta Szold did her best to calm the storms and promote agreement. When the extended Jewish Agency was founded in 1929, on the eve of the riots, Henrietta Szold was elected a member of its executive. The tragic events that caused the loss of human lives and brought destruction to both centers of the old Yishuv and to new agricultural villages enraged her. She was furious that the mandatory government was not fulfilling its obligations and was not defending the lives of Jewish citizens. Relations between her and the labor movement during her period of service on the Zionist Executive were not particularly friendly. Nevertheless, she did derive some satisfaction from the fact that she was elected to the executive of the National Council after the labor movement had ceded to her a seat that it could claim in accordance with the balance of power within the Yishuv. This gesture indicated the esteem in which she was held. During her tenure on the National Council Executive she constructed modern, well-planned social services despite the meager resources available. Henrietta Szold laid the foundation of the Women's Zionist Organization in Palestine, and cooperated with the other women's organizations and volunteer groups active in social work. She was seventy, the age at which most people retire, but Henriette Szold was full of energy, initiative, and freshness.

Independence of thought and action was apparent in whatever she undertook. Henrietta Szold built Youth Aliyah in Eretz Israel, and left the imprint of her personality in this socio-educational institution. Her previous experience in education and social work, her personal connections in the United States and other countries, and her outstanding organizational talent combined to contribute to its success. She put together a team of devoted workers but she herself remained at the center of the operation. She did not abandon the personal touch, traveling herself to welcome the youth on their arrival at Haifa port. She was present at meetings of the youth leaders, read reports on the organization's activities, answered every letter and request, and received in her Jerusalem office anyone who wished to pour out his troubles to her. She could be seen late at night sitting in her office writing letters, and in the morning she would rise early to resume her work as though she were endowed with hidden sources of energy. Her maternal instinct had been awakened, enveloping the hundreds of thousands of children and youth who had been saved. Youth Aliyah gave her inestimable satisfaction, when the first young girls had completed their training, and when the graduates of Youth Aliyah founded Alonim and Matsuba, she went to visit them. No one could have been happier than she to see Youth Aliyah's children's children.

When World War II broke out Henrietta Szold fought to obtain a greater number of immigrant visas and to find new rescue routes. One of the things which upset her most—she was now an old woman in frail health—was the affair of the "Teheran children." Rescued from Poland, these Jewish children had followed a tortuous path from Russia, through Persia, to Palestine. From Persia they were obliged to travel by sea because Iraq refused to allow them to pass overland. Miss Szold then established a new objective: to rehabiltate not only youth, but also orphaned children who had been rescued from the war and had been left defenseless and alone. Youth Aliyah then became a bureau for both child and youth immigration. The arrival of the "Teheran children" aroused fierce public debates that split the Yishuv and the Zionist movement, driving a wedge between the religious and labor parties. They all rushed to the rescue, each declaring faithfully that it was the sole party capable of fulfilling the educational needs of the children and of inspiring them with its spirit. At that time the bureau for child and youth immigration became a special department of the Jewish Agency. A board of management was set up, and norms fixed for the classification of the immigrant children. Committees of enquiry were sent to find out from the children who their parents were; what had been the accepted way of life in their homes; whether they used to pray, lay tefillin, light the sabbath candles, etc. The children did not know why they were being asked all these questions, but accepted the enquiry as a necessary evil.

All this activity, accompanied as it was by unhealthy party fanaticism, gave Henrietta Szold the impression that certain Yishuv circles, in particular the religious sector, regarded her with suspicion. Henrietta, daughter of a rabbi, was herself imbued with deep religious feeling. She lit the sabbath candles in her home, and deeply cherished and respected the tradition of Israel. She therefore refused to accept this suspicious attitude, and it infuriated her. The affair of the "Teheran children" gave her no peace, even after it had been satisfactorily concluded. The children grew up to become members of the defense and security forces, farmers and kibbutzniks, rabbis, teachers, and nurses. They founded families in Israel. But all that was to come later, when Henrietta Szold was no longer alive to see it. *Children of Teheran*, by Ben-Zion Tomer was published in 1971 by the Zionist Library as a memorial to Henrietta Szold, the real mother of those children.

Henrietta Szold initiated another great project. After the outbreak of World War II immigration dropped, and very little rescue work could be done. She therefore agreed to integrate youth from Eretz Israel into the kibbutzim, in collaboration with the pioneer youth groups. A new chapter of Youth Aliyah began—the "town to village" movement. Thanks to

Youth Aliyah, Henrietta Szold was able to implement the idea she had advocated when she was a member of the National Council: the integration and participation of youth from depressed areas in creative pioneering. Scores of pioneer villages were established by graduates of Youth Aliyah groups, together with groups of local youth. Henrietta Szold was of course aware of the need to give special attention to marginal youth with complicated problems. To that end, she set up a special department within Youth Aliyah.

When Henrietta Szold died at a ripe old age, one of the loftiest figures of the twentieth century passed away. Her coffin was followed by her "children"—her pupils, her graduates, her trainees at the Hadassah nursing school, the doctors and the social workers. The entire Yishuv was in mourning, for it had loved and admired her. Zionist organizations throughout the world eulogized her. She died shortly before the end of World War II, when a new challenge was facing Youth Aliyah: rescue of the children who had survived the war. Henrietta Szold's enterprise was ready—as she was undoubtedly aware—for the tremendous rescue undertaking.

She knew that "her" thousands of children would not shrink from difficult tasks. And indeed they fought in the War of Independence, and even prior to that, as members of the Jewish Brigade, in the war against the Nazi oppressor. The health institutions she established in her lifetime served the entire Yishuv in times of trouble and siege. The organization she operated, and the great army of professionals she formed stood the test, and the great efforts she invested were to prove their worth in years of trial.

Henrietta Szold was one of the greatest figures of the Jewish and American people. In the light of her spirit future generations will be educated.

Vera Weizmann

I met Vera Weizmann in the mid-1930s when Dr. Weizmann resumed the presidency of the World Zionist Organization at the nineteenth Congress in Lucerne. After the war, I was elected chairman of the Youth Aliyah Board at the twenty-second Congress in Basle, and in 1948 I was elected head of the department and a full member of the Agency Executive. From then on I was in regular contact with Vera Weizmann; she had been connected with Youth Aliyah from its inception and was the chairman of the Friends of Youth Aliyah in Great Britain. Vera Weizmann succeeded in obtaining the agreement of Prime Minister Jan Smuts to act as patron of Youth Aliyah. In her book *The Impossible Takes Longer* she writes: "When the persecution of Jews in Germany was in full flood, we formed Youth Aliyah, of which I later became the president. Rather timidly, I asked Smuts, who was in London at this time, if he would become the patron of this organization. His immediate reply was, 'Of course.' Before I knew what I was doing, I jumped up and kissed him on both cheeks."

Vera Weizmann also obtained the agreement of Elizabeth, queen of Belgium, to accept the patronage of Youth Aliyah in Belgium. Vera had known the queen since the mid-1920s when, together with her husband, King Albert, she had visited Eretz Israel. The royal couple had been the Weizmanns' guests. During the nineteen years in which I was responsible for Youth Aliyah, I always received help and encouragement from Vera Weizmann. When we agreed to win friends for Youth Aliyah, she was always willing to write to people, meet them or invite them to her home in Rehovot. During her visits to London she maintained her close links with the Friends of Youth Aliyah there, and helped them raise funds and form friendships. She also encouraged the Canadian and South African WIZO (Women's International Zionist Organization) Federations, with whom she had been in contact since her visits to those countries, to support Youth Aliyah. I was often invited to Vera Weizmann's home, for she wanted to hear details of Youth Aliyah activities; she was particularly interested in educational and budgetary questions. She claimed that Youth Aliyah was not receiving a sufficient sum from the treasury in return for its foreign currency earnings, and she tried to take the matter up with Israel's ministers of finance.

During the decade that Eleanor Roosevelt acted as world patroness of Youth Aliyah, she used to call on Vera Weizmann when she visited Israel. I often participated in, or was present at, their meetings; I would sit and listen, and refrained from joining the conversation when it did not concern either myself or my work. On a number of occasions I accompanied Vera Weizmann on visits to Youth Aliyah centers so that she could meet the children. An especially enjoyable experience was her visit to the youth village Alonei Yitschak in Samaria. The children assembled, and she went up to one who was standing in the front row and asked him his name. "Chaim Weizmann," the boy replied. She was very touched. On another occasion we accompanied Eleanor Roosevelt on a visit to the Eleanor Youth Centre in Beersheba, and to the day center for youth, Ofakim, which was named after Vera Weizmann. On that occasion both women signed a petition calling for support of World Jewish Children's Day and of Youth Aliyah.

At my suggestion, Vera Weizmann agreed to accept the honorary presidency of World Jewish Children's Day, whose aim was to reinforce the solidarity between Jewish children throughout the world and the children of Israel, particularly those who were in Youth Aliyah's care. When the International Union of Child Welfare, of which Youth Aliyah was a member, declared its intention to hold World Children's Day, we created the educational framework for World Jewish Children's Day which also served as a fund raising day for Youth Aliyah.

I do not recall Vera Weizmann ever refusing a request I made in connection with Youth Aliyah. She once told me about the beginnings of World WIZO—she and Rebecca Sieff had been among its founders— and why she gave up the copresidency of that organization. She was not on good terms with Rebecca Sieff, something I already knew from conversations with each of the two women separately. On the other hand, Vera Weizmann had an excellent relationship both with Hadassah Samuel, chairman of the World WIZO Executive, and with Pioneer Women. Not far from her home in Rehovot lies the youth village Ayanot, which was founded and run by her friend, Ada Fishman-Maimon. Vera Weizmann held Ada Maimon in high esteem as a pioneer and as one of the founders of the working women's movement in Israel. She often visited her at the youth village. Ayanot was run on traditional lines, for Ada Maimon was religious. She was a sister of Rabbi Yehuda Leib

Maimon, one of the leaders of Mizrachi, and Israel's first minister of religions.

When the friends of Youth Aliyah in Great Britain visited Israel, Vera Weizmann made a party for them in her home. She was very fond of Lorna Wingate, cochairman, together with Dr. Israel Feldman, of the British friends of Youth Aliyah. She greatly admired Sam Goldstein, one of the pillars of Youth Aliyah in London; he had greatly assisted her when she was chairman of Youth Aliyah there. She had many friends among the Youth Aliyah family in Britain, among them Lady Wolfson, Lola Hahn Warburg, and others. Vera Weizmann had been in contact with Lorna Wingate in the thirties when her husband, Orde, was serving in Eretz Israel.

It was then that he trained the striking force of the Haganah, and the couple visited the Weizmanns regularly, both in Rehovot and in London. Vera had retained her London flat, for the couple used it on their visits to London on political Zionist business, and lived there during World War II.

In her book Vera Weizmann wrote about the foundation of WIZO:

My first visit to Palestine was made in the autumn of 1919 and lasted little more than a month. Mrs. Eder, Mrs. Sieff and I, as we toured the country, were very impressed by the hard work done in rebuilding Palestine by the devoted *Halutzot*, a new name at that time for our pioneering working-women. But we were no less perturbed, even appalled, by the arduous physical conditions of their lives. . . .

On our return home, therefore, we decided to form a women's organization, the purpose of which would be to fill the gaps and shortages which had faced us so disturbingly when we were in Palestine.

Thus it came about that in 1920 we three—Mrs. Eder, Mrs. Sieff and I—enlisted the help of Mrs. Romana Goodman and, later, Mrs. Olga Alman, both of whom were active in the English Zionist Federation, and proceeded to work out our plans. . . .

The first international meeting of Zionist Women's groups in Europe took place in London in July, 1920, at the time of the first post-war Zionist Conference. The first steps were taken at this gathering towards the establishment of WIZO (Women's International Zionist Organization.) Having had some experience, as a medical officer of health, in infant and pre-natal care in Manchester, I read a paper to the women's conference on this subject, an understanding of which was essential in such a primitive land as Palestine was at this time. As a result a home for infants and a domestic science school at Tel Aviv were among the first projects created and supported by WIZO. . . .

From the early 1920s onwards, when the able and dedicated women of the executive committee in London were extending WIZO's scope and enlarging its membership by correspondence, I was fortunate enough to travel with my husband on his Zionist mission to various countries. While he was active in political Zionism and in fundraising, I had the opportunity to make personal contact with the women in the lands we visited, and was thus able in the course of these visits to sponsor the creation of WIZO groups in Canada, France, Egypt, Portugal, Italy and South America. . . .

"In Canada I spoke at many meetings of the purpose and objectives of WIZO, in the creation of a Jewish National homeland in Palestine. In the end I succeeded in winning them over, and the Canadian women joined WIZO. They later made themselves responsible for the wonderful project of the agricultural and domestic science school at Nahalal. Thus WIZO became a great force, created many progressive welfare institutions in Palestine, and later in Israel.

Some little while after WIZO was founded a group of intelligent and enlightened women in Palestine formed the *Histadruth Nashim Zioniot* (Organization of Women Zionists) which later joined forces with the world body. Mrs. Hadassah Samuel, daughter-in-law of Herbert Samuel, was elected chairman, and under her competent leadership the Palestine group carried out admirably the program adopted by WIZO at its annual conference. Hadassah Samuel, attractive, capable, intelligent, and successful in her work, was a great friend of mine for almost half a century.

I myself was a member of the world executive committee for two decades, from 1920 to 1940. During that time, Mrs. Rebecca D. Sieff and I were joint-chairmen, serving alternate years. For some months before I was compelled by pressure of work and other reasons to resign in 1940 from WIZO, I was joint president of that body with the 1st Viscountess Samuel. Thereafter I devoted myself to Youth Aliyah (rescue and rehabilitation of children and youth organization), of which I became president. . . .

Looking back over some forty-five years, I think we have every reason to congratulate ourselves on taking the step in 1919–1920 that led to the inception of WIZO, an achievement of which we can be proud. More than that, WIZO has assumed a place and a meaning in Jewish life the world over. It has created social values and established standards which are indispensable for our Jewish existence.

Vera Weizmann undoubtedly won a place in history when in 1913 she persuaded her husband to refuse to leave Manchester for a position in Berlin. In her memoirs she writes:

At about the same time, Chaim received a pressing invitation from the Actions Committee in Berlin to uproot himself from Manchester and join the committee as a paid Zionist official. Disappointed and frustrated over his lost professorship, Chaim was tempted to accept. But for perhaps the first time in my married life I was adamant and flatly refused to go to Germany. Apart from my fear that everything was *verboten* in Germany, I was not prepared to take my medical degree for the *third* time after having completed my examinations successfully in Manchester! But, far worse, I could not contemplate the idea that Chaim should give up his beloved science to become a paid Zionist civil servant. "Our road to Palestine will never go through Berlin," I said firmly.

Chaim did not speak to me for three weeks!

Looking back, I dread to think what would have happened to us all, with the advent of Hitler, if we had gone to Germany. Who would have had the intuition, courage, persuasive power and charm to convince Balfour, Churchill, Lloyd George, Smuts and so many others of the need for the Balfour Declaration without which, after so many struggles and disappointments, trials and errors, and such despair, the Jewish State would never have been proclaimed in 1948?

There is no doubt that Weizmann's continued presence in Manchester, and later in London, had an enormous influence on Zionist history, if not on the history of the entire Jewish people. The Balfour Declaration was first and foremost Weizmann's personal achievement. Ze'ev Jabotinsky, Weizmann's future opponent in Zionist politics, and Vera and Chaim's friend, wrote to Weizmann in Russian in August 1922, a month after the League of Nations had ratified the British Mandate in Eretz Israel:

Dear Friend,

I have re-read the Mandate very carefully; a colossal document and absolutely ineffaceable. Its failings you yourself know, but on the other hand there is nothing in it, not a single sentence which in a severe judicial analysis could exclude our most remote goal—even a Jewish State. This Mandate is almost an idealistically elastic receptacle for our energies. No matter how much we put into it, how much we fulfill, it will not burst. When I remember the beginning: Manchester and Justice Walk in London, and how all this was built up like children's toy bricks—and *sucked out of the thumb of one man*—I must say to you—and I flatter myself that I know a little of history—that this process is without parallel as a personal performance. You need neither congratulations nor compliments.

I wish you a good rest and embrace you warmly; also Vera Issayevna and the children if they are with you.

My family sends you its warmest regards and congratulations.

Yours, Z. J.

Life for Vera Weizmann in Manchester was not easy. Her husband was frequently away for lecture tours on weekends, and often traveled to Europe, leaving her alone. She practised as a doctor, brought up their children, was occupied with Zionist affairs and kept an open house. And then began the great epoch in Zionist history, the days of the Balfour Declaration. When the Weizmanns moved to London, they invited to their home some of England's most important statesmen, scientists and Jewish leaders. The house hummed with social and political activity; Vera supervised the household and acted as hostess.

During World War II, Vera went though difficult times. She assumed tasks in the field kitchen during Nazi bombardments and worked as an ordinary woman soldier. At the same time she was struck by personal tragedy: the Weizmanns' beloved son Michael was shot down in action with the Royal Air Force. That was the hardest blow that ever befell the Weizmann family. Vera did not break down; she continued to accompany her husband on his trips to America during the war and stood by him during the fight against the White Paper, and for a Jewish state. She was a great strength to him in his internal struggles in the Zionist movement, and during the crisis with Ben-Gurion, chairman of the Zionist Executive.

The crisis with the British government was a terrible trial for Chaim and Vera. Chaim Weizmann's reactions were often sharp and angry, and Vera also expressed herself caustically when she met British leaders who had betrayed their mission and the obligations they had assumed toward the Jewish people and the Zionist enterprise. When the declaration of the state was mooted, rumors spread that Weizmann was opposed to it. The opposite was the case. Vera wrote:

> A little later, he asked Sharrett to take a personal message to Ben-Gurion and his colleagues: "Moshe, don't let them swerve, don't let them spoil the victory—the Jewish State, nothing less." Chaim followed this up by telephoning to Sharrett at the aerodrome before his flight, telling him to repeat his message to Ben-Gurion: "Proclaim the Jewish State, now or never!" B-G wanted Meyer Weisgal to contact Chaim and discover his attitude towards the Proclamation of the State. He arranged air passage for Meyer, with a stop-over in Nice. From Nice Meyer telephoned Chaim.
>
> He was about to launch into a lengthy explanation, telling him that B-G had asked for his opinion, when Chaim cut him short. "What are they waiting for?" he demanded in Yiddish. Meyer then sent a cable to B-G.: "The answer is 'Yes.'"

Weizmann brought his influence to bear on President Truman to be the first to recognize the State of Israel after its proclamation, and later he was recalled to Washington to persuade Truman not to detach the Negev from the state and to include Eilat, our only outlet to the Red Sea, within its boundaries.

Thus, Vera traveled the long hard road together with her husband. With that, she was often justifiably criticized for not bringing the president into closer touch with the general public. On the contrary—the Weizmann home was far removed from the people. Officials of the mandatory government, diplomats, visitors from abroad, leaders of the Yishuv, and personal friends were the only guests at the dinners and gatherings held there. Vera never learned Hebrew, and that, too, handicapped her in her contacts with people. I remember a ceremony at the Mossinsohn School in Magdiel when she came to open the Eleanor Rathbone House; it was to be named after a British member of Parliament who had fought in the House for the rescue of Jewish children, and had been financed by the British branch of Youth Aliyah. Vera spoke in English, and afterward a boy came up to me and asked, "Doesn't our queen speak Hebrew?" Thus, Vera Weizmann's visits to Youth Aliyah centers could not take on an intimate character for she had no common language with the youngsters. When she returned to Israel in the spring of 1953, she wrote:

> I found that my two "separate selves" were beginning to merge into one person again as I devoted myself to charitable and social work in Youth Aliyah, the rehabilitation of war-wounded soldiers, and in the Magen David Adom (our Red Cross) of which I am president. Youth Aliyah has become a living proof of the vision which inspired its founders. At Youth Aliyah's twentieth anniversary celebrations in 1953, I recalled that over sixty-four thousand orphaned children had found a home and a "mother" in Israel through the devoted work of the organization. Today, the number of charges is over a hundred thousand. "Of such is the Kingdom of Heaven," said the great hearted Field Marshal Smuts in a message he once sent to Youth Aliyah. "Let this remnant be planted in the soil drenched with blood and tears, hallowed by the prayers of their ancestors." To every Jew and Gentile, I record my thanks and admiration for the work which has been done in this mighty rescue operation.

During Chaim Weizmann's term as president of the State, diplomats, ambassadors, and members of the scientific institute came to the presidential residence. Vera took a great interest in war invalids, and worked for the establishment of a hospital for invalids in Nahariya.

In the conclusion to her memoirs she wrote: "As for myself, I believe, as my husband did, in the ultimate triumph of moral values—although people must get a little push now and then so as to see them more clearly.... And I believe that no power on earth can balance the oil and political rivalries of the Middle East against the fate of two million and more Israelis. For it is said in 1 Samuel, XV, 29—'And also the Strength of Israel will not lie nor repent: for He is not a man, that He should repent.'"

She could have not have foreseen the world oil crisis which followed the Yom Kippur War, and the importance oil was to assume in world politics, particularly in our region.

Vera Weizmann was born in Rostov-on-Don in Russia, a town far from the centers of Jewish life. Her life, though difficult at times, was a fascinating one, and had important results for her people and her land.

Rose Halprin

Rose Halprin was one of the most colorful figures in the World Zionist Organization and the Jewish Agency, and she left her mark on the leadership of Hadassah in the United States upward of twenty-five years. In the mid-1930s the Halprin family was living in Jerusalem and Rose attended the meetings of the Zionist Actions Committee. My friendship with her dates from after the Second World War, when we were both elected to the Jewish Agency Executive at the first Zionist Congress held after the Holocaust, in Basle in 1946. Rose was the first representative of Hadassah on the Jewish Agency Executive. Although Mrs. Rose Jacobs had been elected to the Jewish Agency in the thirties, at the historic Zionist Congress of 1929 when the Jewish Agency was founded, she represented the non-Zionists on the Executive, not Hadassah. Rose Halprin was the leader of Hadassah, its president from 1932 to 1934.

Within Hadassah, a debate raged between the supporters of Weizmann and Ben-Gurion, who advocated a Jewish state in part of Eretz Israel, and the supporters of Yehuda Leib Magnes, who favored a binational state in Eretz Israel. Rose Halprin was loyal to Weizmann and Ben-Gurion, and she succeeded in rallying around her most of Hadassah's leaders. She held central positions in American Jewish and Zionist organizations such as the American Zionist Emergency Council, the United Jewish Appeal, and the World Confederation of General Zionists.

I well remember our meeting in Paris immediately after World War I when, together with Zvi Herman, we convinced Rose Halprin and Judith Epstein, then president of Hadassah, to support the establishment of the Constructive Fund of the World General Zionist movement. The primary aims of the fund were to assist the settlements of the Zionist Youth and the Working Zionists in Eretz Israel, and to help in the absorption of the Holocaust survivors. Rose Halprin played an important role in the world conference of General Zionism that was held on the eve of the Zionist Congress in Basle in December 1946; it was on that occasion that the

United Confederation was founded. At the congress she fought, together with Nachum Goldmann, for the reelection of Chaim Weizmann as president of the Zionist Organization, and against Ben-Gurion and Dr. Abba Hillel Silver, who tried to prevent Weizmann's reelection because of the crisis in relations with the British government. Within the Confederation of General Zionists we made common cause with Rose Halprin, and she supported me in my capacity as head of Youth Aliyah even when I was at odds with Ben-Gurion, who was chairman of the Executive. We became close friends and I knew she could be relied upon.

At Zionist congresses and meetings of the Executive, Rose was one of the leading orators. On more than one occasion she expressed views I did not agree with, particularly her opposition to the centrality of immigration from the free countries, and more especially from the United States. Though she was a great admirer of Ben-Gurion, Rose came into conflict with him over the question of aliyah, and, specifically, over the phraseology defining the central role of Zionism: aliyah to Eretz Israel.

At meetings of the Jewish Agency Executive she was always listened to attentively. In the Yishuv, too, she was known for her independence. Whenever she visited Israel she would turn up with a huge suitcase packed with hats. They were the last word in fashion, and she would change them several times a day. People used to joke about Rose's hats, but they knew that underneath them was an active mind, and that this fashionable woman was a staunch defender of her ideas.

As chairman of the American branch of the Jewish Agency, Rose Halprin was a great success; the men in the organization learned to respect her firm stand and her authority. Emanuel Neumann headed the General Zionists of the American Zionist Organization who, joined by like-minded members in Eretz Israel, decided to identify the World Confederation of General Zionists with their party in Israel. This led to a split in the federation. The majority led by Dr. Israel Goldstein and Rose Halprin declared its nonidentification with the party in Eretz Israel. The heads of this nonidentification federation drifted away from the Progressive Party and later from the Independent Liberals; they even broke ties with our settlement movement. In this, Rose and the heads of the confederation dissociated themselves from the creative, pioneering settlement work of the Zionist Youth. They began to develop an ideology of Diaspora Zionism—a far from encouraging innovation at a time when there was a need for greater identification with the struggle for a more active, fulfilled Zionism. We suggested to them cooperation in our constructive enterprises—youth villages, kibbutzim and moshavim—and coordination of our positions on Zionist issues only, not official affiliation. But the proposal was not accepted. As an alternative, they sought nonparty youth movements that, in fact, were connected with the Union of Collective Settlements in Israel of the Labor party. For as long as I was a member of the agency executive and the head of Youth Aliyah, Hadassah in the United States supported my positions and I was able to serve as a link between our movement and Hadassah because of the personal friendship and reciprocal confidence that existed between myself and the leaders of Hadassah, whatever their shades of opinion.

When I was appointed minister of tourism and development in 1966, Hadassah and our movement drew apart because of the growing friction between the two confederations, and we finally lost the direction of Youth Aliyah as well.

Rose Halprin was highly respected in the Hadassah organization and in the American Zionist movement, and the contributions she made to Zionism and Judaism over such a long period were greatly appreciated.

Rose Halprin was born in New York and studied at the Teachers Institute of the Jewish Theological Seminary, then at Hunter College and Columbia University. She was happily married to Samuel, a businessman, and had much joy from her children. During the stormy period in American Zionism before the establishment of the state, during the struggle for the state, and after its creation, she played an important role and was a partner to historic decisions. It is to be regretted that she did not find time to write her memoirs or her impressions of those great days.

Rebecca Sieff

Rebecca Sieff was the representative par excellence of Zionist women throughout the world, and was one of the important representatives of the London Zionist Marks-Sieff-Sacher family. When I was at kibbutz Hamefales near Kfar Saba, I served in the late thirties as secretary of the board of settlements in the Sharon. It was then that I heard of the establishment of Sieff House at Tel Mond in the heart of the orange groves, in the employment of which Jewish labor was the rule. Dr. Chaim Weizmann, president of the World Zionist Organization, was greatly assisted by the Sieff-Marks family both in his political work and in fund raising for the Jewish National Fund and the Zionist enterprise in general. In 1934, Rebecca and Israel Sieff founded the Institute for Agricultural Research in Rehovot; it was named after their son Daniel. But Rebecca Sieff was best known for her work among Zionist women in Eretz Israel and throughout the world: she founded the Federation of Zionist Women in Great Britain in 1919, and a year later she established World WIZO together with Vera Weizmann. For a time the two women were copresidents of the world organization; when Vera Weizmann retired, Rebecca Sieff remained sole president and served World WIZO for forty-three years.

My personal relationship with Rebecca Sieff began in London after World War II, when I attended the first Zionist Congress held after the Holocaust. I asked her to raise a sum of money for the children's homes that the Honoar Hazioni-Akiva Youth had set up in Poland. Her reaction was immediate and affirmative. I also asked her for a sum to be devoted to the rescue of an important colleague who was imprisoned in a Soviet camp because of his Zionism. She invited me to her home and gave me a long lecture about her Zionist activities, her connections with labor leaders in England, and her grievances against Vera Weizmann. She then gave me the money I had asked for, and wished me success in the liberation of my colleague.

It was then that the Labor Party came to power in Britain. Churchill, who had led England in the war, had been defeated. Like many others, Rebecca Sieff hoped that she would be able to influence Labor government policy, for she had friends in key positions—Aneurin Bevan, for example, leader of the left-wing labor group. At the World General Zionist Conference that was held in London at that time, two delegations of Zionist women participated: Hadassah leaders from the United States, with Rose Halprin and Judith Epstein at their head, and World WIZO leaders, with Rebecca Sieff at their head. Mrs. Sieff was greatly respected and very popular.

After I was elected head of Youth Aliyah, I had close contact with Rebecca Sieff. She complained bitterly that her contribution to Youth Aliyah at its inception, when the anti-Jewish laws were enacted in Germany and Central Europe, was not sufficiently recognized. At that time she had firmly supported Recha Freier, the woman who initiated Youth Aliyah and laid the foundations of the enterprise. Recha Freier wrote of that period in her book, *Yisharesh* (It Will Take Root):

> In addition to the 1,500 Youth Aliyah permits, I decided to ask for 1,000 entrance permits to England for the Hehalutz movement. "You will never obtain 1,000 entrance visas to England for agricultural workers of Hechalutz," I was told by all those whom I approached on the matter. I heard that Rebecca Sieff was looking for me. Maybe she would be able to help us? I called on her, and found her with the Englishman, Dr. Mallon. In reply to a question I said, "I must receive entrance permits for members of Hehalutz." There was no need to explain, and I was asked nothing more. Dr. Mallon took out his notebook and began to write down the details. He discussed with Rebecca Sieff which of them would call on the Home Office, the Trade Unions and the Colonial Office. That same day I told Dr. Weizmann that they had set to work, and I requested that the Zionist Executive provide the guarantees required by the British government for the 1,000 members of Hehalutz before the permits could be granted. Dr. Weizmann took care of the guarantees, and I waited weeks for a message from Rebecca Sieff that the 1,000 entrance permits to England for agricultural workers had also been granted. At this point, Rebecca Sieff's energy and devotion stood her in good stead. When she was told at the Home Office that the permits had been refused, she sat down on the steps and refused to budge as long as the Home Office persisted in its refusal. The permits were granted. . . .

Rebecca Sieff was one of the initiators of the Women's Appeal in England; it united all the Jewish women's organizations in an effort to help rescue Jews from Central Europe. She was also one of the first women to visit the displaced persons camps in Germany right after the war. To make it possible, she was given a temporary rank in the British Army, for civilians were not permitted to visit the area. So it was that she spent Rosh Hashana of 1945 among the survivors of Bergen-Belsen. When she appeared before the Special United Nations Commission on Palestine in 1946, together with Rachel Katznelson-Rubashov (Shazar), she made a great impression on its members. She forcefully demanded that the thirty thousand children who had survived the Holocaust and were now in the camps of Europe, and the two thousand children in the youth village in the internment camps on Cyprus, be permitted to immigrate to Eretz Israel and to settle there. She demanded this in the name of human rights, and said: "We will give you no peace until we get our children back home." At that time I was chairman of the Committee for the Cyprus Internees that had been set up by the Zionist Executive and the National Council, and I twice visited the camps on Cyprus. I heard many of the internees congratulate Rebecca Sieff on her impressive appearance, and on her demand for the immediate immigration of the children in the camps through Youth Aliyah.

Rebecca Sieff was born in 1890 in Leeds. Her father, Michael Marks, was the founder of the huge Marks and Spencer firm, and her brother, Simon Marks, together with her husband, Sieff, were firm supporters of Chaim Weizmann in all his undertakings. From her youth, Rebecca Sieff was involved with Zionist activity in England; the family's connection with Weizmann began during his Manchester days. Following the Balfour Declaration, Weizmann left for Eretz Israel at the head of the Zionist Committee, and Israel Sieff was appointed political secretary of the delegation. Rebecca Sieff and Vera Weizmann accompanied the group, and Mrs. Sieff, by opening the delegation's house, provided an important meeting place where leaders of the Yishuv and members of the delegation could make closer contact with officials of the new British administration. Together with Vera Weizmann and Edith Eder, the wife of a member of the delegation, they studied life in the Yishuv, health and education problems, and social conditions. On their return to England, they decided to found the Woman's International Zionist Organization. World WIZO came into being in July 1920.

Rebecca Sieff was very much involved with social and cultural life in England, and she did much to foster cultural and artistic life in the Yishuv. She helped to encourage Branislaw Huberman to found the Philharmonic Orchestra. The Daniel Sieff Institute served as the nucleus for the Weizmann Institute, and Rebecca was made an honorary institute member. But she will be remembered in Zionist history as the WIZO leader, a humanitarian who fought for her people, who helped rescue children during the darkest period in our history, and who championed the just cause of Zionism among upperclass British society. The hundreds of thousands of Zionist women active in WIZO federations, and devoted to Israel heart and soul, constitute an army which, for over fifty-five years, has faithfully fulfilled the Zionist aims of World WIZO. There is no doubt that these organizations and the tasks they accomplished in Israel—educational projects, pioneer training, social and cultural work, support of Youth Aliyah, assistance to the needy, and a humane presence in some of the most depressed, out-of-the way neighborhoods—have contributed and continue to contribute much to the quality of life in the Jewish state.

Rebecca Sieff was a militant, and she represented, both in her person and in her activity, the humane values of Judaism. All the benefits she had acquired from British culture she wished to impart to the Yishuv in Eretz Israel. She was one of the most gracious figures among the generations of Zionist giants.

Kurt Blumenfeld

Yehuda (Kurt) Blumenfeld was without doubt one of the most original personalities in the Zionist movement. He was a spiritual leader par excellence, an ideologue who won over his interlocutors or his audience by his profound analysis, and by his passionate belief in the justice of his words. Blumenfeld's speeches were impressive, especially when he spoke in German, and they were an unforgettable personal experience for all his listeners. He spoke Hebrew and also lectured in Hebrew later on, but he never attained in Hebrew the brilliance of expression that he displayed in German.

Blumenfeld belonged to the progressive wing of World General Zionism; he was one of its leaders and a follower of Chaim Weizmann. For the Zionist world and the Yishuv in Eretz Israel, Yehuda Kurt Blumenfeld represented German Zionism at its finest. He won over many prominent personalities in German Jewry—and those in other countries—to the renaissance movement, the World Zionist Organization and the Jewish Foundation Fund. Blumenfeld's main weapons in converting people to the Zionist cause were his rich spiritual resources, his fine analysis, and his extensive knowledge of history, literature, and art. He was a profound, thorough orator who knew how to carry his audience along with him, and he was considered one of the leading propagandists of the movement. Neither among his teachers nor his followers was there anyone else with his powers of persuasion.

Kurt Blumenfeld's Zionism was "Palestine-centered." He had absolutely no interest in the fight for Jewish rights in the Diaspora because he did not believe in the possibility of a bridge between his people's culture and that of the people among whom they lived. He did not believe in assimilation, and preached to German Jewry for many years—even before the first signs of Nazism had emerged and before anti-Semitism had manifested itself in public life—that there was no future for Jews on German soil and that their only hope was Eretz Israel. Blumenfeld did not believe in a harmony or synthesis between Judaism and Germanism. For him, Zionism was first and foremost the personal answer to all the Jews' problems. He guided the individual Jew to observe reality carefully, to see it in the proper perspective. Thus he enlightened the Jew as to what actually was happening around him, and presented him with a view of his future at a time when it was still concealed both from the eye and from the consciousness.

Since he was completely at home in German culture, Blumenfeld had innumerable possibilities for influencing his colleagues. First and foremost he succeeded in attracting the Jewish students in German universities to Zionism, and so became the real leader of the young generation. That was his first step in his "conquest" of the German Zionist Organization. At first he was only its secretary, but later he was appointed editor of *Die Welt* and eventually was elected president of the German Zionists. It was only natural that a man who regarded the development and construction of the Yishuv in Eretz Israel as the central Zionist ambition should have been one of the creators of the Keren Hayesod (Jewish Foundation Fund), the instrument created at the end of World War I for the building of Eretz Israel. He succeeded in collecting large donations from wealthy capitalists, attaining records similar to Weizmann's. He attracted to the fund complete strangers to the national movement, and won them over to the Zionist idea.

Blumenfeld was highly esteemed in Jewish and Zionist circles in Germany. Personalities such as Albert Einstein, Walter Rathenau, Oscar Wasserman—the chairman of the Jewish Foundation Fund in Germany whom Blumenfeld had convinced to accept this high position—as well as writers, artists, and public and political figures were influenced by him. Einstein and Blumenfeld were in close contact; Einstein undertook Zionist missions, traveling to the United States to meet with personalities and politicians, as a result of Blumenfeld's influence. The two men maintained contact for many years; indeed, after Einstein left Germany for the United States, Blumenfeld used to visit him frequently at Princeton. At an afternoon tea party I heard Kurt Blumenfeld talk about his correspondence with Einstein. It would certainly reveal many things of particular interest to Zionism if it should ever be published.

When Kurt Blumenfeld immigrated to Eretz Israel he became one of the heads of the Keren Hayesod administration, and continued to work with Arthur Hantke, the man who had drawn Blumenfeld into the activities of the Zionist center in Germany when he was still a university student. He worked together with Leib Yaffe, that noble-spirited man who also did much for the Keren Hayesod. Leo Herman joined them. This group of Keren Hayesod leaders worked in harmony and friendship.

Hantke headed the Jerusalem headquarters of Keren Hayesod, while Blumenfeld and Leib Yaffe traveled throughout the world on the fund's business.

Although Blumenfeld was one of Weizmann's followers, when the discussions multiplied over Zionism's political aims and the "final objective," differences arose on more than one occasion between Weizmann and Blumenfeld. But Blumenfeld was always able to master his feelings and, in the final analysis, to accept Weizmann's opinion and authority.

Kurt Blumenfeld was greatly influenced by the Russian Zionists, in particular by Shmaryahu Levin and the Zionist students who were studying at German universities. They were of his own generation, and with him they occupied a central place in the Zionist movement. When the Zionist Executive was located in Berlin, Russian Zionist leaders were also members of it, and a profound friendship grew up between them and Blumenfeld, the secretary. He admired Russian Jewry's authenticity and way of life. In personal conversations he would frequently recall the great friendship between the German and Russian Zionists, citing his own family as an example. His wife, Jenny, who was later to become one of the leaders of WIZO and was a personality in her own right, was originally of a Russian-Jewish family from Minsk.

After his immigration, Kurt Blumenfeld tried to organize the Hakidma Party, consisting mainly of German Zionists who had immigrated to Eretz Israel. In this he failed. The General Zionist Federation already existed in Eretz Israel (though it was to split later into Zionists A and B). The Progressive Zionist wing in the country was headed by Dr. Moshe Glickson, and included the pioneering Zionist Youth and the Zionist Workers, who saw no reason to join the Hakidma Party. When the German Zionists immigrated in greater numbers and organized the New Aliyah party they were far more successful. The perfect combination—of the German and Eastern European progressive Zionists, the veteran democratic Zionists of the Yishuv, and the Zionist Workers—was eventually achieved in the Progressive Party, but only after the establishment of the State of Israel.

In the thirties, and until the outbreak of World War II, meetings and talks were held among the various groups of Progressive General Zionism, principally among those who belonged to the World Confederation of General Zionists established in Cracow in 1935 following the split in the General Zionist movement (which had been provoked by its right wing). Blumenfeld had been one of the leading speakers at the Cracow conference and one of those responsible for the split, joining the radical Zionists from Poland, the progressive General Zionists, and the Zionist Worker in Eretz Israel.

Blumenfeld, who was loyal to the alliance between progressive and democratic Zionism and the labor movement, regarded the attempt to break up the Histadrut as a turnabout in the direction of Revisionism, and as a contradiction of all that he had taught and advocated throughout his life. At that conference an alliance was formed for the first time between the progressive and radical Zionists from Poland on the one hand, and Zionists A, Weizmann's followers, the Zionist Worker pioneers, and the progressive Zionists in Eretz Israel on the other. This camp became the decisive majority in World General Zionism, for it was joined by most of the American and British Zionists. The headquarters of the World Confederation of General Zionists was in London, and a second center was established in Tel Aviv. The meetings between Blumenfeld and his colleagues who immigrated in the thirties, and the veteran Russian Zionists and members of the Zionist Workers, were always overpowering. The debate was on a high level at all times, even if stormy on occasion. Those were the years of the disturbances—1936 to 1939—of the struggle against British rule on the one hand and Revisionism on the other. Controversy raged over the aims of Zionism in the years that preceded and followed the Peel Report—a document that recommended the establishment of a Jewish state in part of Palestine. Proposals were also made for the establishment of a binational state in Israel. Kurt Blumenfeld was a friend of the Zionist Youth kibbutzim in Eretz Israel and he tried, among other things, to induce Shlomo Zalman Schocken to come to their aid.

Indeed, Blumenfeld was among those who elevated the Zionist movement. He was one of the great revolutionaries of the national renaissance movement both in thought and in action. His life was full, rich, and interesting, and he lived to a ripe old age, witnessing both the tragic realization of many truths and the fulfillment of hopes and dreams. At the end of his life he lived in Jerusalem, the capital of the State of Israel.

His book, *The Jewish Question as an Experience* was written in an original form: it contained a diary, memoirs, character sketches of personalities, and original analysis. It was published by the Zionist Library to commemorate the end of the thirty days of mourning after his death. Blumenfeld saw the original German version of his book in his lifetime, but he was not privileged to see the entire Hebrew translation. He did, however, manage to write a few lines of the introduction to the Hebrew edition. The book deserves to be widely read, especially by the young generation. Blumenfeld was among those lofty personalities who paved the way for the Jewish state.

Selig Asher Brodetsky

The life story of Professor Selig Brodetsky, one of the central personalities of contemporary Judaism and Zionism, is something of a wonder tale. His life was rich in scientific, Jewish, and human content—the life of a versatile Jewish personality of great charm.

Son of an Orthodox Jewish family, Selig Brodetsky arrived in London from the Ukraine when he was five years old. He was educated at a Jewish primary school and a Talmud Torah of the Jewish ghetto in the East End of London. His father, a synagogue beadle, supported the family with great difficulty. Selig Brodetsky, through his own efforts and his great talent, attained a high position in the scientific world, played a central role in Jewish life in England, and became an influential figure in world Zionism. While he was still a youth his mathematical genius became widely known, and he was awarded a scholarship to continue his studies. It was not easy for the young Jewish lad from an Orthodox family in the East End of London to reach Cambridge. But all the obstacles were overcome, and at the age of twenty he won the title of Senior Wrangler, awarded to the highest first-class honors student in the mathematical tripos at Cambridge.

He continued his studies in mathematical astronomy at Leipzig, and in 1913 was awarded his Doctorate of Science. A year later he was appointed lecturer in applied mathematics in Bristol, and by 1924 he was professor of mathematics at the University of Leeds. He was an expert in the General Theory of Relativity and did a considerable amount of work in aerodynamics. In 1920, when he was only thirty-two, he published a paper on the mechanical principles of the airplane. He also wrote a book on Newton's theories which was well received in Britain, and his book *What Is Mathematics?* also appeared in Hebrew, Spanish, and Dutch.

Had Brodetsky devoted himself entirely to mathematics he would have made major contributions for he was a genius in opening up new fields in the scientific world. But he went through the same experiences as did many other young Jews of his generation who were living at a time of political and social unheaval. World War I changed the face of nations, among them the Jewish people. The revolution that took place in Jewish life left its imprint on this young Jewish professor who, while still an adolescent, had already been influenced by Zionist theory.

In 1907, when the Zionist Union was formed at Cambridge, Brodetsky was elected secretary. In Leipzig he had been chairman of the Zionist students' organization, and while still a young man he was elected to the executive of the Zionist Federation in England. He was only forty when he was elected by the Zionist Actions Committee to the Jewish Agency Executive. Until the State of Israel was established, he headed the political department of the Jewish Agency in London, serving under Chaim Weizmann, president of the Zionist Organization. Brodetsky's rapid rise in the Zionist world may well have taken many by surprise.

During the days of perfidious British rule and its attendant disappointments, Brodetsky faithfully carried out his professorial duties at the University of Leeds. However, this did not prevent him from playing an active role in British and Anglo-Jewish society. He traveled frequently to Jewish communities throughout the world, made a stay in Eretz Israel, traveled on behalf of the national funds, and labored on behalf of the Hebrew University, on whose board of trustees he served. Dr. Nachum Goldmann was correct when he wrote in his introduction to Brodetsky's memoirs that Brodetsky lived a number of parallel lives which fused into a rich and interesting existence. He was a professor at Leeds; he was active in the University Teachers' Organization in England; he was guest lecturer at other universities; he published papers, did research, and took a personal interest in the Hebrew University.

Selig Brodetsky was a member of various national scientific associations in England and he had extensive connections with scientists and intellectuals in British society. Parallel with his scientific activities he lived a rich and animated Jewish life as head of the British Board of Deputies. He took a great interst in Jewish education, loved and respected Jewish tradition, and argued unceasingly with Jewish assimilationist and anti-Zionist circles. But all that did not prevent him from being a friend and companion to many people who opposed his views.

On one occasion his personal friend and public adversary, Neville Lasky, tried to present a proposal to the board of deputies in accordance with which a man who held a leading position in the Jewish Agency and the World Zionist Organization, and who had assumed obligations toward international Jewish and Zionist organizations, could not at the same time head the board of deputies, whose loyalties lay first and foremost with British Jewry and the British Crown. Brodetsky forcefully rejected this attempt to create a contradiction between his world Zionist and Jewish commitments and those he assumed as head of British Jewry. The British Board of Deputies accepted his approach by a large majority. Brodetsky explained on many occasions that it was the Jews who created the artificial problem of dual loyalty; other people saw no contradiction between a Jew's obligations as a citizen of the country in which he lived and his relationship and identification with the ancient homeland of the Jewish people, the State of Israel, and the people of Israel throughout the world.

Parallel with his scientific and Jewish life, Brodetsky was immersed in active Zionist work and in the stormy discussions that took place during the British Mandate period and the War of Independence. Brodetsky was loyal to Weizmann and his approach but at the same time retained his independence of thought and action. He was to suffer for that more than once.

He had his own way of bridging yawning gaps and of reconciling contradictions, and was a master in the art of preventing crises. But above all, he harbored no personal bitterness and never sought revenge on his opponents. By nature he was a man of synthesis—a builder, an amalgamator and a unifier, and at the same time a man of principle. Brodetsky belonged to the progressive wing of World General Zionism and remained faithful to that outlook all his life. In his personality he combined eastern European Jewish tradition and loyalty to his religion and his people with western social and cultural values, primarily those of Britain.

He was a good-natured man who knew how to win people's affection and influence them. He was a compromiser but only up to a point. He headed the great Jewish demonstration in Trafalgar Square, for he saw no contradiction between his struggle as head of British Jewry and Zionism, and his role in British society. On the contrary: he believed that this struggle could save Britain's honor and rescue its just commitment to the Jewish people and to the Yishuv in Eretz Israel. Both Jews and non-Jews held him in great respect at that time. He was at one with himself, with his people, and with his British citizenship.

It is regrettable that his memoirs are only a general summary and are not in diary form: a diary would have contained pages of enormous interest. The memoirs, which were published in 1959, were written in the twilight of his life when he was already a sick and bitterly disappointed man.

When the State of Israel was established there was not a happier man than Brodetsky, his dreams had been fulfilled, his struggles successful. He had succeeded in putting a resolution in favor of the Jewish state through the British Board of Deputies some years earlier. He now realized that the time had come for him to live and work in the state for whose establishment he had done so much. Many years earlier when he was still a young man, Professor Albert Einstein, who recognized his talents, had insisted that he assume the leadership of the Hebrew University in Jerusalem. Einstein's desire was that a scientist should preside over that institution. Brodetsky, now Professor Emeritus at Leeds University, immigrated to Israel, and was elected president of the Hebrew University. With his rich experience both in the scientific world and in public life, and his extensive personal contacts, he had everything necessary for success in that position. But soon after his arrival in Israel he suffered a heart attack from which he never completely recovered. A strong, healthy man was needed to fulfill the important but difficult task he had assumed. The university was growing constantly and needed a president who could cope with the problems of study and research, and at the same time further construction of the university campus.

Brodetsky had transferred his home to Jerusalem and was happy there with his wife, Mania, née Barenblum, and with his son and daughter, but he was obliged to return to England for treatment of his heart condition, and was never to return. He died in 1954 in London. For some reason, he believed that his closest friends had forgotten him.

Abba (Albert) Schoolman

Dr. Abba Schoolman was a pioneer of Jewish educational camping in the United States. For over sixty years he devoted himself to the construction of Jewish summer educational camps, and for his contribution to this educational enterprise he won the esteem and gratitude of every sector of American Jewry.

Dr. Schoolman was born in Suwalki, Poland, and reached the United States at the age of thirteen. Jewish education became the ideal of his life, and he considered the summer camp the most effective and successful means of dispensing a Jewish education faithful to Jewish tradition and American culture, with Eretz Israel and the Zionist idea holding an important place in its consciousness. The Cejwin camps were the central undertaking of Albert Schoolman and his wife, Bertha. These camps were on a high educational and cultural level; they were imbued with Jewish tradition, and the individual youngster, as well as his behavior within the juvenile society, were carefully fostered. Here the Schoolmans, their colleagues, and their staff brought up thousands of Jewish youngsters who, as adults, became devoted to the Jewish community and to Eretz Israel. A considerable number of American Jewish leaders were trained there.

Schoolman worked on the assumption of Dr. Samson Benderly, architect and builder of Jewish education in America, that in the camps it was possible within the space of two months to devote to Jewish education and study the same number of hours as throughout an entire school year. Hence, the Schoolmans worked out a comprehensive educational program for the camps. In one of his articles, Schoolman wrote with admiration of the Eastern European Jewish townlet, which provided the young Jew with his family home, the synagogue, and an environment that was imbued with a Jewish way of life. Thanks to those three elements, the youngsters grew up as good Jews who maintained their centuries-old tradition. The school was seen as an addition to the child's life, the institution that imparted knowledge. Schoolman oriented the education given in the Cejwin camps so that it would provide the youngster what the little town once did, though under different conditions and within a different reality. Camping was to him an educational challenge. In a camp, the educator creates, administers, and directs all that happens in his surroundings, and he influences both the campers and the educators. The camp is a small community for the duration of the summer months, the long vacation, and this period is to be exploited in order to achieve important results in the moulding of the character and outlook of the young camper. Jewish educators in the United States consider Schoolman's enterprise an excellent example of Jewish camping, which was to a large degree an American creation and contribution to the educational world.

Schoolman's friend and colleague, Alexander Dushkin, who worked together with him in the development of Jewish camping and education, wrote that it was at the initiative of Albert Schoolman that the Berksons, the Dushkins, and the Schoolmans first built Camp Modin in 1922 as a Jewish private camp for the children of middle-class families. This was another model for the Cejwin camps to follow in developing Jewish camping. Later, in 1951, Schoolman was invited by the president of the Jewish Theological Seminary, Louis Finkelstein, to act as advisor to the "Ramah" camps organized by the Conservative movement throughout the United States and Canada. Thus, Albert Schoolman came to be regarded as the highest authority in the sphere of Jewish camping. He represented all that was fine and lofty in American Jewry, and Alexander Dushkin was right when he wrote of him that his life was a benediction—a life that fulfilled the Lord's promise to Abraham: Be Blessed.

Schoolman considered himself a disciple of Rabbi Mordecai M. Kaplan, from whom he learned much, and by whom he was greatly influenced throughout the course of his life and educational activity. He belonged to the Conservative movement and together with his wife Bertha, fulfilled in his lifetime the principles of traditional Jewish philosophy held by Dr. Kaplan.

Abba Schoolman contributed much to other spheres of Jewish and Hebrew education as well. In 1932 he responded to the call of the rector of the Hebrew University, Yehuda Leib Magnes, and, through the National Council for Jewish Education, raised funds for the establishment of an education department and a teachers' seminary on Mount Scopus. Dushkin and Kaplan were among the founders of those enterprises within the Hebrew University. The other project that Schoolman helped to implement at the Hebrew University was connected with the Institute for Contemporary Jewry. Within this department Dushkin was requested to establish a branch for Jewish education in the Diaspora. The execution of this project was made possible thanks to the efforts deployed by Schoolman and his friend Judah Pilch to convince the National Council of Jewish Education to establish the Dushkin Foundation for the training of Jewish educators for Jewish communities in the Diaspora. Schoolman was also instrumental in equipping the Hebrew University Secondary School with a physics laboratory of a very high standard.

Bertha Schoolman arrived in Jerusalem in 1947, just before the War of Independence, to collaborate with me in the reorganization of Youth Aliyah following the decease of Henrietta Szold, but she remained here throughout the hostilities. Schoolman revealed great understanding of her important mission, and did not press her to return home even during the days when news of attacks on the roads and settlements were being published daily in the American press. She regarded her mission as a mission of piety. From then on, her husband began to take an interest in Youth Aliyah, and the Schoolman home became an important center not only for Jewish education in the United States and matters pertaining to Jewish camping, but also for the discussion of the problems of Youth Aliyah in Israel. Abba Schoolman would accompany his wife on visits to Youth Aliyah villages and schools together with Dushkin and his wife, for we were all involved in the great task of absorbing and educating the children who reached us after the Holocaust, as well as those who came from the Arab countries. I considered Schoolman an expert in educational matters, and Dushkin and I were always happy to seek his advice. There is no doubt that his wife, who was later elected cochairman of the Youth Aliyah Management Board, was guided by his counsel concerning the manner in which to cope with the difficult problems confronting that body.

The Schoolmans took a particular interest in the kibbutz movement, mainly thanks to their daughter Judith, who was among the founders and builders of Kibbutz Sassa in the upper Galilee. Schoolman saw his second home at Sassa and was familiar with all the details of the kibbutz's development. To the best of his ability, he also assisted the kibbutz members in achieving the aim they had set themselves. Bertha and I made it possible for the kibbutz to establish the "Anne Frank Haven" for the absorption of Youth Aliyah children. This educational enterprise developed extremely well, thanks to the kibbutz members, whose policy was to raise the Youth Aliyah children to a standard that would enable them to live and study together with the kibbutz children. Thanks to this integration many of the children who were raised in the "Anne Frank Haven" were absorbed as members of the kibbutz.

Albert Schoolman had the privilege of seeing his first great-granddaughter at Kibbutz Sassa in the last year of his life. Thus, the Schoolman's life was rich in Jewish and Zionist content and the couple identified completely with the challenges of establishing and maintaining the young State of Israel. I received great encouragement from Albert Schoolman in my struggle for religious pluralism within Israel. He could not tolerate the extremism and fanaticism that can bring disaster in their wake. He repeated to me many times, both orally and in writing, his assumption that Jewish unity between the state and the Diaspora and within the state itself could be constructed only on the basis of pluralism, which would enrich our spiritual life and enable the mass of Jewry to give expression to their Judaism as they saw fit. When his wife died, Schoolman brought her remains to be interred on the Mount of Olives, and in accordance with the terms of his will his daughters buried him alongside their mother.

Albert Schoolman's life and his blessed enterprise deserve to be the subject of a comprehensive monograph: perhaps his students and friends in the United States will carry out this project. In the last year of his life he was depressed for he was not certain that Cejwin camps would continue to exist. I visited him at camp, and he told me that not a single Jewish public body in the United States was prepared to accept the responsibility for the continuation and development of the camps. This was a source of deep concern to him. He did not want the camping venture, which contributed so much to Jewish education in America, to come to an end with his passing.

As I write these lines in his memory, there is still no solution to that problem.

Yechiel Charif

A life full of spiritual and intellectual activity, a life of action, initiative, and vision, was cut short before its time. Yechiel Charif combined within himself knowledge, courtesy, and extraordinary organizational and executive ability. He was a man with a mission who identified himself completely with the lofty aims of a nation.

He died on Yom Kippur night 1967, at his home in the youth village of Alonei Yitschak, which stands on one of the lovely rises of the Shomron between Kibbutz Kfar Glickson and Givat Ada. That village was his life's work.

Thousands of friends—veterans of the Zionist Youth and the Zionist Workers, his students, personal friends and admirers—came to pay their last respects. His sudden death shocked them all deeply; they had seen him brimming with energy, initiative, and action, and could not accept the fact that he was now silent forever. Those who had been near him during the Kol Nidrei prayer, and after the service, said that he had radiated spirituality in his conversation, and that he had talked only of the future of the Alonei Yitschak school. But those who had seen him a few months earlier, after his first heart attack, feared greatly for his health and his life. He knew no respite and refused to accept the careful regimen that his heart condition demanded.

Yechiel died at the age of sixty-four. Mourning and orphanhood enveloped the children's village he had built, and the great family of children to whom he had been a father. Together with his wife, Shifra, he had made his home and his village into an educational center full of love and warmth.

Yechiel Charif—his original name was Pandler—was born of a rabbinical family whose genealogy goes back to the famous sixteenth-century rabbi and cabbalist Yehoshua Halevi Horowitz. Both his father and grandfather were rabbis and his brother is a rabbi in Tel Aviv. Yechiel was born in a townlet of the Ukraine in 1902. When he was still a child his father died. He studied the Bible and the Talmud and was an expert in Halacha. He was fluent in modern Hebrew, and qualified as a teacher. He also studied other languages, and thus both Hebrew and world literature were well known to him.

In 1919, after World War I, he tried to cross the border between Russia and Poland, but was caught. He then acquired false papers: Yechiel Pandler became Yechiel Pooss.

Between 1920 and 1932, the year he immigrated to Eretz Israel, he taught at the Tarbut school in the Galician townlet of Gorlice, and greatly influenced the youngsters of the town, most of whose population was Jewish.

When the Jewish Youth Association—later to become the Zionist Youth—was organized, he joined, and for many years participated in their summer sessions and seminars. His wealth of Jewish knowledge gave him a priviledged status in the camp.

The Zionist Youth movement in Gorlice was divided into two separate groups, one for boys and one for girls. He was the senior teacher and educator, and served as the authority for the education of both groups.

I remember his visit to my town of Pinsk, when he came to get to know the Zionist Youth movement there. At that time discussions were underway between the movement in Congress Poland and the movement in Galicia, and there was much talk of establishing a united movement. However, doubt and suspicion existed on both sides, and Yechiel Charif was sent to visit us in Pinsk, and then to the movements in Lodz and Warsaw. His colleagues at the head of the movement in Galicia rightly thought that he, the man with Jewish roots, would find it easier to win us over to his idea. I met him then for the first time, and from that time on—for thirty-six years—we made our way together.

Yechiel immigrated to Eretz Israel in 1932 together with a group of pioneers from Galicia who were absorbed into the Zionist Youth's first kibbutz in Petah Tikva. Individual members also gathered around the kibbutz, and the Zionist Youth Association was established.

I immigrated just a few months after Yechiel. We very quickly found common ground and acted within the framework of the Zionist Youth secretariat. I well remember those beginnings, the movement's first steps, the ideological gatherings and the stormy discussions that went on, usually, till dawn. Not a few differences of opinions arose within the General Zionist camp over its relationship to the Histadrut, and the divisions in World General Zionism were reflected in our camp. Life in the Petah Tikva kibbutz was rocked by the two schisms—the first when the Akiva movement was established, the second when the Zionist Youth movement split over the dispute about whether or not to break away from the Histadrut.

Yechiel Charif tried with all his might to prevent the split and to preserve the unity of the camp. He believed in his ability to resolve the contradictions and to smooth over the thorny problems. But he was not always successful, whether within the kibbutz or within the movement. Basically, he was not cut out to be a public figure or a trade union activist. Nevertheless, he was sent as our movement's first delegate to the second session of the Histadrut's fourth conference, for the first time speaking on behalf of our movement at the Israel workers' conference. He also tried to participate actively in the Petah Tikva workers' council. But all that ran counter to his inner being. By nature he was a teacher and an educator, a man of vision and thought, and he was disillusioned on more than one occasion when he tried to express his opinion on matters in which he had had no experience. Kibbutz life did not satisfy him; nor was he capable of physical work. He was destined to teach and guide, and in that area the future was to hold much for him.

In 1934 he moved with a group of spiritually close friends to Kvutzat Geva in the Jezreel Valley, where he remained for a whole year. There, on one of the veteran kvutzot, he could work quietly, relax from his intense activity at Petah Tikva, and feel his way toward the future. By nature he was a man in search of a path. Once he was seen wandering among the orange groves in Petah Tikva, and when his friends asked him what he was doing there, he replied that he was looking for the Zionist Youth movement that had been uprooted on its way. Though he spoke with a humorous smile, what he said was true.

Yechiel was not the type of person to accept things ready-made. By nature a man of independent thought, he was an endless source of original propositions into which were woven fine and lofty ideas. He dreamed of our movement as a great force which would contribute much to the construction of the country. I well remember his brilliant debates with the supporters of the class struggle. His questions to his opponents were phrased thus: "Who are those classes who will risk their lives in that war, and where is that great capital that the proletariat will fight against? And most important, everything, after all, depends on the Jews of the Diaspora; what will be their part in that struggle?" He did not hesitate to stand up to the strong men of the group, whether from the General Zionist or the labor camp. At Geva, Yechiel married Shifra and they continued their life together at the Ben Shemen Youth Village, where they lived from 1936 until 1947. They moved to Kfar Glickson and then to Alonei Yitschak, where Yechiel died.

At the founding assembly of the General Zionist Workers' group within the Histadrut, which was held at Ra'anana in November 1935, Yechiel Charif was one of the outstanding personalities. Later, he was one of those active in the group's first secretariat. In the first party program published by the Zionist Worker in 1936, he wrote a polemical article in which he took issue with Berl Katznelson, who had spoken at Ra'anana. Charif wrote:

> I do not doubt for a moment that the Zionist Youth will continue to exist as an independent movement. . . . We are convinced that many of the workers in Eretz Israel harbor our thoughts. We must faithfully fulfill the tasks we have assumed: to rebuild the nation and ourselves; to physically realize pioneering Zionism; to organize the people and to demand Zionist acts. Our role in the Histadrut is to preserve its pioneering and Zionist character, and even if many Zionists attribute "leftist" deviations to us because of our sin in belonging to the Histadrut, and even if our situation as a feeble minority within the Histadrut is not exactly brilliant, we will nevertheless not recoil or retreat from our path; we will succeed in faithfully fulfilling our role, and we will raise it to the level of a great historic destiny.

This article, which makes interesting reading even today, was signed "G. P."—Gavriel Pooss. Over the years Yechiel wrote many articles under this pseudonym. He had a natural talent for writing though he never had the time to devote to it. Nor did he have the patience for it. He found it easier to express himself orally. He was a brilliant debater—passionate, convincing, interesting and captivating. His own special qualities and originality were always discernible. Among other things, he published a grammar book, and he had intended to continue working in that direction. Those literary plans were never fulfilled for lack of time; the youth village absorbed him completely.

As I have noted, Yechiel was a linguist: he knew Russian, Polish, Hebrew, German, and Arabic. He also learned English and was, of course, fluent in Yiddish. He read every book in its original language, enriching his mind with works of fiction and philosophy. He read scientific works and he still dipped into rabbinical literature. When I brought him, as a gift, the Talmudic Encyclopedia, he was delighted with it, as he had been on previous occasions when I had given him other Talmudic works.

Yechiel and Shifra—the ideal couple—found their place at the Ben Shemen youth village, and there an important and decisive period in their life together began. At that time—from 1936 until the War of Independence—Ben Shemen was an important educational center. It was also an absorption center for immigrant youth from Germany, parallel with kibbutzim. The founder of the village, Dr. Siegfried Lehman, knew how to draw around him people after his own heart. In Ben Shemen, Yechiel Charif found a field in which to express his forceful educational spirit. Lehman drew Yechiel close to him, seeing in him the learned Jew, familiar with the sources of authentic Judaism. Charif also served as Lehman's translator from German, influencing him and being influenced by him simultaneously. The Jewish world from which Yechiel came was scarcely known to Lehman; to the extent that he knew Eastern European Jewry it was from Lituania, where he had spent World War I and had founded the children's home in Kaunas (Kovno). But he had had absolutely no contact with Hasidism, or Russian and Ukrainian Jewry, whose representatives he met in Berlin.

Yechiel Charif made great educational and cultural contributions to Ben Shemen. His conversations with Lehman on the relations between Jews and Arabs in Eretz Israel encouraged him to continue with his study of the Arabic language and culture.

During Yechiel's stay at Ben Shemen an important development took place within our movement: it became an independent, crystallized trend within the Histadrut. With Dr. Glickson's group and Greenbaum's radical Zionists, we established the General Zionists Association, which followed Weizmann and fought for progressive social ideas within the Yishuv. We held talks with Kurt Blumenfeld and Felix Rosenbluth (Pinchas Rosen), the spokesmen of German Zionism who had immigrated to Eretz Israel. Yechiel, though he agreed with our political initiative, did not work with us. He was completely immersed in the world of Ben Shemen. At times he disagreed with Dr. Lehman: his ambition as to create a youth village that would reflect his own spirit and implement his original ideas. But the time for that had not yet come.

I often used to visit Yechiel at Ben Shemen after a youth group from our movement in Poland was integrated into it at the end of the thirties. It is worth noting that all the youth groups affiliated to the Histadrut found their place at Ben Shemen. Dr. Lehman respected the educational and movement autonomy of each one, although they were all obliged to accept the principles common to all at Ben Shemen. A group of members of the Petah Tikva kibbutz—some of the first members of our movement, who knew Yechiel and Shifra—were also integrated into Ben Shemen and there they continued to weave the tapestry of friendship that went back to the early days. Yechiel and Shifra saw in their joint work with immigrant youth at Ben Shemen a pioneering and educational mission. They continued to belong to the movement, and dreamed of its expansion into a large-scale force.

On the eve of the War of Independence and the outbreak of violence throughout the country, the Ben Shemen youth village found itself isolated; it had no direct contact with the Jewish home front and was entirely surrounded by Arab villages. There was deep concern for the welfare of the children and youth. Ben Shemen faced a crisis. It was decided to evacuate the youngsters, transfer them to a military base near Kfar Vitkin, and house them on the site where the Ne'urim youth village now stands. Dr. Lehman knew difficult times, not only because of the dangers that menaced the village and the victims who fell, but also because of the defeat of his political ideal, which had come to a cruel and unexpected end. At Kfar Vitkin everything had to be rebuilt from the foundations.

Yechiel Charif drew his conclusions from the situation. He now became fully aware of something he had long suspected, namely, that the great challenge confronting our movement was to absorb immigrant youth on a large scale—members of the movement in the Diaspora, refugees from the Nazi sword, and survivors of the Holocaust; to establish educational institutions and youth villages of its own, and inspire them with its spirit. He knew no respite until that program was carried out. And he succeeded in drawing the movement toward the new educational objectives he conceived.

Already in 1938 negotiations had begun between our movement and Henrietta Szold on the need to establish an agricultural training institution at Magdiel. But Yechiel was not yet prepared to accept the responsibility for it because at that time he was completely bound up with Ben Shemen. The state was established and with it came mass immigration, which included a large contingent of young people. At that time, our movement's educators got together—Yechiel and Shifra, Yerachmiel and Sarah, Gershon and Mania—and moved to Kibbutz Kfar Glickson. They began absorbing immigrant youth in the hope and belief that there, on the rise near the kibbutz, our movement would establish a youth village that would educate its pupils and mould their character according to its ideals. It was only natural that Yechiel should be at the center of the initiative to implement this idea. So began the second great chapter in Yechiel's life in Eretz Israel—a chapter that continued for over eighteen years. The youth village Alonei Yitschak was founded on his initiative, and we all considered him its spiritual guide.

The youth village became the essence of his life. All the spiritual wealth he had absorbed in his parents' rabbinical home, at the Tarbut school abroad, on the kibbutz and in the party, in his public activity, in the education movement and the labor movement, and in particular the broad educational preparation he had received at Ben Shemen—all combined to form the basis on which the wonderful youth village of Alonei Yitschak was built. He poured into that enterprise all the powers of his being—and he succeeded.

At first the village was housed in wooden barracks and tents near the kibutz, and its beginnings were rough, as were those of any other pioneering enterprise. I was then head of Youth Aliyah and I was pleased that the opportunity had been given to our movement to establish youth villages and various other educational institutions. Thus our movement became an equal partner in the construction of Youth Aliyah's great educational enterprise. Youth Aliyah was in need of new absorption and educational facilities, and I was delighted that from within our movement came members worthy of the name, Yechiel at their head, who saw this task as the aim of their lives. World General Zionism, of which we were the pioneering wing, then established the Construction Fund, which enabled us to build and develop settlement and educational enterprises in accordance with our spirit and principles. The Palestine Colonization Association (PICA) placed the rise beside Kfar Glickson at our disposal. It was barren, covered with scraggy bushes—the remains of oak trees that the Turks had felled during World War I to use as fuel for their steam engines. On that hill, the building of the village began. Forests of oak trees (alonim), began to grow there again as in days of yore, and in honor of the great Jewish and Zionist leader of Polish Jewry, Yitschak Greenbaum, the educational institution was called Alonei Yitschak.

Slowly, as the years passed, the new educational enterprise took shape. Alonei Yitschak, headed by a great personality, acquired a prestigious reputation throughout the country. We knew that Yechiel could be relied upon and that the children and youth who were absorbed into that village were in good hands. There was maternal love there, and a paternal eye to watch over the standard of education at the school, to ensure that aesthetic considerations were not overlooked, and to see that every tree and flower was nurtured. A home was created that radiated family warmth, and attention was given to every individual.

Yechiel succeeded in drawing around him young, fresh forces. But above all he knew how to educate his pupils to become partners with him in the work of the youth village, and not only to find their own happiness there but also to help in the education and absorption of new children.

Yechiel was not only a great educator and a teacher who inspired his pupils with his beliefs; his greatness lay in the fact that he was also practical and realistic in his administration of a great undertaking that required a thorough understanding of financial matters and the organization of buildng plans and agricultural training. This task, too, he fulfilled with complete success. He knew no rest until he realized all his objectives. In time, the village reaped high praise both in Israel and abroad. Parents from distant countries, as well as from Israel, requested us to educate their children at Alonei Yitschak. Yechiel continued his search for ways in which to impart the Jewish experience and tradition, and to deepen Jewish consciousness in the education of both boys and girls—a search he had begun at Ben Shemen. He fostered in the children the positive social qualities of identification with the needs of society as a whole, and with the good of the nation; he taught them to fight negative phenomena in society and to seek the unifying elements within the Jewish people, and between Israel and the Diaspora. Every child at the institution knew that he could come to Yechiel and Shifra's home whenever he wished to pour out his feelings, and that he would find there an open heart and an attentive ear. The barriers fell between educators and educated. No one was happier than Yechiel when the Alonei Yitschak alumni gathered in their hundreds of holidays and festivals, or on other commemorative occasions. How his face shone on the sabbath eve when, as was his habit, he explained the weekly portion! Whoever saw him during the Shavuot night liturgy, at Purim parties or Chanukah festivities at the village, on Seder night or at weddings of alumni, could not fail to see the great happiness that filled his heart.

Every new project that was established at the village, every new house that was built, every addition and every innovation were for him not only an achievement for the village and the enterprise, but above all, and rightly so, his own personal achievement. He established the regional school where kibbutz and moshav children born in the country could study together with immigrant children from different Diaspora communities. He considered such contract highly beneficial, and continued to ensure that a satisfactory standard of studies and of teaching staff was maintained. Recently, about half the pupils at the village have been children sent by their parents from abroad (their expenses are covered entirely by their families), as well as Israeli children whose education is also paid for by their parents. The other half are Youth Aliyah children. Yechiel wanted to encourage Jewish children from the Diaspora to come to study in Israel, even if they did not assume an obligation to immigrate permanently.

When I brought before the Jewish Agency Executive the proposal to set up a committee, together with members of the government and the Secondary Schools Association, for the establishment of boarding facilities for Jewish children from the Diaspora within the secondary school framework, I had in mind the experience Yechiel had acquired. It was therefore only natural that when the committee and the Center for the Diaspora decided to establish two boarding schools—one general and the other religious—for Diaspora children, Alonei Yitschak should be chosen as one of them. Yechiel was wildly enthusiastic at the idea and saw it as a new experience in bringing Diaspora and Israeli youth together. He also worked together with World Zionist Organization's Department of Education and Culture in the Diaspora in order to bring children from the United States to summer vacation camps at Alonei Yitschak.

The camps were held regularly for several years. Though they deprived Yechiel of his own summer holiday, his satisfaction grew as the new project was consolidated. He constantly looked for new educational paths for Jewish youth from the Diaspora who, in the end, would come to Israel.

At one time he put the accent on agriculture. Later he tried vocational training. But he quickly came to the conclusion that at the center of his mission at Alonei Yitschak must stand humanistic education—education toward a combination of nationalist and human principles. He gave special attention to the gifted, tried to work for their progress, and encouraged them to carry on to secondary school. He also requested his pupils to volunteer for service with Nahal. He asked them to remember well the source of their education, reminding them of their duty to serve loyally in any national or government function they might be called upon to fulfill. His alumni, scattered throughout the country, hold positions in economic life, in politics, in education, in public and health services, on kibbutzim, moshavim, and in the army. They consider Alonei Yitschak their real home, and Yechiel and Shifra their mother and father. Frequently, even after they left the village, they would come to Yechiel to seek advice and support.

Throughout the years of the construction and development of Alonei Yitschak, Yechiel did not abandon his political action within the Progressive Party, the Liberal Party, and later the Independent Liberal Party, as well as in the labor movement in the Histadrut. He was also chairman of Yesodot, which united all the youth villages and educational institutions of the movement. He was outstanding among the directors and educators and was regarded by all as the ultimate authority on educational matters.

On more than one occasion we argued over matters of principle concerning the movement and education. I used to spend days at a time at his home in Alonei Yitschak which, for me, was like a second home. We talked for hours about politics and the state, about the children of the village and their future, and then back to world problems and those of world Jewry. We went into the stamp and image to be given to the youth village of our movement—the Zionist Youth. We searched for an acceptable way of life; asked ourselves what place tradition should hold in education, and what were the rules of Zionist fulfillment in accordance with which today's youth should be educated, given the profound changes taking place in the life of the state.

Before his death I used to visit him in his new home at Alonei Yitschak. I found him, as usual, full of energy, conceiving new plans of action and prodding me, as Minister of Tourism, to lay the groundwork for the establishment in Israel of camps for Jewish youth from the Diaspora, this in light of the experience gained so far. He promised to present a detailed plan, into the preparation of which he would pour all his experience. I remember that in our last conversation we also touched on this problem.

On the hilltop of Alonei Yitschak, Yechiel lit an educational beacon whose light sprang from his belief in, and love of, the child. All his life was devoted to others. He paid little attention to himself. His private life merged with and became one with the life of the village he established. His personality did not change substantially even as he grew older. Thus he was when he arrived in Gorlice after World War II, and thus he remained during the various stages of his life on the kibbutz, at Ben Shemen, and during his later years at Alonei Yitschak. His image will remain engraved in the hearts of his friends, his colleagues and his thousands of pupils: a scholar immaculate in every way, an original man with a comprehensive education and wide culture. He was and remained a noble man, a lover of beauty and morality, one of the most wonderful educators of Youth Aliyah and of the educational enterprise in Israel. He was one of the founders and builders of our movement, a Zionist, a pioneer who lived Zionism in every fiber of his being.

He passed away before his time, but he left a rich educational heritage at Alonei Yitschak.

Moshe (Ossi) Biderman

Ossi Biderman, one of the best educators in our movement and one of the most faithful to it, passed away at the age of fifty-two. His life may be divided into two main periods: one spent among Hungarian Jewry during and after the Nazi defeat, the other at Kfar Glickson and Alonei Yitschak after his immigration to Israel in 1948.

Ossi was very young when he set about the rehabilitation of the Zionist Youth movement in the shattered Hungarian Jewish community, hundreds of thousands of whose members had been exterminated by the Nazis and their Hungarian fascist collaborators. There were families without children and children without families. Ossi organized the young people—children and youth who had been deeply affected both physically and mentally by the horrors they had undergone—into children's homes, and into branches of the Zionist Youth movement. A fine team of devoted colleagues worked with him during those difficult days, and the friendship that grew up between them at that time continued to the end of his life. It found expression in the interesting gatherings held in Israel every year by former members of the Zionist Youth of Hungary.

Many of the friends Ossi had made then accompanied him on his last journey, and spoke of his fruitful work. Yehuda Talmi, who was then in Hungary as an emissary from Eretz Israel and had worked with Ossi to rehabilitate the movement and to organize both legal and illegal immigration, recalled those difficult days and praised Ossi's complete identification with his role and his ability to unite the movement's team and build an exemplary collegial spirit.

I remember Ossi when he came from Budapest as a delegate to the Zionist Congress in Basle—the first to be held after the Holocaust—and spoke of the trials of Hungarian Jewry during the war. He himself had been in the underground, and along with our other active party members had made sure that the glowing embers did not die out—that Zionist Youth would be able to emerge from the ruins and rebuild itself. Within

Hungarian Jewry fierce debates were raging over the behavior of its leadership during the Nazi occupation, and the Eretz Israeli office was being criticized for the manner in which it distributed assistance funds that arrived from the Joint Distribution Committee. I served on the Immigration Committee of the congress.

I had confidence in Ossi's reports. He was the one sure source of information on which I could base my stand on these questions in the committee. It was then that he told me about our large movement in Hungary, about the children's homes and our members' work in the rehabilitation of the young generation of Hungarian Jews. Our Hungarian members participated in the illegal immigration organization and sailed in the illegal immigrant ships. They had decided to speed up the rate of immigration because of their concern about the future of the Hungarian regime and its attitude toward Zionism. Indeed, in the spring of 1949, the very day I reached Budapest from Warsaw after my second visit to the movement in Poland, the Hungarian government announced its decision to put an end to the activity of the Zionist organization. My visit to Hungary was short, but I was very impressed by the way the movement had grown and developed, not only among the children and youth but also among Hungarian Jewry in general.

Ossi was no longer in Hungary at that time. He had immigrated to Israel in 1948, after having organized the recruitment of young people who were to immigrate and then participate in the War of Independence. He came straight to Kibbutz Kfar Glickson. The kibbutz had been established by pioneers from our movement in Transylvania who were later joined by members of the movement from Hungary and Latvia. Most of the years Ossi spent at the kibbutz were devoted to educational work. He was employed as a teacher at the neighboring youth village, Alonei Yitschak, and, being the intellectual he was, proved outstanding in his job. He read and studied much, always striving to learn and broaden his horizons, for he knew that an educator who wishes to succeed in youth work in our times must be familiar with world literature and current events. He himself had his roots in Judaism, for he had attended the secondary school run by the rabbinical seminary in Budapest, and even in Israel he read and studied the treasures of Jewish literature and the traditions of our people. He knew many languages and was able to read the world's great literary creations in the original text.

When Yechiel Charif, the founder and director of Alonei Yitschak, passed away, I considered Ossi the most suitable candidate to succeed him as director of the village. Charif was one of the greatest educators in Israel, and in our movement Ossi was a worthy successor. During his tenure as director of the village, it absorbed many young people from

Soviet Russia; indeed, it was Alonei Yitschak that paved the way for the absorption of youth from that country. Alonei Yitschak later absorbed American youth, too: they came on a program I had drawn up during my last year as head of Youth Aliyah that consisted of bringing American youth to study here without obliging them to immigrate. We felt that if their education was successful, most of them would want to remain and make their lives with us.

The American youngsters brought with them serious problems. Some of them had been sent by parents who hoped that Israel would cure their children of ills induced by American society. In addition, some of them had a bad influence on the other children of the village. What had happened was that the screening of candidates in the United States before they were authorized to join the program was inadequate, and we had to send some of them home. Stories appeared in the press, but Ossi, who was at the center of the public debate, overcame the problems.

Alonei Yitschak was later charged with the absorption of youth of quite a different kind—children from the disadvantaged population groups in Israel. It was thus called upon to contribute toward the bridging of the social gap—the central task of Youth Aliyah once immigration from abroad had declined. Changes had to be made in curriculum and a way found to build bridges between youth groups of various levels within the same educational institution. Ossi lived those problems with all his being. Together with the school board, the youth leaders and the staff, he made sure that the Alonei Yitschak youth village would not only maintain its tradition, but would also innovate and change.

At the same time Ossi did not for a moment cut himself off from the problems of Kfar Glickson, the kibbutz to which he belonged and where he and his wife, Irma, raised their sons. But he had to spend long hours at the youth village, for it is generally desirable that the director of such an educational institution live on the premises. Ossi thus lived at both Alonei Yitschak and Kfar Glickson, a situation that demanded additional mental and physical effort and increased the strain in his already full and interesting life.

Despite the burden that was imposed upon him, Ossi managed to take an interest in the problems of the movement and the party in Israel, as well as in the other youth villages within the framework of Yesodot, in the Massuah enterprise, and in the Foerder Liberal Seminary. He lived the problems of the Holocaust survivors and helped in publication of the Massuah yearbooks. Thus, his activity was ramified and not confined to the village in which he lived and the educational institution he directed. He expressed himself impressively and thoroughly on every subject. I was in close contact with him, and he frequently came to discuss the problems that arose at Alonei Yitschak. At the same time he continued to maintain personal ties with his friends from the movement in Hungary.

When he first became ill and we learned the nature of the illness, we were greatly concerned. After a long illness, he seemed to have recovered and was able to return to his position as director of the village. But he was not the same man, despite the enormous effort he made to conceal his difficulties. The illness struck again, felling that flourishing, deeply rooted tree in its prime. I used to visit him in the hospital. He would look at me through his big dreamy eyes, filled with tears; he was no longer able to speak.

Ossi was fully conscious to the end. In a note to a close friend who visited him he wrote that he did not wish to go on living. Now that he is gone his absence is sorely felt. He was a captivating personality. Intellectual honesty, an open mind, broad horizons, and an inner tranquility and equilibrium were the qualities that characterized him. The fact that the best directors of our educational institutions died in their prime indicates how great a physical and spiritual effort is required of men in such positions. Another reason for their untimely death may be that those same colleagues, who built exemplary enterprises and distinguished themselves in the fulfillment of their functions, were members of the generation that lived through the Holocaust and the rebirth of Israel; it was a generation that had more than its share of suffering.

Ossi was one of those men who lived their lives to the full. He was one of a group of people with exceptional qualities, the flower of the young generation that built the state and its society, our movement with all its various branches, and, in particular, the pioneering and educational institutions.

One month after Ossi's death the friends who had known him in Hungary and in Israel gathered and talked about him. From what was said it was clear that Ossi had been an extraordinary figure among the young leadership of the Zionist movement in Hungary after the Holocaust. Some expressed surprise that he had not occupied a position within the movement's leadership after his immigration to Israel, for he had been a brilliant intellectual as well as a man of action.

I reminded our friends of the article Ossi had published in the Massuah yearbook, "A Zionist Youth in Hungary." In it, he described the history and ideological and organizational course of Zionist Youth there, including the period of World War II and the absorption of members from the Polish movement who arrived in Hungary as refugees in 1943—to them Hungary seemed the land of salvation. Ossi's article also contained details of the rescue operations initiated by our movement, which was then the leading pioneering Zionist youth movement. Ossi was then at its head. As a kind of epilogue to the article, he wrote: "A member of the movement said to me recently: 'Tell me, did we do all that for others, or for ourselves? Perhaps we are exaggerating a little?' And another member asked: 'Tell me, where did we find the strength and the daring to do things that today I wouldn't dare to even imagine myself doing?'" Ossi's answers can be summarized thus: First of all, our members were guided by a great belief in the Zionist vision and by the hope that they would have the privilege of living in Israel and realizing their dreams. Second, they were not educators who merely followed the commandments and the way of life of their society, but who lived education. Third, they believed in the movement's ideal and in the prospects for its realization, convinced that it could serve as an example for its members. They were extraordinarily daring, ready to take risks, and not fearful of the consequences. But the risks they assumed, extraordinary as they were, had been weighed carefully, and were taken with a sense of responsibility.

Ossi wrote and spoke much about Natan Otto Komoy, leader of the Hungarian Zionists during the most difficult days. Both he and Natan risked their lives at that time. Komoy was a symbol and example for Ossi, and he may have learned from the older man how to act when he reached a parting of the ways. Ossi was both a friend and a leader. In reply to the question about why he did not turn to public and party life in Israel, I said that Ossi was a man who lived the Zionist principles of his life. He knew that to found a family on a kibbutz, and to educate a young generation at Alonei Yitschak in Zionist and human values, was more important at the time than was public life. Indeed, there have recently been many candidates for public and party work, but there is a dire lack of people of stature to devote themselves to the construction of the pioneering and social infrastructure—people who possess the qualities necessary to mould the character of the young generation and prepare it for the decisive missions that the state and society must fulfill. Too many people in Israel believe that the work of construction is complete and that they may now hasten to reap the fruits of the labor of the pioneering generations. But we are only at the beginning of the road. We must continue developing and strengthening the foundations. Ossi believed in that approach to life; he practiced it and remained faithful to it until the very end.

Daniel Brisker

Daniel Brisker was only thirty-seven when he died as the result of a malignant disease. He was still in his prime, a young man full of energy. Only a year had passed since he had returned, together with his wife, Jean, from his mission on behalf of the movement to the United States. The young couple hoped to build a home at Alonei Yitschak with which Daniel had been connected, physically and spiritually, for many years as one of its outstanding educators. "Now I too will have a home and I will be able to receive guests and friends," he wrote to me on his return from America. Less than six months after his return the illness was diagnosed; four months later he was dead.

Daniel was thirsty for life and creativity; he was tall, broadshouldered, handsome, and powerfully built, and he was full of plans and ideas in the educational and social spheres. He combined the qualities of a typical Jewish and Zionist pioneer with the characteristics of an educator and humanist who saw as his main role in life the care of children and youth—his contribution to a better world. Daniel wanted to continue his studies during his mission on behalf of the movement, the United Jewish Appeal, and the youth village. He had high hopes but they were not fulfilled.

I met Danny some thirty years ago when he immigrated from Transylvania as a member of the Zionist Youth movement. He had joined the movement as a child in his hometown, and his parents had acquired lofty Jewish, nationalist, and Zionist values. His father, Dr. Yechezkel Brisker, was one of the Zionist leaders of Transylvania, but his roots were deep into the soil of Judaism, and he educated his only son in the love of Zionism and the Jewish people. The Brisker home was also that of a doctor with a broad European culture, and from it Danny absorbed universal human values as well. He took his pioneering Zionist education seriously, and when he immigrated to Eretz Israel he decided not to remain at home with his parents but to follow his own path to an agricultural kibbutz. He was among the builders of Kfar Glickson, in the Shomron. During World War II he enlisted in the British Army, prepared to fulfill his obligation as a Jew.

His service with the British Army and his knowledge of the English language fitted Danny for his first mission on behalf of the World Zionist Youth movement to the United States. Following the destruction of the movement in Europe, the Zionist Youth secretariat decided to try to establish a similar movement in North America. Danny was chosen as the emissary for this task. He had had experience as a member of the youth movement, he knew English, and he possessed all the requisite personal qualities of a successful emissary. During that period, which lasted nearly four years, he established the nucleus of the Zionist Youth movement in the United States, acquired the agricultural training farm at Poughkeepsie, and became very friendly with the members of the youth and pioneering committee, which was run jointly by the Zionist Organization and Hadassah. When I was in the United States I was Danny's guest at the training farm, which in time became the center of the movement. Here the nucleus was formed that later immigrated and settled at Kibbutz Hasolelim near Tzipori. Here, too, study days, courses, summer sessions and meetings of the movement's youth leaders were held. The farm served as Danny's headquarters, and from it the movement network spread out. He found the way to the hearts of American Jewish youth. They had affection and esteem for him, considering him a leader, companion, and friend. This was one of the most successful of his many missions. He ploughed the first furrow on that great continent, bringing our movement to American Jewry among which it had not been active hitherto. His mission completed, Danny returned to Kfar Glickson, but only for a short time. He did not resume kibbutz life, but he did not seek occupation in town either. Because of his knowledge of languages, diplomatic posts were offered to him. However, he preferred to move from the rise of Kfar Glickson to the neighboring rise on which the Alonei Yitschak youth village had been established.

Danny—the pioneer, the settler, the emissary, the graduate of the movement—decided to assume educational functions and to prepare youth for village life, thus creating reserves for the movement's settlements. Into the village he introduced innovations he had learned in America. He helped put into operation the youth council—the self-government of the young generation; he developed the broadcasting network in the village; and he confided to the youngsters all kinds of independent tasks. In time, he was appointed youth leadership director. He knew the names and character of every child and youth, and became attached to them.

Danny loved children, seeing his vocation in the rehabilitation of immigrant youth and disadvantaged youngsters from the Yishuv. He was familar not only with the children in his charge but also with their homes and families. He was never satisfied with the knowledge he had acquired, and sought both to complete his formal education and further his studies in education and social work. With the help of the youth village and the movement, he went once again to the United States to study at the School of Social Work at Columbia University. Besides his work as a student, he brought the message of Youth Aliyah and the Alonei Yitschak educational enterprise to his fellow students and teachers, and multiplied his professional connections. His graduation paper was devoted to his work in education and rehabilitation at Alonei Yitschak. At the university he met his future companion, Jean Douglas; she decided to follow him to Israel and make her home at Alonei Yitschak.

During his stay in the United States, the United Jewish Appeal "discovered" Danny; he was a brilliant speaker who had a tremendous influence on donors. Hadassah, the Keren Kayemet, and other organizations also knew his qualities. He would tell of his life, and his experience in Israel. The heads of the appeal affirmed that Danny was one of the most successful UJA emmissaries, and one after the other invited him to the United States. He would fly from one large community to another, speaking to them in his eloquent style. On those trips he won many admirers who made special visits to his home at the youth village when they came to Israel. Even when he was on his sickbed he received requests from Jewish communities in the United States imploring him to visit them again. He deserved his success, for he knew how to touch hearts and open doors that had remained locked to others. He appeared to his audience as the archetype of the Jewish pioneer, the educator whose roots are in the soil and who draws his inspiration from a deep human source.

Despite these successes, Danny really wanted to be at home, at Alonei Yitschak, and to devote himself to educational and social work. A position was offered him within Youth Aliyah as the coordinator of social and rehabilitation work in the youth centers in his area. Youth Aliyah had discovered in him a talented youth leader and educator who made a fine contribution to every educational discussion in which he participated. He succeeded in whatever he undertook, whether in the village, in the movement which raised and fostered him, or in Youth Aliyah, in Israel or abroad. The delegation of the International Union of Child Welfare that visited Alonei Yitschak was intrigued by the direct, friendly relationship between him and his charges, and the president of the organization, Mr. Leonard Mayo, devoted special attention to it in his report on the visit.

Daniel Brisker's life was rich and full of substance—a wonderful dynamic life. It was all too short.

Abba Barditchev

For a long time after Abba Barditchev's disappearance in December 1944 in the mountains of Slovakia shortly after he had parachuted into that region, we knew nothing of his end. There was fragmentary rumor and supposition, but no reliable information. For many years we searched for traces of him in vain. In the late 1960s I applied to Israel's military attachés in the United States and Great Britain, requesting them to inquire from the military archives of the United States and Britain whether they had any knowledge of the fate of the group of British and American parachutists to which Barditchev had belonged. The group had fallen into the hands of the Nazis or their collaborators in the Slovakian mountains. I also applied to our embassy in Austria, as well as to the Jewish community there. Chaim Chermesh, a member of Kibbutz Kfar Glickson, had been a parachutist in World War II and had met Abba Barditchev then. They had been colleagues on that mission, and Chaim kept prodding us not to give up our search. Then, on 23 January 1971, I received a letter from Moshe Raviv, the counselor at our embassy in Washington, with a detailed report dated 19 January 1971 and the copy of a letter and report dated 2 February 1971 from the Pentagon to Colonel Eliyahu Zeira, military attaché at the Israel Embassy in Washington. The American report solved the mystery of the death of Abba Barditchev and the parachutists.

Abba Barditchev and his colleagues were caught on 26 December 1944 near Polumka in Slovakia, and were imprisoned at the Gestapo prison in Banska Bystrica. In January 1945 they were all transferred to Mathausen, the notorious Gestapo camp in Austria. There they were interrogated and tortured for eight days by the Gestapo, and on 26 January 1945 they were shot by a firing squad by order of Ernst Kaltenbrunner, who had arrived from Berlin. One of the German interrogators, who was later caught and questioned, admitted that they were tortured during their interrogation. The interrogators were sent from Berlin and the interrogation was brutal, according to another interrogator who was also caught after the overthrow of the Nazis. After the prisoners were shot, their bodies were burned in the crematorium—this according to the account of an eyewitness. Abba Barditchev's name—as a British parachutist—was Lieutenant Robert Willis, and he appears under that name on the group roster.

At the end of February 1971, I received a letter from Mr. Haim Goma of the consular division of our Embassy in London, in which he informed me that the British War Office report confirmed the details we had received from the Pentagon. I forwarded photocopies of all the material to the Barditchev family in Haifa, to Abba's colleagues at the Alonei Abba moshav, which bears his name, and to his close friends in the Zionist Youth movement from Romania, Yehuda Sha'ari and Yitschak Artzi, as well as to Chaim Chermesh at Kfar Glickson. The details were also communicated to the Israeli press, and when the news of Barditchev's death was published, articles appeared describing his personality and mission.

Abba Barditchev is engraved in my memory as he was on that morning at Magdiel when he came to take his leave of me before dawn, prior to setting out on his mission. He was in uniform, handsome, tall and strong, with a refined, pleasant, captivating expression on his face. He was well aware of the gravity of the mission and the extent of the risk. Fully conscious of what he was doing, he went out to fulfill his objectives: to make contact with the movement in Romania, help in the rescue work, encourage immigration to Eretz Israel, bring the message of Eretz Israel to the suffering Diaspora, and see his family. Only men of strong character with the force to withstand tough tests were accepted for such operations, and only very few were chosen for this parachute mission into enemy territory. Abba Berditchev undertook it only four years after his immigration—a difficult enterprise in itself, for he had escaped after the Iron Guardists had taken over Romania following the outbreak of World War II. Thereafter, German influence grew and the political situation deteriorated. The Jews of Romania became the victims of pogroms and the gates of Eretz Israel had been locked.

The answer was illegal immigration, and it was on board the *Darian B.* that Abba Barditchev decided to make his perilous way to the land of his destiny. The ship sailed but turned back, was held up at various ports, and took on extra passengers on the way although it was already packed to capacity. Food and water were short, sanitation was inadequate and there was danger of illness, there were storms and moments of despair. The captain disappeared at one of the ports of call: he was terrified of German submarines. Another was found. Strong nerves and outstanding qualities of leadership were needed to control the heterogeneous group of passengers, who were in an emotional turmoil, having suffered to the limits of their endurance.

The ship arrived in Eretz Israel but was caught by the British, and the illegal immigrants were transferred to the Atlith camp where they were interned for a long time. They suffered much, but it was paradise compared to what they had endured on the ship. I well remember my visits to Atlith and my meetings with members of the movement there. We came to encourage them, for they were impatient, and were not convinced that we were doing everything possible for their release. At the camp, too, Abba was among those who calmed and moderated, trying to prevent outbreaks that could lead to a clash with the British soldiers who guarded the camp, and to further bloodshed.

Then came the wonderful day when Abba and his friends decided to form the nucleus of a new kibbutz belonging to our movement. They went first for preparation to Kibbutz Geva in the Jezreel Valley and from there to Kibbutz Ashdoth Ya'acov. After their tribulations in Rumania, on the boat, and at the Atlith camp, they were intoxicated by the beauty of the valleys and the pioneering atmosphere that enveloped them. Happy with their lot, they dreamed of the day when more of their friends would join them, and together they would establish the new settlement. It was during that period at Ashdoth Ya'akov that Abba was chosen for the fateful mission from which he was never to return.

At that time I was a member of the Histadrut executive secretariat, and I dealt with matters connected with rescue work and with channeling assistance to members of the pioneering movements and the Zionist youth in embattled Europe. I maintained contact with members in occupied countries, and I collaborated in organizing the parachutists. To me it was inconceivable that members of our movement would not be among the parachutists that would be dropped from Eretz Israel into the occupied countries. Abba Barditchev was among those who were authorized at once. When he would come to the Histadrut executive to meet the people responsible for preparing the emissaries, he would come into my room for a chat. He was calm and quiet, but there was sadness in his eyes. He did not accept the mission lightly. He was not a veteran among us and had not yet absorbed the essence of life in this country. He dreamed of founding a home and family, and thought much about his parents and family in Rumania to whom he was greatly attached. Later he sent me regards from Egypt, where he did his training. The last I heard from him was a note from Yugoslavia, where he had been parachuted with the transmitter. He used to transmit from there, adding greetings to his messages. There, too, he met up with his parachutist colleagues, and waited impatiently to carry out his mission.

After Rumania surrendered to the Red Army and the trails along which Abba had planned to enter Rumania were sealed, he sought other ways, through Slovakia and Hungary. He knew that the risk in following such paths was extremely high, but he on no condition wished to abandon the full accomplishment of his mission.

In his book *Operation Amsterdam*, Chaim Chermesh recounts his conversation with Abba after Rumania's surrender. They met in the soldiers' club in the Italian port of Bari.

"What will you do, Abba? Will you go to Bucharest, or return home?" asked Chaim, as Abba sat alone looking out of the window into the night, his dreamy eyes staring into the eternal darkness. He felt terribly lonely. Abba replied: "I would very much like to get home . . . I have good friends there . . . ."

On the club radio the theme tune of the B. B. C., the V for Victory of Beethoven's Fifth Symphony, was heard. "Ah, Beethoven," said Abba as he hummed the theme. "How I admire him . . . He's terrific at evoking storms. When I listen to his music I too feel as if I were in one; I hear the wind breaking branches and uprooting trees, I see the lightning and shudder from the thunder. Then comes the sign, the redemption, the universe returns to its pastoral idyll, to the sounds of the harp, white clouds in a blue sky . . . As for me, the storm within me is at its peak and the redemption has not come . . . I cannot return to Eretz Israel without completing my mission. They need me in Rumania."

[Chaim Chermesh adds:] I left Abba with a heavy heart. He remained alone with his thoughts, because for him the "sign" had not yet been given. He listened in his loneliness to the confusion of the storm raging in his spirit, and I knew that in the depths of his heart he envied me . . . From the door I threw him a last glance. Abba smiled a last soft smile of farewell, but in his eyes a strange fire glowed. At that moment I knew that he would not give up, that he would go on to the end. He had to hear the "sign." Even if, after it, the calm did not come.

Chaim and Abba met again, this time at the Tari-Dovy airport in Slovakia, in territory that had been liberated by the partisans. To the astonishment of his parachutist friends who were already there, Abba arrived by plane. His colleagues wondered why he had come since he did not speak the language of the country. When they asked him he replied, "I won't be able to reach Batcheka because Tito's partisans won't let me into Rumania, lest I increase the 'imperialist influence' in the land of Mihai, the Red King. On Major Stepha's path into Hungary everyone was caught. Yoel Peretz is in prison. It's certain, I'm afraid, and there are rumors that Stepha has been executed. Even the two Canadians from the Sixth Corps who crossed the border were caught and murdered by the Hungarians."

"I understand that you didn't want to return to the arms of Tito, but what do you hope to find here?" his colleagues asked.

"You're not satisfied? Then I'll pack up and go," he answered jokingly. "I have my own logic. My plan is to get into Hungary with Rafi and Chaim and from there to enter Rumania illegally. Imagine: the Zionist movements are already working there, and our parachutists are working with them. I can't bear the idea of not making it. Meantime, I am entirely at your service. What would you like me to do?"

Chaim Chermesh concludes:

> Abba made an excellent impression everywhere. The rescue committee appreciated the summaries he brought with him, and at headquarters they treated him as befitted his rank. His first job was to convince Siehmar to make room in his office for us. After Haviv's bitter experience we wanted to operate in a secure place. I was charged with communications, and with the help of the little suitcase, I managed to establish a good, clear line to Bari and Cairo.

After the Hungarian Nazi party overcame Hungary and Franz Szalasi's government was set up, our parachutists held a meeting on October 15th to decide whether to cross the border at once, or to wait until the situation cleared. There were five of them. Opinion was equally divided, two for and two against. Abba had to cast the decisive vote. His decision was that this was the time to enter Hungary.

Abba Barditchev rose early. He hurried to headquarters and rushed in to see Major Siehmar, the superior officer and commander of the Allied Military Mission. They obtained a car that would bring them to the Hungarian border. Abba requested another but didn't get it.

He asked for a seat for himself in the car and convinced his colleagues of the justice of his stand. Somewhat depressed, we loaded the packages onto our shoulders and accompanied Abba to the car. Last handshakes and the driver revved up the engine. Abba's face shone with happiness. As if to say, "One step further . . . "

The car he traveled in was caught, and the fate of all those in it was sealed at Mathausen by the Nazis.

Abba Barditchev

Abba Barditchev symbolized the very best in the Rumanian Zionist Youth movement. The first members of that branch of the movement whom I met in Eretz Israel belonged to the kibbutz nucleus who were being trained at kibbutzim in the Jordan and Jezreel valleys and affiliated to the Kibbutz Association of those times, as well as at the movement's kibbutzim at the workers' camps in the villages of the Sharon and Lower Galil (in HaiGalil at Yavniel and Lamakor at Herzlia). My first visit to the movement in Rumania was in the summer of 1934, and in August I arrived at the Zionist Youth camp in the Gura Humorului mountains in the Bucovina Carpathians. This was after the split in the movement and the establishment in Poland of the separate General Zionist Workers B organization. I was then at the movement's council in Warsaw, and from there I set out for the first time for Rumania. I participated in seminars and summer sessions and visited our movement's youth groups.

The Zionist Youth movement in Rumania was outstanding for its serious approach to preparation for pioneering, and to educational and cultural activities. Further, it was faithful to the course of Progressive General Zionism. It opposed the alliance concluded at that time by the right-wing General Zionist workers B and the Revisionists, trying to break up the Histadrut in Eretz Israel. Soon after the split in 1934 it became clear that most of the national Zionist Youth movements in Eastern Europe had remained faithful to the movement's original path, and together we saved the soul of the movement from grave deviation.

I continued to maintain contact with the movement in Rumania until World War II. I saw the training farm at Palorska near Bucharest, I met General Zionist leaders, and I witnessed the great political struggle of Rumanian Jewry against the growing anti-Semitism in that country. The national Jewish party led by the Zionists played a great role in that struggle, defending Jewish interests and preserving Jewish national honor. Our movement was concerned with education, training, and winning over to Zionism and immigration the young generation of Jews in Rumania's vibrant communities. The friendships I established with numerous members of our movement in Rumania during my visits were to stand the test in Eretz Israel, in the Histadrut, in the Zionist movement, and in independent Israel.

In 1934 Abba Barditchev was still a youngster, one of those who attended the summer camp in Bura Humorului. As the years passed he grew up, studied, and developed. When he came to work at movement headquarters in Bucharest he was disappointed by the state of things in the Zionist leadership, and returned home. When he told me about this, I replied that the same thing had happened to me when I came from

Pinsk to Warsaw to work at the movement's center in Poland, and that I had had no desire to remain in the capital. One evening I packed my things and took the train home. Abba Barditchev did the same, and returned to his home in Galati. When he went to the training farm he did not want to be a leader but to work like any other member; he refused to accept a privileged status. He knew that he must serve as an example and observe the commandments of pioneering Zionism himself.

Abba Barditchev's personality was formed in his home in Galati. He was born of a Hasidic family in an important Jewish community, and from his youth he fought in the Zionist movement to defend the honor of young Jews against the anti-Semitic youth of Rumania. He learned languages, read much, and loved music. Since Galati was a port city, Abba had the opportunity to observe all kinds of strange phenomena during his early school years. He had every chance to grow and develop. His short life ended in the war against the great oppressor, but thanks to his bravery he will be remembered forever in our people's history as one of the most inspiring examples of courage during that somber period.

At the Alonei Abba village and in the world Zionist Youth movement as our children read the chapters devoted to the parachutists in the Holocaust literature of World War II, they will learn about Abba Barditchev, a wonderful young man who, in full awareness, sacrificed himself for his suffering people—a man who believed in the great ideals of the renaissance of the people and the redemption of its land.

To mark the twenty-fifth anniversary of his death, a combined house of culture and community center was set up at Alonei Abba. There, all the material about Abba Barditchev is concentrated so that whoever wishes may learn of his courageous acts—so that the children of the village which bears his name, and those who come after them, will always be aware of the great merit of that young man in defending and fighting for the lives and honor of the Jews.

David (Dado) Elazar

I first heard of Dado Elazar during the War of Independence, when I was in Jerusalem during the siege. I knew he had commanded one of the most difficult battles for the liberation of the city, and his superiors were full of praise for him. Over the years he filled important posts in the Israel Defense Forces: Divisional Commander in the Sinai campaign, Commander of the Armored Corps, and in the Six-Day War, GOC Northern Front. The Six-Day War was Dado's finest hour: on the last day he liberated the Golan Heights and the Shomron, putting an end to the perpetual menace that had hung over the villages of the Galilee and the Jordan Valley. More difficult days were to follow—the war of attrition waged by the guerrillas and the Jordanian Army in the Jordan and Beth Shean valleys and on the Lebanese border. Great presence of mind was required to cope with the tough problems that this war posed.

During that period, an alliance was forged between Dado and the settlers in the valleys who held the front line and whose children spent most of their lives in bunkers and shelters. Dado was one of them, and he was admired by them as he was by the men of Galilee who had held out against the Syrians during the long years of Syrian domination of the Golan Heights prior to the Six-Day War. He knew what was going on in every village, and he felt himself a part of the body of front-line settlements that defended our borders in the Jordan Valley and in the Galilee. In those days he was outstanding as much for his personality as for his loyalty to the values of the Haganah and the Palmach, which guided him throughout his military career.

Personal ties had grown up between Dado and myself from the time when I was still at the head of Youth Aliyah. Dado had come with Youth Aliyah to Eretz Israel from Yugoslavia in 1940. His father was an officer in the partisan army Tito had formed to fight the Nazis. He remained in the Yugoslav Army after the war, and retired with the rank of major. He then came to visit his son, a colonel in the Israel Army.

Dado was to settle in with a Youth Aliyah group at Kibbutz Sha'ar Ha-Amakim. In 1941, when he was fifteen or sixteen, the kibbutz youth leader Moshe Rado visited the immigrant center in Haifa to prepare the youth group for integration into Sha'ar Ha-Amakim. Dado proved to be an intelligent youngster, on good terms with his friends, monitors and teachers. Though he did not always do his homework satisfactorily, he learned quickly and made a great effort to perfect his Hebrew. As a youth Dado possessed a fine social sense and did much to unite the group. He was a natural leader. During his two years at Sha'ar Ha-Amakim Dado matured. He was outstanding as an actor and a creator of theatrical pieces and an impressive speaker.

Dado wanted very much to join the Palmach, but he was not included among those authorized to join. When his group joined Kibbutz Ein Shemer, Dado joined the Palmach nevertheless—contrary to the wishes of the kibbutz. Dado always remembered what he owed to Youth Aliyah, and to the fact that his first two years in the country were spent with Youth Aliyah and on the kibbutz. Although he was to hold positions of great responsibility, he never forgot the values he acquired during that period. When he was appointed commander in chief of the Israel Defense Forces, he replied thus to Youth Aliyah's message of congratulations:

> I would like to thank you, and the institution you head, for your kind letter. As one of those who had the privilege of being educated by Youth Aliyah, I would like to extend my best wishes and thanks to that wonderful enterprise. Yours very sincerely,
> David Elazar
> Lieutenant-General
> Chief of the General Staff
> 22.1.1972.

In 1973 he sent greetings to the Hadassah Conference in the United States, the organization that represents Youth Aliyah in that country. He wrote:

> As one of the graduates of Youth Aliyah, I would like to send warm greetings to the leaders and members of this important organization. Thanks to your cooperation, dating back to Henrietta Szold, Youth Aliyah has been able to provide an excellent education for 140,000 citizens of Israel. I share Hadassah's hope that Youth Aliyah will enable every young immigrant and every youngster in difficult circumstances in our country to receive an education that will fit him for a decent life.

Dado was a faithful disciple of Yitschak Sadeh. Throughout the years in which he held IDF commands, he remembered the principles that Sadeh had inculcated in his subordinates in the Palmach and the IDF. On 28 August 1973, Dado addressed the Yitschak Sadeh Prize Award Ceremony at the Tel Aviv Museum. Among other things, he said:

At the very beginnings of the Jewish force in Eretz Israel, the phrase "purity of arms" was coined. This would seem to be a contradiction in terms: Lethal weapons do not seem to have anything in common with purity. And yet, then as now, there is no contradition. The arms were clandestine and expensive, acquired and maintained at great danger, and they were the only concrete barrier between life and its loss. Those who sat in the yard of Tel Hai and waited, arms in hand, for those who were coming to kill them, knew that there was nothing more just, and therefore, more pure, than to press the trigger in defense of life. In time we went beyond the limits of passive self-defense. Yitschak Sadeh, who preached the purity of arms, himself preached going beyond those limits. We went out to attack the enemy, to ambush them at the approaches to their village and to strike at them in their homes. Methods of warfare changed without a change in values. Combat became offensive; the means to wage war improved, but the aim remained defensive and the arms remained pure.

Today we are a sovereign state. Our military force is no longer an underground movement but a regular army, amply equipped with sophisticated armaments . . . . One of the components of that force, and, indeed, the most important among them, that which gives us a qualitative advantage and bridges the quantitative gap, is the fighter, the man and his spirit, the fighter with a fighter's ethic. One could well ask whether in contemporary warfare it is possible to maintain the ethic of purity of arms. Modern warfare is comprehensive. It is a tragic struggle which is not fought only between strongholds of the opposing forces. . . . But even in this type of war the finest possible distinction must be made between the operative enemy and the helpless. On that distinction as on the point of a blade stands the purity of arms. We would not have been able to maintain the ethics of warfare had our aim not been just. The existence of the people of Israel in the land of Israel, the Jewish renaissance, which is not built on the destruction of others, is a just aim. The ways and means of achieving it must also be just. Not all means are justified. We maintain our fighers' ethic despite the bottomless hatred that still smoulders among our neighbors; despite their longing for a third destruction.

We maintain the ethics of warfare in the face of hypocrites and men without morality, whose law states that anything is permissible against the Jews.

We maintain the ethics of warfare for ourselves and for those who will come after us. The IDF is the melting pot and the formative school of Israel's future citizens. The moral values of the fighter become the moral values of every citizen in our democratic society. These values inspire us with hope for a better world, a more ethical world, a world of peace.

With these words Dado expressed his belief in and his adherence to the values in which he was educated and to which he remained faithful to the end. He delivered the speech only a short time before the tragic Yom Kippur War, the most difficult Israel has ever fought. Dado, the IDF's ninth chief of staff, was outstanding in this war. I saw him stand like a rock, a man who believed in our ability to win, a fearless fighter who did not falter in the most difficult trial of his life.

Dado appeared at cabinet meetings and reported with exemplary precision on the situation on all fronts. With that, he gave us hope that we would overcome once the reservists were organized and reached the fronts. He believed we would be able to carry the war to enemy territory, as indeed we did toward the end: the IDF conquered new territories on the Golan Heights and crossed the Suez Canal. Had Washington and Moscow not interfered, Israel's forces would have liquidated the Third Egyptian Army, which was already surrounded. In that terrible war, Dado distinguished himself as a fighting leader; as commander in chief much credit for the IDF's victory was due to him.

After the war, the Agranat Commission was appointed to inquire into the circumstances that had prevailed on the eve of the war and during the first days of the fighting. The commission was composed of Supreme Court judges, former chiefs of staff and the state comptroller. The commission's conclusions concerning Dado were extremely severe and stunned many. Everyone knew that Dado had demanded a full call-up of the reserves and that there had been a fierce discussion of the matter on Yom Kippur morning between Dado and the minister of defense. The prime minister decided in favor of a full call-up as the chief of staff had requested, but precious hours had been lost in discussion. Dado had also asked permission to bombard the Syrian Army on the Golan Heights and not to wait until it attacked, but the request was rejected by the prime minister and the minister of defense.

Dado particularly resented the fact that the Agranat Commission did not apply the same criteria to him and to his superior, the minister of defense. The commission was harsh in its judgment of Dado. He drew the inevitable conclusions and resigned. He left the army with a heavy heart, and with the conviction that he had been done a grave injustice. When he took his leave from the soldiers of the IDF he said, in his Order of the Day:

For two years I have commanded you. We have traversed a stormy period, a period which included the reinforcement and strengthening of our forces, a campaign to eradicate omission and oversight; the liquidation of terror within and beyond our borders and, above all, the Yom Kippur War, which we fought and won. It was a cruel and difficult war at the start, but by the time it was over we had, as always, carried the fighting into enemy territory. I end my command after twenty-eight years of service. I regret, my comrades-in-arms, that I must take my leave of you thus.

I had formed a very positive opinion of Dado during his tenure as chief of staff; I came to know him closely through cabinet meetings and personal contacts with him. We talked frequently about crucial issues and I sometimes criticized him. But Dado told me more than once that he accepted criticism from me with understanding and friendship because he knew that there was no personal prejudice in my remarks. He neither could nor would reveal to me his opinion prior to an operation, whether mounted on his own initiative or decided upon by his superior. In this he behaved nobly. His words to the cabinet before his resignation, though uttered out of a searing sense of injury, were extremely restrained. He spoke the truth as he saw it, but refrained from leveling accusations against others.

After his retirement from the IDF he went through a difficult period of soul-searching. He lived constantly with the feeling that he had been the victim of injustice. The memorandum that he later wrote on the conclusions of the Agranat Commission concerning him, which was published after his untimely death, is a distressing, thought-provoking document. It penetrates the depths of a soul, and reflects the nobility that marked the personality of one of the finest, most talented of our commanders—a man who was at one with himself and his beliefs.

People were stunned by his death. Many believed his heart had collapsed under the strain of being forced to leave his post as commander-in-chief of the IDF after its great victory—a victory that stands out all the more when one recalls the terrible Day of Judgment on which the war began.

Dado's life and his period of service in the army will no doubt become the object of historical research. From his memorandum it appears that hundreds of telegrams concerning the possibility of the outbreak of war and the danger of a surprise attack never reached him. As is well known, the view of the intelligence branch was that "the probability of the outbreak of war is lower than low." It is also not clear what information was channeled to the chief of staff from Intelligence and from the fronts. From General Kahalani's book *Oz 77* it appears that General Avigdor

Ben Gal (Yanush) was of the opinion—a week or more before it broke out—that there would be an all-out war. This was also the opinion of the Northern Command. In the south, too, there were a few who had doubts and suspicions; we heard of them and particularly of one called Simantov, afterwards. During the week prior to Yom Kippur there were very worrisome signs. The air force was ordered to stand by and top alert was declared. Just what that state of alert meant, and to what extent the orders were fulfilled—on that the Agranet Commission reported extensively. On the eve of Yom Kippur the prime minister held consultations with a number of ministers who happened to be in Tel Aviv. It was then known that the Russian families were being evacuated from Egypt and Syria. This was a danger sign, but it was not sufficient to convene the entire cabinet to make a decision. Even early on the morning of Yom Kippur, when war was certain, the cabinet was not convened. It finally did meet at noon.

The report of the Agranat Commission is highly confidential and will remain so for many years. The cabinet did not discuss it. But a great tragedy had occurred: Dado's heart was silenced forever.

After his death, many people wrote letters to the press and made their comments, but even after the publication of his confidential memorandum no discussion was held in the cabinet, and apparently none will be held. Much will be said about him; he will not be forgotten. Each individual in Israel will form his own judgment in accordance with his conscience. We will remember Dado as one of IDF's finest commanders, a man of strong character who did not bend, but was broken and fell.

Glossary

AGUDA: The non-Zionist, right wing Orthodox Movement in Israel and the Diaspora.

AGUDAT ISRAEL: A political party in Israel, represented in the Knesset, continuing their fight against Zionism. Translation: "United Israel."

DEMOCRATIC ZIONIST FACTION: Created in the first Zionist Congresses to oppose the policies of Theodore Herzl, and headed by Chaim Weizmann.

ETZEL: Military underground movement of the Revisionist Zionists, called in Hebrew: Irgun Tzvai Le'umi. Their leader was Menachem Begin.

GAHAL: A parliamentary block created in 1965 by the Herut and the right wing General Zionists, called "Liberals" since 1961. Gahal is an acronym of the words: "Gush Herut Liberali."

HAGANAH: Underground military major organization of Palestine Jews during the British Mandate. "Haganah" means Defense.

HAPOEL HATSAIR: Zionist Labor pioneering political party. Translation: "The Young Worker."

HERUT: Present political nationalistic party represented in the Knesset since the formation of the State. Herut means "Freedom."

INDEPENDENT LIBERAL PARTY: Progressive liberal political party, representing social liberalism, created in 1965.

LECHI: Underground military organization that broke away from "Etzel" at the time of the Second World War. Acronym of the words: "Lochamei Herut Israel."

LIKUD: Present parliamentary block under the leadership of Menachem Begin, continuing the "Gahal" block. "Likud" means "Unity."

NAHAL: Military settlement movement of the Israel Defence Forces. Acronym of the words: "Noar Halutzi Locheim." Translation: "Pioneering Fighting Youth."

PAOLEI ZION: Zionist Socialist Party, represented at the Zionist Congresses. Translation: "Workers of Zion."

PROGRESSIVE GENERAL ZIONISTS or PROGRESSIVE ZIONIST SYNTHESIS MOVEMENT: Political party of progressive liberal Zionists, created in 1948, represented also at the Zionist Congresses as a part of the General Zionist World Movement.

WORLD CONFEDERATION OF GENERAL ZIONISTS: World movement of all General Zionists represented at the Zionist Congresses and Zionist Executive and Jewish Agency.

ZIONISTS A: Progressive General Zionist wing within the World Movement and Confederation of General Zionists.

ZIONISTS B: Right wing of General Zionists within the General Zionists World Movement.

Index

Adler, Dr. Cyrus, 133
Al Hamishmar (On Guard), 49, 56
Allenby, General Edmund, 136
Alonei Yitschak, 60, 178, 179, 180, 183, 184
Arlosoroff, Chaim, 129

Bakshtansky, Levi, 25
Balfour Declaration, 25, 28, 29, 33, 47, 62, 78, 79, 81, 136
Bank Leumi, 88, 90, 127
Barditcher, Abba, 186–92
Barth, Lazarus, 77, 78
Baruch, Shalom ben, 32
Beilinson, Moshe, 69, 70
Benderly, Dr. Samson, 163
Ben-Gurion, David, 26, 28, 36, 42, 57, 83, 84, 88, 92, 93, 94, 98, 102, 116, 124, 126, 145, 148, 149
Ben-Zvi, Yitschak, 35–38, 42, 44, 98
Berlin, Eliyahu, 36, 71, 72
Bevan, Aneurin, 152
Bevin, Ernest, 27, 102
Bialik, Mosad, 40, 56
Bichovski, Arieh, 71
Biderman, Moshe (Ossi), 177
Blumenfeld, Kurt, 50, 78, 79, 80, 155–58, 171
Borochov, Dov-Ber, 35, 39, 42
Brandeis, Judge Louis, 135, 136
Brisker, Daniel, 182–185
Brodetsky, Professor Selig, 25, 159–62

Caro, Joseph (rabbi), 40
Charif, Yechiel, 60, 167–76, 178

Chermesh, Chaim, 187, 189, 190
Churchill, Winston, 26, 144, 152
Cohen, Hermann, 64, 65

Dayan, Moshe, 93
Danziger, Dr. Felix, 80
David, Aharon, 121
Davidson, Michael, 17
Diaspora, 36, 40, 41, 42, 46, 60, 64, 79, 80, 96, 105, 112, 149, 155, 165, 169, 172, 174, 175, 176, 187
Dobkin, E., 59
Dushkin, Alexander, 164, 165

Einstein, Albert, 156, 162
Elazar, David (Dado), 193
Eliad, Nissim, 93
Ellenberg, Dr. Shmaryahu, 118
Epstein, Judith, 152
Eshkol, Levi, 84, 88, 91–96, 124, 125, 126

Feldman, Dr. Israel, 142
Fishman-Maimon, Ada, 141
Foerder, Dr. Yishayahu, 127
Freier, Recha, 41, 152
Friedlander, Professor Israel, 135
Frischman, David, 32

Ginsberg, Louis, 134
Glickson, Moshe, 32, 50, 52, 61–75, 80, 108, 119, 157
Goldblum, Y. K. (rabbi), 56, 82, 103, 104, 149
Goldsmith, Gertrude, 135

Goldstein, Dr. Israel, 149
Goldstein, Sam, 142
Goma, Haim, 187
Gottheil, Richard, 133
Greenbaum, Yitschak, 25, 32, 45–60
Greenberg, Chaim, 41

Ha'am, Ahad, 63, 74
Ha'aretz, 31, 50, 61, 74
Haas, Jacob de, 135
Hadassah, 135, 136, 148, 150
Haganah, 27, 35, 36, 58, 59, 100, 102, 123, 142, 193
Halacha, 14, 39
Halprin, Rose, 148–50, 152
Hantke, Dr. Arthur, 78, 156
Harari, Chaim, 71
Hartglass, A. M., 54
Hartzfeld, Avraham, 118
Hatsfira (the Epoch), 32, 33, 34
Helsingfors Conference, 46, 79
Herman, Zvi, 148
Herut (Progressive Party), 84, 85, 86
Herzl, Theodore, 62, 63, 71, 77, 112, 113, 114
Histadrut, 40, 41, 49, 51, 56, 58, 67, 71, 72, 81, 99, 108, 109, 110, 115, 117, 118, 119, 120, 124, 125, 170, 175, 188
Hitler, Adolf, 30, 120, 144
Holocaust, 14, 41, 120, 165, 172, 181
Huberman, Branislaw, 153

Israel Defense Force (IDF), 95, 94, 103, 193, 195, 196, 197, 198

Jabotinsky, Ze'ev, 25, 31, 49, 94, 144
Jacobs, Rose, 130, 148
Jacobson, Victor, 78
Johnson, Lyndon, 94, 95

Kagan, Dr. Helena, 135
Kahn, Jacobus, 78
Kaplan, Eliezer, 91, 93
Kaplan, Mordecai (rabbi), 164
Kaplan, Rose, 135
Katznelson, Berl, 40, 67, 74, 75, 98, 106–114, 116, 170
Keren Hayesod, 31, 34, 156, 157
Keren Kayemeth, 111
Kfar Glickson, 73

Kfar Habad, 40
Kfar Juliana, 37
Kfar Saba, 15, 123, 151
Kibbutz Degania B, 91, 92, 93, 95
Kibbutz Gan Shmuel, 45, 46, 59, 60
Kibbutz Hamefales, 15, 151
Klausner, Professor Joseph, 18
Kolodny, Alter (rabbi), (Pinchas Eliyahu), 13–23
Komoy, Natan Otto, 181
Krol, Jacob, 116

Landauer, Dr. George, 81, 129, 130
Landey, Rachel, 135
Lavon Affair, 83, 84, 93, 103, 126
Lehman, Dr. Siegfried, 130, 171, 172
Levin, Shmaryahu, 78, 135, 157
Lipsky, Louis, 135

MacDonald, Ramsey, 53
Magnes, Dr. Judah Yehuda Leib, 131, 136, 148, 164
Maimon, Yehuda Leib (rabbi), 52
Maimonides, 64, 70
Mapai (Labor Party), 84, 85, 86, 93, 99, 103, 126, 127
Marshall, Louis, 133
Meir, Golda, 125
Michaeli, Zvi, 117
Mossinson, Ben-Zion, 71

National Council Executive, 36, 37
Nazis, 20, 25, 26, 30, 36, 74, 123, 129, 130, 139, 177, 190, 193
Neumann, Emanuel, 149
Nixon, Richard, 95

Olienkov, Michael, 71

Peel Commission, 25, 27, 101, 158
Peretz, Y. L., 32, 55
Pinsk, 13, 14, 15, 16, 17, 18, 21, 22, 23, 24, 104
Poalei Zion, 42, 98

Rabinowitz, Joseph, 58
Rado, Moshe, 194
Rapaport, S., 71
Rathenau, Walter, 156

Index

Remez, David, 98
Rokach, L. Y., 71
Roosevelt, Eleanor, 14
Roosevelt, Franklin, 26, 59
Rosen, Pinchas (Felix Rosenbluth), 50, 76–90, 93
Rosenbluth, Martin, 78
Rothschild, Baron, 136
Rothschild, Lord, 33
Ruppin, Dr. Arthur, 139

Sadeh, Yitschak, 195
Saint Petersburg, 17, 46
Sapir, Pinchas, 91, 123–28
Schiff, Jacob, 133
Schneider, Bezalel, 19
Schoolman, Albert, 163
Sejm (Polish Parliament), 47, 48
Sieff, Rebecca, 151–54
Sharett, Moshe, 97–106
Shazar, Zalman, 39–44
Shiber, Dov, 75
Shoham, Z., 71
Silver, Dr. Abba Hillel, 101, 149
Six-Day War, 93, 94, 95, 128, 193
Slonimsky, Chaim Selig, 32
Smuts, Prime Minister Jan, 140, 144
Sneh, Dr. Moshe (Kleinbaum), 58
Sprinzak, Joseph, 82, 115–22
Sokolow, Nachum, 30–34, 78
Szold, Henrietta, 129–39, 173, 194

Talmi, Yehuda, 177
Tchlenow, Yechiel, 78
Tel Aviv, 24, 34, 45, 46, 53, 59, 72
Ticho, Dr. Albert, 135
Tomer, Ben-Zion, 138
Truman, Harry, 27, 145

Ussishkin, Menachem, 78

Verlag, Klal, 17

Warburg, Prof. Otto, 78
Wasserman, Oscar, 156
Weizmann, Chaim, 24–29, 31, 33, 36, 44, 49, 50, 52, 53, 62, 78, 79, 81, 89, 100, 101, 120,1 21, 127, 129, 136, 146, 151, 153, 158, 160
Weizmann, Vera, 140–47, 151
Wertheim, Avraham, 58
Wilhelm II (emperor), 77
Wise, Stephen, 133, 135
Wolffsohn, David, 78
Women's International Zionist Organization (WIZO), 140, 142, 143, 151, 152, 153, 154
World Confederation of General Zionists, 49, 149
World War I, 22, 33, 47, 48, 98, 134, 151, 160, 173
World War II, 16, 22, 25, 26, 27, 28, 36, 43, 47, 53, 58, 91, 101, 138, 139
World Zionist Organization, 26, 27, 28, 30–31, 34, 56, 57, 60, 78, 79, 88, 97, 99, 103, 140, 151, 155, 160, 175

Yaffe, Eliezer, 117
Yaffe, Leib, 156, 157

Zalman, Rabbi Schneur, 40
Zemora, Dr. Moshe, 80
Zionist General Council, 24, 25
Zionist Youth, 24, 30, 70, 71, 75, 98, 107, 108, 109, 115, 127, 168, 176, 180, 182, 183, 191
Zuchovitzky, Shmuel Zakif, 58